"Does Wednesday Mean Mom's House or Dad's?"

The Community Enhancement Grant

Tennessee General Assembly

2008.

"Does Wednesday Mean Mom's House or Dad's?"

Parenting Together While Living Apart

SECOND EDITION

MARC J. ACKERMAN

WILEY

John Wiley & Sons, Inc.

For general information on our other products and services or for technical support, please contact our Customer Care Department within the United States at (800) 762-2974, outside the United States at (317) 572-3993 or fax (317) 572-4002.

Wiley also publishes its books in a variety of electronic formats. Some content that appears in print may not be available in electronic books. For more information about Wiley products, visit our web site at www.wiley.com.

Library of Congress Cataloging-in-Publication Data:

Ackerman, Marc J.
 Does Wednesday mean mom's house or dad's? : parenting together while living apart / by Marc J. Ackerman. – 2nd ed.
  p. cm.
 Includes bibliographical references and index.
 ISBN 978-0-470-12753-7 (pbk.)
 1. Parenting, Part-time–United States. 2. Divorce–United States–Psychological aspects.
3. Children of divorced parents–United States. 4. Children of divorced parents–United States–Psychology. I. Title.
 HQ755.8.A25 2008
 649′.1–dc22   2008001382

Printed in the United States of America.

10 9 8 7 6 5 4 3 2 1

This Book is Dedicated to:

Aaron, Adam, Alexandra, Amy, Andrea, Angela, Anthony, Brandon, Brian, Caitlin, Cameron, Casey, Christian, Christina, Christine, Christopher, Chuck, Daniel, David, Elizabeth, Eric, Evan, Grant, Jamie, Janine, Jason, Jennifer, Jonathan, Jordan, Joseph, Julia, Katherine, Kelly, Kenneth, Kevin, Lawrence, Lindsey, Marcy, Mary, Maureen, Megan, Melissa, Michael, Patrick, Raymond, Robert, Ryan, Scott, Shannon, Stacy, Todd, Vincent, William...

This book is dedicated to the above-named children and to all other children who have been forced to endure their parents' fighting for years about custody-related issues. To those, and all others, whose parents believe that winning is more important than the well-being of their children, I hope you overcome these obstacles, and best wishes to you.

Contents

Preface   xiii

Acknowledgments   xvii

Chapter 1 A House Divided   1
Facts about Divorce   2

Chapter 2 Moving Ahead:
Telling Children about Your Divorce   13
Concrete Thinkers in an Abstract Situation   17
When Your Child Is No Longer a Child   24
Academic Performance   26
Boys and Girls React Differently   26
Adjustments Abound   28
Mourning the End of a Marriage   29

Not Enough Hours in the Day, Not Enough
   Friends in the World   32
One Magical Wish   34

Chapter 3 Custody Options: The Best Interest of the Child   35
Joint versus Sole Custody   37
Chronic Mental Illness Leads to a Topsy-Turvy
   World   39
Active Alcoholism or Other Drug Abuse and
   Children Don't Mix   41
Physical or Sexual Abuse: Confounding
   Dilemmas   42
Violating Orders, Communication Failure,
   Obstructing Visits   43
Endangering Your Children   44
Separate Lives under One Roof, Then the Great
   Divide   46
Giving Up Placement   48
Grandparents: Help or Hindrance   49

Chapter 4 Navigating the Legal Waters   51
Finding an Attorney   51
Don't Be Attracted by Unrealistic
   Promises   55
Avoid "Hired Guns" and "Dirty Tricks"
   Attorneys   56
Switching Attorneys   58
Telling Your Story in Court   59
Acting as Your Own Attorney   60
Mediation as a First Step   61
Collaboration   64
Arbitration   68
The Court Process   69
Custody Disputes   72
The Guardian ad Litem   72
The Custody Study   76

Custody Evaluation 76
To Supervise or Not to Supervise 83
Relocation Cases 85
Going Back to Court 88

Chapter 5 Two of Everything? Dealing with the Practicalities of Placement and Custody 93

Placement of Young Children 96
The Ackerman Plan 98
Bad Schedules 100
General Rules 101
Separating Children 105
Uninterrupted Time 106
Different Cities: Creating a Placement
  Road Map 107
Making Things Work under New Rules 109
The Master Schedule 109
The Parenting Plan 111
Visits and Flexibility Work Hand in Hand 114
Dividing Property with an Eye on Details 119
Parents' Rights 121
College Education 125
Religious Training 126
Phone Calls 127
Presents 129
Vacations 129
Finances 130
Parents Working after a Divorce 131

Chapter 6 How to Parent Apart 132

The Family Conference: Increasing Avenues of
  Communication 133
A United Front 134
Making Placements Better 134
Power to the Children 138
Children as Coequals 139

Sleeping Arrangements   140
Children in the Middle   140
A Different Sort of Communication   143
Fighting in Front of the Children   144
Where to Live   146
Problems with the Other Parent   147
Parents Who Won't Visit   148
Lack of Cooperation   149

Chapter 7 Maltreatment   152

Physical Abuse   154
Who Will Be the Abusers?   154
Proving Abuse   156
Consequences of Childhood Physical
   Abuse   157
Family/Domestic Violence   159
Domestic Violence and Custody   161
To Stay or Not to Stay: Is That Your
   Quandary?   164
Emotional/Psychological Abuse   165
Sexual Abuse   167
Who Are the Sexual Abusers?   169
Evaluating Sexual Abuse   169
If You Think Your Child Has Been
   Sexually Abused   170
Sexual Abuse Allegations: True or False?   172
Devastating Effects of Sexual Abuse   176
Warnings!!!!!!!   181

Chapter 8 The Only Certainty in Life Is Change   183

Move-Away Placement Plan   186
Longer Lasting Reactions   187
A Plan to Make Everyone Feel Better   188
The Challenge of Additional Adjustments   188
Remarriage   192

The Role of the Stepparent   194
Disciplining Children   195
Cementing Relationships   197
The Other Extended Family   197
Change as Children Grow Older   198

Chapter 9 Custody Do's and Don'ts   200

A Boy Named Chris   201
Custody Do's   207
Custody Don'ts   217

Chapter 10 Resources Abound   224

Psychiatrists   225
Psychologists   226
Social Workers   228
Professional Organizations   229
Current Resources on Child Custody/Divorce
  231

Index   241

Preface

Divorce is one of the most difficult transitions you will ever make in your life. It is a dramatic, time-consuming, frustrating, stressful process, which leaves many adults reeling from the extreme changes it creates in their lives. Swings in financial and social status, emotional upheaval and grief over failed expectations and the loss of the marriage partner have a tremendous effect on lives.

As difficult as divorce is for adults, it has the potential to be absolutely devastating for children. Divorce impacts all children, regardless of age. It shatters their underlying security and throws them into a state of limbo because from one day to the next they don't know what to expect from life or from their parents. They feel as if they can count on nothing and no one.

Depending upon their age, children experience guilt, believing the divorce is their fault; anger sometimes bordering on outright rage; sadness; confusion; and a sense of helplessness that makes them anxious, forlorn and frightened. They even have bouts of feeling abandoned and rejected, especially when one parent moves out of the home. Divorce adversely affects their school work, method of play and even their health.

As the divorce and custody processes unfold (they are inseparable if you have children), children's emotions and reactions to their situations change. These swings generally dissipate as some of their fears are alleviated. For example, when a child feels abandoned because mom or dad has moved out, over the course of the next few weeks or months, if that child sees that you are still around through planned visits, that you can still help with homework, play basketball and so on, the feelings of abandonment and rejection normally disappear.

The extent to which your child is affected by divorce depends largely on you. You are the operative figure in this picture, but you are not the most important person to be considered in it, even though you and/or your spouse are responsible for triggering the process. If you have children, they are the single most important considerations in the divorce and custody processes.

Most separations or divorces occur when children are under the age of 12 and are still concrete thinkers, meaning they don't understand all the subtleties and underlying influences on such abstract things as falling in and out of love. Many occurrences must be explained to them, even things, which as an adult you may not see the need to explain. Children can be made more comfortable at each stage of the divorce and custody processes if you tell them specifically what you expect to happen and how it will happen.

How and what you tell them and under what circumstances is critical to the way they react to the information and accept or reject it. For example, it is okay for children to know that the separation is taking place because you and the other parent don't love each other anymore. However, it is not necessary but destructive to go through small details about affairs or other problems.

It is important for you to consistently assure your children that although you and your spouse have fallen out of love, you have not fallen out of love with them. Explain to them that the love bond between children and their parents occurs at birth and that it will last throughout their lives, that you will not unlearn to love them.

Knowledge is one of the keys to lessening the impact of divorce on children. You must learn from the outset of your divorce how to handle children. You must know how to inform and approach them to lessen their emotional load and help them deal with rapid changes in their lives as they occur and, whenever possible in advance of their occurrence.

This book is designed to guide you through the divorce and custody processes with the best interests of your children as your primary concern. You will discover that it takes a good deal of focus, self-control and selflessness to keep children in that number one priority space. You will find that if you and your spouse can exercise enough self discipline to contain your anger toward each other and work things out based on what is best for your children, you will also benefit.

As you read on, you will find information that will help you break the news of divorce to your children, keep them informed without overburdening them and enable you to anticipate behavioral and emotional responses at various ages of your children and stages of the divorce and custody processes. This book will even help you simplify their lives and yours through the use of highly adaptable schedules and plans for visitation.

As you move through your divorce, and find yourself repeatedly tested and stretched to and beyond your limits, if you have any doubts about keeping your children first, just look at their faces and really hear what they are saying when they ask you where they are going to live, with whom and for how long. I have dealt with more than four thousand children in my practice who were in the midst of custody and placement battles. One need only look at and listen to them to understand what divorce does to them and to realize that winning is never more important than the well-being of your children. This message is repeated throughout these pages. Keep it in mind as you help your children figure out if Wednesday means mom's house or dad's house.

Over the years a number of terms have been used for the time that children spend with each parent. These terms include: visitation, placement, access, and accommodation. This text will use the term placement interchangeably with all of the other labels, depending upon which term is used in your state.

Two major changes have occurred in the landscape since the publication of the first edition of this book about 10 years ago.

The issue of maltreatment (abuse) has taken the forefront in the area of custody evaluations. A completely new Chapter 7 has been added to discuss these areas of concern in detail.

Another new area of interest is the mushrooming in use of the internet and its resources. Chapter 10, "Resources Abound," lists dozens of web sites available to parents, and also dozens of books that can help parents address the many troublesome issues that arise in divorce and custody cases.

The previous edition listed the custody Do's and Don'ts. In response to requests of readers, that list has now been expanded to include a narrative that discusses each of these custody Do's and Don'ts in detail.

M.A.

Acknowledgments

This is the second edition of this book. The success of the first edition was made possible by those individuals who helped with the initial project more than 10 years ago. They included Kelly Franklin, my editor at the time at John Wiley & Sons, and attorneys Lee Calvey, Martin Gagne, Susan Hansen, James Podell, Peggy Podell, and Nina Vitek. The most important contributor to the success of the initial book was Toni Reinhold, who brought life to the text at that time. I have a deep appreciation for the work these individuals did in making the first edition successful.

The second edition has also benefited from the work of a number of individuals. Patricia Rossi, senior editor at John Wiley & Sons, Isabel Pratt, and Linda Indig were very helpful and understanding during difficult times in the preparation of this manuscript. Again, I was able to rely on the help of several attorneys, especially in revision of the new chapter on legal issues.

These attorneys were Susan Hansen, Peggy Podell, and Carlton Stansbury.

Recognizing the extraordinary benefit of working with Toni Reinhold 10 years ago, I conducted an internet search to redis-cover her whereabouts. We worked together again, and it was instantly a hand-in-glove fit. She made useful suggestions for updating the manuscript, and was particularly helpful in working on the chapters that were completely rewritten.

Further thanks go to Colleen Drosdeck, a doctoral student, who spent seemingly endless hours on the internet and in book-stores accumulating information for the resources chapter. Most of what is included in that chapter is a result of her diligent work.

Over the 17 years that I have been doing this type of work, my wife, Stephanie Ackerman, has willingly allowed me time away from other activities so that I could accomplish these tasks. With-out her continued cooperation and understanding, I would not have been able to work on these projects. Lastly, as always, I must thank my office manager, Roseanne Rech, who organized and typed all the additions to the second edition and spent hours cut-ting and pasting, along with me, to produce this finished product, all without complaining.

"Does Wednesday Mean Mom's House or Dad's?"

A House Divided

The end of your marriage is in sight, but you still live with the hope that somehow, some way, you'll be able to resolve the problems and differences that are wrenching you and your spouse apart. You deny that your difficulties are insurmountable or could be so overpowering that they would nullify the investment of time, energy, emotions, and money you've made in your spouse and the two of you as a couple. You wonder what else you might do to make your marriage better and restore the love that brought you together in the first place.

You think about your children, recognizing that (in all probability) they love both of you and would be better off in a whole family instead of a broken one. You are torn by indecision and guilt, born of questions about whether it is better to stay in a marriage void of happiness and fulfillment for the sake of your children.

Before you have a chance to resolve these issues, you open the mail or answer the door or have a discussion with your spouse and discover that what you've been dreading has now become your reality—*You are getting divorced.* For a moment, the world seems to stop on its axis. What will you do? What about the children? How will you survive? Where will you go? What will people say? You wonder if life is over and if things will ever be the same.

Although your life and the lives of your children and your spouse will never be the same, life does not end with divorce. You will survive. Sometimes it is in everybody's best interest to live apart, but if children are involved, your household must continue standing, albeit under different roofs. You face a long and probably difficult road along which many decisions will have to be made, including determining custody and placement for your children, placement times, discipline issues, financial arrangements, and schooling.

Throughout the divorce process, you will become involved in counseling, mediation, and court hearings. You will also need professional advice from lawyers, psychologists, social workers, and judges. You will be called on to be strong when you feel weak, to advance when you are tired, and to repeatedly put your children's interests before your own. The focus of this book is the well-being of your children. This is one of the facts about divorce—children must come first.

Facts about Divorce

If you are going to negotiate a divorce with your children's best interests as your focal point, you must be aware of some other important facts about divorce.

Fact 1:   Divorce is always painful for children, no matter how old they are.

You cannot change that, but as parents, *you* will determine the degree of heartache your children will experience. In my practice, I speak with many parents who are concerned about how their divorce will affect their children and want to protect them from its negative impact. Sadly, I have to tell them that they cannot protect their children from the pain and grief of divorce, but they can keep the hurt and damage at a minimum through their own behavior. The more fighting, hatred, and lack of cooperation that exist, the harder it will be on the children.

Fact 2:   Divorce does not end the relationship between spouses, it just changes the rules of the relationship.

Many people get divorced with the notion, "I'm going to finally get rid of this guy" or "I'm not going to have to listen to her anymore." The fact is that if you have children under the age of 18, you will be required to have some sort of relationship with your ex-spouse until your child reaches 18, and even after 18 for special events.

Although your relationship will continue on some level, children must learn that life will never be the same after the divorce. It is not uncommon for children to fantasize that someday life will return to the way it was before. This is not possible and the sooner everyone understands that, the easier life will be. If your children have difficulty grasping this, it may be necessary to get outside help such as counseling.

It's important at this time to give your children as much stability as possible. Direct your energy toward helping them adjust to their new life.

Fact 3:   You are not the only parent going through divorce.

Parents become very self-focused during the divorce process. They often feel they are the only ones having to change their daily routine, work schedule, and time with the children. Your former partner is going through the same changes. Recognize that every change you must make, he or she must also make. In addition, the moving parent will have to make significantly more changes than the parent who remains at home, and may actually be going through more adjustments.

Fact 4: You do not have to hate your spouse to get divorced.

It's not unusual for a parent midway through the divorce process to question whether the divorce should even take place. The assumption that people often make is that if they are getting divorced, they should hate their spouse. Extending that logic, if they don't, they question whether they should be getting divorced at all.

There are things you are apt to still like about your partner even if you are getting divorced, and those ambivalent feelings can lead to confusion about the impending separation. If the things you don't like about your partner outweigh the things you do like, the decision to divorce is probably a sound one. However, when the things you disliked have changed, then questioning the divorce may be reasonable. A therapist can help you sort through this dilemma.

Fact 5: The divorce takes place psychologically for children on the day of the separation.

The divorce occurs for children the day their parents separate. Visitation and placement schedules and support payments begin around that time, and the rules of the relationship also start changing with the separation. The legal divorce only solidifies those changes.

Fact 6: Two people living apart cannot live as cheaply as two people living together.

The first major reality of separation and divorce is financial. I'm sure that it's not news to you that two households are more costly to maintain than one. This can be a major problem for some families and can add to the stress and strain of divorce.

The financial impact of divorce on a family is several-fold, and much of the severity of it depends on the ages of your children. It may necessitate both parents working, when before the divorce only one worked outside the home. Psychologically, children perceive this as a second loss (the first being when one parent moves out of the house).

The immediate financial impact is on short-term, daily finances. The crunch begins when attorneys ask for retainers of $1,000 to $5,000 or more (sometimes even up to $25,000) just to begin a divorce action. Parents must turn to savings, if they have any, and in some cases they borrow against credit cards or from relatives.

Once a divorce action has begun, parents usually live in different places. They must pay two rents, or a mortgage and apartment rent, and two sets of utility, grocery, and insurance bills; their budget gets stretched to its limit or beyond. Many people living in one household are overextended, but if they must support two homes, they experience a tremendous change in essential versus nonessential expenses.

For children, a limited budget may mean a reduction in recreational activities and an end to ballet or karate lessons, or leaving private or parochial school for public school. They may have to wear clothes longer than before or wear hand-me-downs. Children may become bitter, resentful, disappointed, and unhappy. They may also have problems at school if they cannot dress to be socially acceptable or if they cannot attend school outings because of a fee that divorcing parents cannot afford.

Ironically, one of the common causes of divorce is financial irresponsibility on the part of one or both parents. If a parent is already financially irresponsible and his or her responsibilities increase because of divorce, the financial impact on the family is even greater.

When both parents are employed outside the home, the husband often makes more money than his wife, and this fact becomes a basic conflict in many divorces. One parent generally thinks the ex-spouse has the children too often, and the other parent thinks the ex-spouse has too much disposable income.

One of the long-term plans that is usually upset by divorce is saving for college. If a divorce drags on and involves many court appearances, you may have to spend the equivalent cost of several college educations. I was involved in one case in which, between the attorneys, psychologists, and other professionals, the couple spent $1,000,000. This kind of spending on a divorce angers children because they may be prevented from attending college at all or have to choose a less expensive school.

Divorce decrees usually don't include a plan for college expenses, because at 18 years of age a child is considered an adult and support payments stop. Also, it is difficult enough for attorneys and courts to agree on what should happen financially to an underage child. They don't want to plan for when a child becomes an adult, so in most divorce cases the college issue is ignored.

Fact 7: Two people living apart cannot see their children as often as two people living together.

Even in the most ideal situations, when parents live apart they will have less access to their children than when they lived together. Typical visitation and placement schedules allow for a quarter- to half-time with each parent. That means you will be spending from three to six months less time with your children than before the divorce.

Fact 8: Divorcing parents generally are upset by any extra time the other parent may have with the children.

Learn to value the time you have away from the children as much as the time you have with them. Save errands, doctor's appointments, and other personal business for when your children are with the other parent. This way, you will have more quality time with them, and you may actually be spending as many hours with your children as you did when they lived with you full-time.

Fact 9: Courts do not want to place children with a parent who is systematically trying to destroy the other parent.

Judges and court-appointed guardians are reluctant to place a child with a parent who feels the need to systematically destroy the other parent. Courts view such desire for destruction as a character flaw. Professionals believe one parent's desire to destroy the other also destroys that parent's ability to be a good role model for children. I heard a guardian say to a father, "Don't tell me the children would be better off with you when your only purpose right now is to destroy their mother."

If you are in the heat of a custody dispute, step back and examine your actions.

- Are you keeping voluminous notes about every mistake the other parent makes?
- Do you call his or her neighbors, employers, coworkers, and relatives for negative information?
- Do you file motion after motion in court to discredit and denigrate the other parent?
- Do you use your children as spies against the other parent?

If any of these patterns of behavior describe you, *stop.* You are hurting yourself, your children, and your chances for reaching a good custody arrangement. If your spouse is that bad, he or she will demonstrate it through behavior. You will not have to prove anything.

Fact 10: Never ask a child to decide whom he or she wants to live with.

Children are generally not concerned with who gets legal custody of them, but they are very concerned with where they will live. By involving a child in this decision, he or she is put under incredible pressure and in a no-win situation by being forced to accept one parent and reject the other. Often, one of the first things children ask is, "Who am I going to live with?" The answer is, "you they are likely to spend time with both parents. The grown-ups will work out the details and let you know what is decided."

This concern is a big stressor for children. Imagine that as an adult you don't know where you are going to be living in three months, where you are going to work, where you will get your recreation and food, and if you are going to be able to see your friends. Even for an adult, this situation would produce great anxiety. Children live under that cloud for the entire period of a divorce and custody dispute.

Children who are especially worried will press the issue. No matter how often they ask where they are going to live, parents have to stand firm and not incorporate children into this decision-making process. Most children under 15 years of age are incapable of making a fully informed decision about what living situation would be in their best interest. The younger they are, the more likely it is that their desires will be based on concrete matters, such as the size of a bedroom or the number of toys available.

Custody arrangements are something you and your spouse must try to work out. If you cannot come to a reasonable agreement about custody and visitation that is based on the welfare of your child and not your own desires, it will be up to the court, with input from guardians and other professionals such as psychologists, to make the decision for you.

Rarely will a court decide that a 16- or 17-year-old should live somewhere he or she doesn't want to, but in most cases the ultimate decision about custody and placement does rest with the courts. Young children simply need to know that you intend for them to be able to spend time with both of you. Teenagers need to know that their wishes will be considered as well.

A custody ruling appeal throws children right back into limbo until the appeal is heard. A child's underlying security is continually tested during custody battles.

Fact 11:   You should be willing to do whatever you want your spouse to do.

Every new situation arising after the separation sets precedents or establishes new rules as to how things will continue. In establishing these rules, recognize that what's good for the goose is good for the gander and vice versa. Don't expect your spouse to do something that you are unwilling to do.

Fact 12:   Unhappy mothers cannot raise happy children.

Although this issue cuts in both directions, since mothers receive placement in most cases they are chosen as the descriptor in this rule. When a father continually undermines, sabotages, and makes life miserable for the mother, she will be very unhappy. Fathers must recognize that it is not possible for an unhappy mother to raise happy children. Therefore, fathers have a vested interest in keeping things on an even keel. The same is true if a father has custody and the mother is the potential saboteur.

Fact 13: Child support payments are intended to support your children, not to serve as extra spending money for your ex-spouse.

Too often a parent will say, "I'm not giving her a dime" or "I'm not giving him money to spend as he sees fit." It may be that not every dime from these payments is spent on supporting your children. Sometimes more money will be spent on the children than support provides, and other times less money is spent. In the end, however, it is your children who benefit from this money. Doing anything to directly or indirectly manipulate support payments affects your children. Do not use anger toward your ex-spouse as an excuse for manipulating support payments.

Fact 14: When parents live apart, children have more opportunities to manipulate them.

When parents live together, children try to take advantage of opportunities to manipulate one parent against the other. It's not unusual for a child to ask one parent if he or she can do something and after being told "no," to ask the other parent the same question. When parents live apart, they have more difficulty coordinating their answers, and therefore it becomes important for you to communicate effectively with one another to reduce manipulation.

Fact 15: "It is hard when children cannot spend time with someone they love."

This is a quote from a little girl with tears running down her cheeks while I was seeing her in therapy. She said she still loved both her parents, but one parent was making it very difficult for her to see the other. In most cases, it is important for children to continue an ongoing relationship with both parents in spite of the anger the parents may feel toward each other.

Children may not be allowed to spend any time or only a small amount of time with the other parent for a number of reasons. They could include allegations that have been made, charges that have been filed, or extended periods of time when no contact was permitted. Even so, the parent with placement of the children must realize that the children probably still love the other parent and want to spend time with him or her.

Fact 16:   A parent should not become a peer and a child should not become a parent or peer.

It is a big mistake when a parent tries to make a child his or her peer or tries to become a child's peer. Children generally have enough peers. They need parents to act like parents, not friends. A parent attempting to be a child's peer loses credibility when the need for discipline arises. Some parents try to compensate for the absence of the spouse by being more of a pal to their children, spending time playing with them, and doing things at the child's level. A parent taking on the role of a child's peer constitutes a change of rules that children don't always understand and that may be interpreted by them as inconsistency on the part of the parent.

Conversely, unless a parent handles the separation well, children may end up trying to parent the parent. They may respond to the unhappy parent by putting their arms around him or her to be consoling, assuring the parent that everything will be all right. Children actually say things like, "Don't worry. I'll always love you" or "You can talk to me about it."

The parent, needing support, may respond inappropriately to this attention by leaning on a child for emotional support, nurturance, and a sounding board for his or her feelings. Children then find themselves taking on the parent's worries and fretting about issues as an adult would. Suddenly, the child *is* a parent and his or her childhood is stolen by being put into that position.

A variation of this occurs when parents turn their children into peers. Parents are accustomed to having each other to discuss ideas and ask for advice. Once the marital partner is no longer present or willing to participate in this exchange, the natural response is for the other partner to look for someone to fill the void. He or she often turns to those closest— the children—and this is another way of overburdening them. Drawing children into the decision-making process permeates all aspects of life, and they find themselves faced with questions about adult issues, such as: Should I date this man or woman? Should I spend this money now? Parents in the uncertain and frightening position of suddenly living alone with children must reassure them that even though the parents appreciate their love and attention, they are still children and must not try to take on adults' problems.

Fact 17: The more consistency parents provide in their children's lives, the healthier the children's adjustment will be.

Changes abound in a child's life during divorce. The more consistency you provide at this time, the more stable your child's life will be. When inconsistency is the order of the day, children will be less likely to adapt well to the divorce process.

Fact 18: The more flexibility a parent has regarding placement and visitation arrangements, the more comfortable children will be.

At the same time that you are trying to be consistent, you must also be flexible and roll with the punches as needed. For example, if Wednesday night is Mom's night with the children, but that night is a father/son activity at school, Mom should let the children go with Dad. Neither parent should say, "You can't have the kids because it's my night" when special activities are concerned.

Fact 19: Divorce is a process, not an event.

Too many people think of divorce only as the date on which the divorce actually occurs. Divorce is a process that begins when you first think about getting divorced but doesn't end when you are through filing, mediating, and litigating. Situations such as children getting married and grandchildren being born will require you to deal with each other for the rest of your lives.

Fact 20: Winning is never more important than the well-being of your children.

If you remember only one fact from this book, remember this: *Winning is never more important than the well-being of your children.* No one wins a painful custody battle. In a custody dispute, it is not unusual for one parent to strongly believe that he or she is superior to the other parent, that the other parent is defective, and placement with the other parent would be detrimental for the children. However, there is a point of diminishing returns. When the pursuit of winning endangers the mental health of your children, you must step back and recognize that your children's well-being is more important than winning.

I am reminded of an attorney named Ted who, in the process of getting divorced, became obsessed with winning. Over the course of five years, he brought his ex-wife back to court three or four times a year, resulting in tens of thousands of dollars in legal fees for her. Almost every decision by the court was appealed, and in several instances Ted took issues to the state Supreme Court. He lost at every turn. He failed to recognize that his children were becoming more and more negatively affected by his behavior, and each child ended up in long-term psychotherapy to deal with Ted's behavior and with the fighting between their parents.

Ted also misperceived his children's anger and thought his ex-wife had purposely turned the children against him, which made him believe that he needed to continue taking the issue to court. He actually alienated them himself by taking their mother to court so many times after the divorce.

Put it on your computer. Put it on your Palm Pilot. Put it on your mirror. Put it on your bulletin board. Put it on your refrigerator. Write it on the palm of your hand:

Remember: Winning is Never More Important Than the Well-Being of Your Children.

WINNING IS NEVER MORE IMPORTANT THAN THE WELL-BEING OF YOUR CHILDREN.

WINNING IS NEVER MORE IMPORTANT THAN THE WELL-BEING OF YOUR CHILDREN.

Chapter

2

Moving Ahead: Telling Children about Your Divorce

With the facts from Chapter 1 in mind, and once you have your priorities in order, you can move ahead with the business of helping your children and yourself deal with the divorce process.

One of the most difficult things you will ever have to tell your children is that you are getting divorced. How you break this news to them makes a big difference in the magnitude of their fears and frustrations from the outset and in the apprehension with which the entire family approaches this major upheaval in their lives.

The ideal way to bring this very private matter between two people into a family forum is to make a formal announcement to your children together, showing a unified front between you and your spouse. There are several things that you need to do and

> **Helpful Hint**
>
> You and your spouse should be together when you break the news to your children.

to keep in mind when telling your children about your divorce. These include:

- Regardless of how much acrimony exists between you, for that brief time it is very important for you to be able to put it aside so that your children see you together and recognize that this is something their parents (in spite of getting divorced) are able to work on together. It's also reassuring for children to see that you aren't coming apart at the seams while making this announcement.

- Give your children hugs and loving touches during this time, and hold their hands to be reassuring. You and your spouse don't need to touch each other, but you should both be affectionate toward your children.

- If you and your spouse cannot sit together to make this announcement without calling each other names or placing blame, each of you should meet separately with the children. In the absence of a visual unified front, however, you should at least decide together what you are going to tell the children so you can say the same thing.

- Whether you make the announcement together or separately, as part of your explanation for why you are divorcing you should avoid blaming each other and you should make sure your children don't think you are blaming them. Don't say, for example, "I'm divorcing your father because he's an alcoholic," or "I'm divorcing your mother because she's having an affair." This is not information children need to know and it will not be particularly useful in helping them understand the situation.

- If children ask why you are getting divorced, you can use carefully selected examples of what has been going on at home in your explanation. You might say: "You may have noticed that Mom and I have been arguing a lot lately and that we aren't sleeping in the same room anymore. That's because we aren't getting along as well as we used to, and we feel it might be better if we live apart instead of living together."

- What you say and how you phrase it depends on the ages of your children. Explanations to younger children should be in simple, brief terms. You may tell them, "You've heard the word *divorce* and you see Mommy and Daddy living in different places. What we are doing is called getting divorced." Older children, who generally know what divorce means, usually want more information about why their parents can't stay together and what will happen next.

   If a child asks, "Are you getting divorced because of Dad's (or Mom's) drinking?" obviously that's the message he or she has received. I always recommend that parents do not lie to their children. You can omit information, but you should not lie. If a child raises a point pertaining to an actual problem, such as a parent's drinking, there is nothing wrong with addressing it. You can say: "Obviously, you've noticed that this is a problem. It is part of our difficulties, but it is not the only problem."

- Another important message to give children is that even though you may have fallen out of love with each other, you will continue loving them. Explain the difference between the kind of love parents have for each other and the love they have for their children. One of the things children can be afraid of, which is not entirely illogical, is that you will stop loving them.

- Assure your children from the outset and over the course of time that they don't have to worry about details of the divorce. Tell younger children: "These are things the grownups are going to take care of, and we're going to try to let you just be children. You continue going to school and playing with your friends. We're going to watch things happen and figure it out in a way that's best for you."

- As best as you can in these early days of the divorce process, tell children what you expect to change and what you expect to remain constant. You might explain, "Dad (Mom) is going to find a new place to live," or "We're going to have to share the car because Mom (Dad) has to drive it to work and we'll only have it on the weekends."

- Avoid incorporating support or maintenance (alimony) issues into discussions with children. This can be very destructive to them. I'll explain more about that later.

Children also need to know that both parents are going to be taken care of during the divorce process. If you are following the most typical scenario, which is that Mom stays in the family house and Dad moves out as soon as is reasonable, the children should be shown where he is going to live so they can see that he has a bed to sleep in, a kitchen to eat in, and a bathroom. Children know how important these basic needs are and need to be sure that these needs are being met for both their parents.

If you have a family in which there are older and younger children, speak with them separately in addition to talking with them as a group, because what you tell a teenager, for example, is going to be different from what you tell a six-year-old.

Even though it is better to tell children about a divorce in a formal setting, they usually learn about divorce in an inappropriate way, either through your anger, communicated by things you say to them, or by being exposed to the hostilities that led to the divorce. For example, when putting your children to bed, you might say: "I don't want you to be surprised, so I'm telling you now that I'm filing for divorce tomorrow." Or you might blurt it out to your spouse in front of your children: "That's it. You've had it. We're getting that divorce." These types of statements have a devastating effect on children.

Most frequently, children overhear their parents shouting at one another late at night or when parents think the children are out of earshot, or they witness arguments that include the word divorce. Divorce adversely impacts all children. The extent to which it affects them, however, is based on their parents' behavior more than anything else. If children are trying to fall asleep and they hear their parents screaming in the living room—"I talked to my attorney today and I'm filing papers and you're going to be out of here before the weekend"—they can be traumatized, and the tone is set for the children to see how negative the divorce process is going to be.

Concrete Thinkers in an Abstract Situation

Regardless of how they have heard the news, once children understand that you are getting divorced, they will soon respond in a number of different ways, depending on their age. Let's divide children into three groups: early childhood (birth to age 6), middle childhood (6 to 12), and adolescents and older children (13 to 18).

Early Childhood (Birth to Six)

Children who are four years old or younger probably don't need to hear more than three or four simple sentences from you: "Your daddy and I are going to get divorced. This means we are going to live in different places. You will still spend time with each of us. We love you very much." They can't handle more than that. If they have questions, answer them as simply as possible.

Remember that actions speak louder than words, and all children, even very young ones, are going to react to what is happening in their environment. Your ability to handle your divorce in a relatively civil manner sends the message that life is going to be okay and not too much different from what they are accustomed to.

Hostility between you and your spouse causes instability in children in the early childhood group, and their immediate reaction will be crying and in many cases regressive behavior, such as bed-wetting, thumb-sucking, wanting to play with baby toys they haven't played with in a while, or not wanting to sleep without an overhead light. If the acrimony between you and your spouse continues, the disruptive behavior in young children will escalate.

Children under six often experience feelings of guilt, thinking the divorce is their fault. They may say or believe things such as, "If I had been a better child, my parents would not be getting divorced."

Middle Childhood: Depression Becomes Anger with Age (Six to Twelve)

To fully grasp reactions of the middle childhood group, you must understand that children don't start developing the capacity for abstract thinking until they are about 11 years old. This capacity is fully developed by about age 15. Issues such as love, falling out of love, and divorce have quite a few abstract aspects, which are lost on younger children.

The best example I can give of concrete versus abstract thinking is how an eight-year-old girl with whom I worked in therapy handled the concept of death. Coincidental to the therapy, the child's grandmother died. I asked how she felt about her grandmother's death and she said she was sad. I asked why she was sad and she replied: "Because now there won't be anybody to cut my hot dogs for me." She took the abstract concept of death and converted it into something concrete that she could understand.

Children in the younger end of the middle childhood group are likely to respond to news of a divorce with a depressive kind of behavior, becoming sullen, perhaps crying, and having reduced appetites. They may answer you in an indifferent, almost passive manner with "I don't care," and when asked what's bothering them, "nothing" may be a common reply.

They often react to divorce with feelings of sadness. What they had relied on as the family structure has collapsed, threatening their security. Emotional immaturity prevents them from protecting themselves against such losses, and because they have not yet developed the capacity for abstract thinking, they will not be able to process problems as they arise. This leads to greater sadness.

Emotional immaturity also means you cannot reassure these children that the loss of one parent does not automatically mean the loss of the other parent. Worrying about losing both parents through divorce is a source of genuine sadness and melancholy in children in this age group. I know of a nine-year-old girl named Vicki who had silently lived with this fear until it surfaced at a party. Vicki was dropped off at her friend's birthday party by her father, who promised to return at a certain time to take her home. As the party came to an end, parents picked up their children until Vicki was the only child left. Fearing that her father was not going to return, Vicki initially cried quietly, but as her fears mounted, she sobbed until she became hysterical. Her father was only 15 minutes late, but when he arrived, she blurted out: "I thought you had gone away and left me, just like Mommy left us."

Even if you try to explain these issues in an abstract way to children under 11 years of age, they will understand only what you say in a concrete way.

Six-, seven-, and eight-year-olds tend to become very depressed about divorce because so many things change. They are saddened by Dad's car not being in the garage anymore, or by the basketball in the corner because he isn't there to play. They often pine for their fathers, because in most divorce cases the father leaves the household.

Some children in the middle childhood group feel hatred toward their parents, which they verbalize. They also experience almost uncontrollable anger and find concrete ways to apply that anger to the divorce situation. For example, a child who is intensely angry over his parents' divorce may say he is angry because his father, who has moved out and taken a weekend job to cover his additional expenses, can no longer take him to baseball practice on Saturdays and games on Sundays. He doesn't understand the subtleties of supporting two households and paying attorneys' fees and other costs associated with divorce. By the time the child is 15 years old, however, the anger dissipates because he understands the abstract elements of what has been going on.

As children get to be 9, 10, 11, and 12 years old, and sadness turns to anger, which can be manifested as rage and hate, they are apt to say spiteful, denegrating, hateful things to their parents and others. I worked with a 9-year-old boy and his brother and sister because a recommendation had been made to change their placement from their mother to their father. I started explaining to the children what was going to happen and why, and the 9 year old looked at me with absolute fire in his eyes and said: "I hope you burn in hell for what you have done to my family." This is the kind of hurtful thing children his age will say, and because of the level at which he was dealing with things, he meant it.

A parent can be overwhelmingly devastated to hear such a comment from his or her child. Parents take these statements very personally because they don't understand the dynamics of what is happening, and they feel hurt, guilty, and often depressed because they believe their children really feel this way.

It is vitally important to help a child deal with and diffuse these angry feelings. If these feelings are not resolved, the child may have serious relationship problems as an adult. A parent may be tempted to take advantage of a child's angry feelings toward the other parent, creating an alliance that may make the parent feel triumphant. This, however, is divisive and prevents a child from resolving his or her anger and moving on. Unfortunately, when a parent uses this kind of anger to form an alliance with a child, the situation often backfires during adolescence and may culminate in even greater anger against the divisive parent.

Loyalty issues frequently develop during this period. Children come to rely most on the parent who remains at home, seeing him or her as the key provider upon whom they are dependent for all basic needs. Even if that parent is not the principal financial provider, because he or she is in the homestead, the child's perception is that primary allegiance belongs with that parent.

If that parent is angry with the other, a child tends to take sides and generally feels it is safer to identify with the parent who provides all these benefits. A child will almost always manifest this loyalty without explaining it in terms of personal security, something that he or she may not even recognize as the motivation. Instead, it generally appears like this:

Bobby comes home from a visit with his father saying, "I don't want to visit Dad anymore." His mother, Marjorie, presumes her son has recognized what a wretch his father is, and she tells him: "I can understand why you don't want to visit with him. If you don't want to go anymore, you don't have to." Marjorie now feels that she has an ally in her son and will continue to bad-mouth his father and not support or encourage visitation.

Regardless of how she feels about her ex-husband, Marjorie should put Bobby's needs to have a positive, loving relationship with both parents before her own needs to vent and form alliances. The scenario should have gone like this:

Bobby comes home from visiting his father and says he doesn't want to go there anymore. If this is the first time he has said this, Marjorie should question his reasons. Has his father mistreated him, offended him, or done something else to alienate him?

If the answers to those questions are yes, there may be a legitimate reason to stop supporting or even allowing visitation. However, if Bobby is vague and says something like, "It's not fun being with him," Marjorie should say, "I can understand that you might have more fun here. However, he is your father, he loves you, and wants to spend time with you. The way he and I feel about each other should have nothing to do with your relationship with your father."

She should also add, "If things aren't going as well as you would like when you visit your father, maybe we should all sit down and discuss it so we can make things better." This position is difficult to take if you are angry with your spouse, in the throes of divorce, and perhaps even fighting for custody. However, it is the best one to take for the child's benefit, and you may even quell some of your own anger by having to focus on being so reasonable and rational.

Marjorie's first response illustrates the type of highly destructive reaction that will interfere with a child's ability to establish appropriate relationships in adolescence and early adulthood. The second type of response, however, will lead to more positive outcomes and better adjustment.

Straddling Two Worlds: The Struggle for Teenage Independence (Twelve to Eighteen)

It is easy to forget in the turmoil of divorce that children are dealing not only with the emotional upheaval and problems associated with their parents' lives, but with changes they undergo as they mature. This is perhaps best illustrated in teenagers.

When children reach their teenage years they need to start separating from their parents. Look at typical adolescent development and you will see that as time goes on teenagers want to spend less and less time with their parents and more and more time with their friends. They begin to straddle the worlds of childhood and adulthood, dealing with a host of emotional and physical changes, as well as challenges presented by a higher level of education.

Parents too often misunderstand what is happening through normal development, and they misinterpret their teenagers' desire to separate from the family as having to do with the divorce.

If a divorce is taking place, teenagers generally want to be even more separate from their families. I recall one situation involving two girls, ages 16 and 18. When the divorce started, they were 14 and 16 years old and the older child was knee-deep in the fight. By the time the divorce finally took place, she was almost 18 and she basically blew it off, saying: "I don't care what you people do. I'm going to college and I don't want to have anything to do with this anymore. I've got my own life."

A different kind of anger develops in teenagers than in the young and middle childhood groups. To understand it, think of the Greek term *sophomore,* which means wise fool. We often accuse high school and early college students of having sophomoric attitudes and a sophomoric way of thinking. A high school sophomore is typically 15 going on 16 years old and has just developed the ability to think in the abstract. These teenagers generally figure they have solved the problems of the world and no one can tell them anything they don't know.

At this age, they use their abilities to reflect back on what happened when they were 9 and 10 years old. Assume that during that period of time, much of the anger they had for their parents was based on one parent saying negative things about the other, doing negative things, subverting the visitation schedule, alienating a child from the other parent. Now the child is a teenager and reasons, "I see what Mom (Dad) was doing all that time and it wasn't nice." Now the teenager becomes angry with one or both parents.

Teenagers generally have no compunctions about saying to a parent, "You ruined my childhood with my father (mother) by doing these things and I don't want to have anything to do with you because of that." Their anger takes on a different form and sometimes adds to a teenager's not wanting to spend time with one or the other parent.

Adolescents are also subject to a kind of pseudomaturity, caused when teenagers become parentified. As I described earlier, this happens when one parent turns a teenager into a parent (this also occurs in intact families) through the nature of responsibilities and demands made on the child. This pseudomaturity robs childhoods, adds to anxiety and depression, and can also increase the level of anger a teenager feels toward his or her parents.

There is a question of how much weight to give teenagers' wishes because they are transitioning from leaving behind their childhood immaturity and entering their early adult maturity. As has been true in the past, the current thinking is that we do not allow teenagers to make decisions for their lives, just as we do not allow them to decide to go to school or not, take their medication or not, or fulfill other responsibilities. However, current thinking also supports the notion that we are trying to teach older adolescents to become independent thinkers. Not to give some weight to their wishes and desires regarding divorce-related issues flies in the face of teaching them to become independent thinkers. Therefore, if the reasons that adolescents are giving to support their positions sound mature and rational, the positions should be given more weight than if they sound immature, child-like, and have little substance.

Despite their roller-coaster ride to maturity, teenage children have an easier time with divorce than do younger children because they have already begun to become independent. However, when telling teenagers about your divorce, remember that trust is important to them and you must be totally honest about why the marriage has not worked out.

If the divorce is the result of extramarital affairs, alcoholism, mental illness, or abuse, teenagers may be told—but spare them the gruesome details. If they suspect any of these issues were problems, they will be relieved to know their perceptions were accurate.

Discussions with teenage children about relationships are very important at this time. When teenagers emerge from divorce feeling that personal relationships are not worth the effort, their own meaningful relationships may be disrupted in the future.

Helpful Hint

You must help teenagers realize that problems in the marriage were related to the relationship between two specific people, and that not all relationships need to be that way.

This concept is sometimes difficult for young people to grasp because children judge all behavior and what is considered acceptable against what happens in their own homes. The way couples communicate or don't, the way they speak to each other, and the manner in which they treat their children are learned at home.

One of the best ways to convey to teenagers that all relationships are not supposed to be disappointing and tumultuous is by saying, "What you see happening at home is not the way life is supposed to be between two people who love and respect each other. They are not supposed to lie to each other, hit each other, or cheat on each other." You can add, "Learn what not to do in a relationship by watching what your father (mother) and I are going through. Don't become bitter or jaded."

Another approach to help reduce the impact of negative parental behavior associated with divorce is by asking your teenager to envision how the relationship between his or her parents should be. You can start by saying: "You know the things your father (mother) and I are doing wrong. It's not difficult to see how they affect both of us and you." Then use specific examples to start an exchange between you and your teenager. "Your father and I spend a lot of time screaming at each other. How do you think couples should communicate?"

This type of communication between you and your teenagers demands that you calm down and focus. If you also have younger children, you may find them joining in at their own level, asking questions and looking to you to help them figure it out. You may actually need some counseling from an objective observer, such as a therapist, to be able to deal with your children on this level, especially if you are in the midst of a super-charged divorce and custody case.

When Your Child Is No Longer a Child

I have already mentioned how divorce can wipe out college plans. However, older children confront more than questions about who will pay for higher education once their parents are divorced. To begin with, people erroneously believe that because college-age children are considered adults, divorce will not seriously impact them. This is not true.

The 20s are an age when children completely separate from their parents and start displaying distinctive characteristics that make them individuals. College-age students are only beginning to identify these traits, and although their bodies and minds are fully developed, they still have not developed a true sense of who they are apart from their families.

While college-age children search for their own identities, they are employing some of that sophomoric thinking I talked about earlier. Consequently, they are more likely to blame one parent or the other for the failure of the marriage instead of recognizing that two people were involved in the process. They also tend to choose sides, since they are having a difficult time establishing a sense of independence from both parents.

Tolerance and patience are just as crucial for dealing with children in this age group as in any other. Here are some guidelines:

- Both parents should discourage college-age children from choosing sides. Remind them that they are no longer little children and that they should be able to look at the entire picture objectively.

- Continue to avoid dirty details of where the marriage went wrong and why the divorce was unpleasant. Talk in general about the reasons for the failed relationship and the roles both of you played in it.

- It is very important, once again, for both parents to be saying the same thing. If you are blaming each other, your child will end up acting as judge and jury, weighing the evidence and deciding who was right and who was wrong. Don't give your child that kind of power over your life, and don't inflict that kind of burden on him or her.

- When dealing with adult children, you can talk more about your personal emotional turmoil and how you felt about ending a marriage, thereby making yourself more of a real person and less of a parent who wounded his or her children and destroyed the family by getting divorced.

- If something as identifiable as alcoholism, adultery, abandonment, or abuse led to the divorce, say so, but don't do it as a way of placing blame. Don't say: "your father was nothing but a drunk who couldn't support the family. He left me no choice but to throw him out." Do say: "Your father was an alcoholic who refused to recognize his disease and get help. I did my best to live with him, but I finally realized that I could not help him and it was better for all of us if he stopped living with us and he and I divorced."

- Always tell the truth to adult children, but be concise and kind in your delivery. Hammering an adult child with the faults of the other parent serves no good purpose and if it affects the way he or she feels or thinks about that parent, the child may eventually resent you, too, for having triggered those negative feelings.

Academic Performance

Much research has been done about how divorce affects children's performance in school. It is not unusual for children to have poor achievement test scores immediately following the divorce. However, as the years go by, the divorce is more likely to affect boys' grades than girls' grades. It is not unusual for the poor academic performance in children of divorce to last for two to three years. The younger the children are, the more the divorce will negatively affect their performance in school. The research has also found that the less time the mother spends at work and the more time the child spends with the nonplacement parent the better the child will perform academically. As children move to the middle school years, significant drops in grade point average occur following divorce.

Boys and Girls React Differently

Just as different age groups exhibit different reactions to divorce, likewise there are differences between the way boys and girls react to the dissolution of their parents' marriage. Initially, boys are more negatively affected by divorce than are girls, and sometimes for longer periods of time. They act out more in school, have more trouble with relationships, and display longer lasting, sometimes more dramatic, poor school performance.

Some traditional stereotypes creep into the way boys and girls see themselves in a divorce situation. These influences may be acquired through parental behavior, entertainment, reading materials, school, and friends and their families. In families where two parents are present, boys tend to feel greater responsibility for the stability of the household and family than do girls. Girls tend to be more nurturing, often assuming caretaker/giver roles within the family.

During a divorce, boys tend to want to assume responsibility for the family in Dad's absence, even to the point where they may get part-time jobs to help support the family. Girls tend to see themselves as the emotional glue, and during a divorce they bury or deny their own feelings while being more concerned about the family's moral and ethical fiber and about other people's feelings. Girls sometimes appear to be taking their parents' divorces better than boys, but looks can be deceiving.

Later on, girls' relationships seem to suffer more from the effects of their parents' divorces than do boys' relationships. Many women with divorced parents tend to marry and divorce early; they may become promiscuous and may have difficulty trusting their partners, heterosexual or homosexual. Girls of divorced parents also tend to have more problems with heterosexual relationships, with instability and abuse being among the major difficulties.

Here again, speaking with your children, getting them to examine and verbalize their feelings, and being as positive as possible about your love for them and their continued relationship with both parents are very effective methods in helping children deal with divorce.

A psychiatrist I collaborated with in the past once said to me that all children of divorce should be involved in therapy. As a young practitioner I cynically thought that this was more for the desire of building a practice than meeting children's needs. However, as the years have gone by I have understood the wisdom in this statement. Because of the negative effects of the acrimony, on children's academic performance, and on their interpersonal relationship skills, there should at least be the opportunity to check out how much, if any, therapeutic intervention is necessary. Schools and community agencies offer support groups for children of divorce, and mental health professionals are readily available for these types of consultations.

Adjustments Abound

The adjustment period to divorce lasts 6 to 12 months after the divorce is final, under the best circumstances. When anger between parents continues, adjustment lasts forever or never occurs. It is critical for parents and children to deal with such concerns as:

- Becoming accustomed to new relationships.
- Becoming familiar with placement schedules.
- Moving to a new neighborhood.
- Going to a new school or job.

Most children are able to make the necessary adjustments to cope with changes precipitated by divorce. Societal issues vary from situation to situation, depending on the reason for the divorce, the home environment prior to it, how lengthy the process is, and, as I've said, a child's age.

To help children adjust, you must be aware of the various areas of their lives that are affected by divorce. Be alert to changes in their:

- Level of play. The child of divorce may not want to play, choosing instead to mope around the house or hang around the parent who is present. They may not want to socialize with friends, opting instead to spend more time playing "alone" games. They may avoid games requiring a fair amount of attention and interaction because they are worried about their home life and cannot properly focus.

- Interaction with friends. They may become hostile, even picking fights with children with whom they had been friendly. They may lose interest in established friendships, or hang out on the periphery of a group of friends, feeling and playing the role of outsider or outcast. They may gravitate toward a new, less desirable set of friends, perhaps children from divorced households or children who are rougher and appear more hardened toward life.

- Physical health. They may become more susceptible to illness. Children who are unhappy and run down and not eating or sleeping properly because of the situation at home tend to be ill more often with colds, headaches, and more serious illnesses such as depression.

- School performance. This is another barometer of how your children are being impacted by divorce. All children's school-work generally suffers immediately after separation or divorce and during custody battles. Declines in grades and lack of interest at school can continue for two to three years and even longer after a divorce is final.

- Outside activities. Children may no longer want to participate in dance classes or the soccer league. They may drop out of extracurricular activities in school such as clubs, band, athletics, and community volunteering.

Look for these signs that the upheaval at home is spilling over into school, and don't wait to act:

- Your child starts coming home without books, homework, or both, and makes lame excuses. Call his or her teacher and ask about homework and your child's performance in general. Explain your concern, and if you have not already told the school about your divorce, you may do so. However, spare teachers and school officials unpleasant details unless they absolutely need to know something specific.

- Work that is generally neat and complete becomes sloppy and incomplete. Again, phone or visit the school.

- Study time is spent daydreaming, there is resistance to studying that did not exist before the divorce, or your child is spending as much time studying as in the past but cannot remember anything. These are signs of a preoccupied mind, and your child may need therapy or to be in a support group. Some schools have support groups for children of divorced parents.

Mourning the End of a Marriage

In addition to all these reactions, divorce presents a host of emotional changes that occur again and again in the form of a grief cycle, affecting children and adults. Most couples generally feel a tremendous sense of loss when their marriage ends, even if both spouses wanted to divorce. When one parent did not want a divorce, however, he or she mourns the end of that marriage, experiencing the same grief that occurs after the death of a loved one.

The grief cycle encompasses:

• Denial of what is happening.

• Sadness or depression, at times bordering on being debilitating because of its potential to be overwhelming.

• Anger over the loss, sometimes with the person who has moved out, and sometimes with oneself for having allowed the loss to take place or for being unable to have seen it coming.

• Resignation and a resolution to go on despite the loss.

A person in a divorce situation is continually reminded of the lost relationship because the other parent is still alive and serves as a reminder of what is gone. As a parent in the throes of divorce, you must deal with all of this while being there for your children, trying to understand their feelings, and helping them cope with their own grief.

Helpful Hint

The grief children experience in divorce is different from what their parents undergo.

Even though they may not fully understand the abstract concept of death, children realize that when a loved one dies, he or she is not coming back to see them, hassle them, or do things with them. However, most children generally expect to see both parents after a divorce, so they do not have the sense of finality associated with death.

Children grieve for the parent who moves out and the reduced interaction with him or her. They are also upset over less interaction with the parent that stays, if he or she is home less because of working extra hours or extra jobs, and over the violation of the family unit and consequent loss of activities as a family. Because of these feelings, a child who cannot access you immediately when he or she needs or wants you perceives this inaccessibility as another loss and engages in a mini-grieving process.

Allow your child to call the other parent or volunteer to drive him or her to see that parent. Don't be negative by saying, "It's too late (or too early) to call" or "You already called your dad (mom) today, so you can't call again" or "You know how much I hate it when you call him (her)." If you respond in an unreasonable fashion, a child may grow sadder and more depressed.

The grief cycle occurs repeatedly for parents and children, coming into play anytime a situation arises in which the parent wishes he or she were still married. For example, if Mom goes to school for open house and the teacher talks about a project that fathers can work on with their children and there's no father around, Mom's grief cycle is likely to resume. She becomes sad and angry, but then reaches a resolution. In this case, her resolution may be to do the project herself with her child, or to ask her ex-spouse or a male relative to do it.

Every milestone that a child reaches where it would be important for the missing parent to be present or participating may trigger grief. This situation is particularly true with adolescents because, whether their families are intact or broken, they usually gravitate toward the same-gender parent. Boys are turning into men and girls are becoming women and they are looking for someone to emulate and turn to for advice and approval.

In the divorcing family, this becomes more problematic for a teenager living with a parent of the opposite gender. The child must make do with whatever that parent has to offer, which may not be enough to fill his or her needs. Under these circumstances, a child may ask to live with the same-gender parent. This doesn't stem from hatred or dissatisfaction, but from a basic need to live with someone with whom he or she has more in common. It is very difficult to let a child go under such circumstances and equally challenging not to take it personally, but it must be done if the other parent is willing and capable of properly caring for the child. If the move is not possible, your teenager is apt to experience more grief.

Certain behavioral reactions to grief may be anticipated in children based on their ages. Very young children generally experience more confusion than actual grief when one parent is suddenly missing. Children between the ages of 6 and 8 are apt to do a lot of crying and become depressed. Children between the ages of 9 and 12 often experience agitated depression, which looks more like anger than depression and may be mistaken for acting out angry behavior.

The Challenge of Role Reversal

All the while that children and parents are dealing with waves of grief, they must also meet other challenges to their emotional stability, including a reversal of roles in parents. In scenarios, for example, where the father moves out and the mother takes on all responsibility for the home, children may see her performing tasks that were previously carried out by their father, such as shoveling snow or making household repairs. When children visit their father, they may see him doing things he had not done when the family was together, such as laundry, ironing, cooking, or arranging a schedule for his children.

In one sense, a reversal of roles is not bad, because I believe adults should be viewed equally and children should see their parents sharing responsibilities. Role reversal becomes a problem for adults and children, however, when suddenly one parent is absent and the task of keeping the home and family organized and operating as close to normal as possible (normal is the operative word) becomes much more difficult. With a change in roles comes a change in the frustration level of the parents, which affects the children. As I have said, if you don't have a happy parent, you don't have happy children. Children end up modeling the sadness, depression, or inappropriate expressions of anger that they see in their parents.

Not Enough Hours in the Day, Not Enough Friends in the World

Another major stressor for adults and children that occurs after one parent moves out—a stressor that is directly related to role reversal—is time or the lack of it. All players in the family find themselves dealing with the feeling that their world has been turned upside down, and rules that were in place in the household are gone. They realize that things they had done together or worked on as a team are now left to one person.

Intact families in which responsibilities fall mostly to one parent because the other is not around to help as much as would be desirable do not experience as much change when divorce occurs as do families in which parents had worked more cooperatively. When change is sudden and the time stressor strikes, the parent with all the responsibility feels overwhelmed: He or she has to get up at 5 A.M., is not finished until 1 A.M., has no time to sleep or read or look at a videotape, and then has to start all over again. This parent needs recreation but generally has no time for it, not even enough money to go bowling or to a movie, because the children require even more attention than they did before the divorce.

The more frustrated and fatigued you become, the more aggressive you are likely to be. Physically inappropriate behavior toward children tends to increase at these times and sometimes escalates to child abuse. Children tend to get hit more by divorced parents than by nondivorced parents.

Another major stressor is social relationships. Although you may need a night out, even if you have the disposable income you may not be inclined to go because you may have to recreate alone. Most friends prior to a divorce choose sides with one parent or the other. Both spouses in a divorcing couple will rarely be able to remain friends with the same people. It is almost as if the parents are fighting for custody of their friends as well as of their children. A woman, for example, may find herself alienated from a neighborhood friend whose husband has chosen her exspouse's side in the divorce. Or, she may find herself isolated from married friends because she is suddenly perceived as being lonely, emotionally needy, and available. Suddenly, people she thought she would be able to rely on for social support are gone, and she experiences another loss.

Be sure you have an appropriate support network during this time, even if it is composed only of relatives and/or friends at work. Be on the alert, however, for deserters from the ranks of your relatives, particularly grandparents and in-laws, which is another big social stressor and yet another loss. In spite of what may have gone on in the home, grandparents tend to ally themselves with their natural child against a son-in-law or daughter-in-law.

The divorce process is really a series of losses—personal, social, or financial—and related grief.

One Magical Wish

Through all this confusion, sadness, and insecurity, children often carry with them, even into adulthood, the wish that their parents will magically be reunited. One of the questions I ask children during custody evaluations is: "If you had three wishes, what would they be?" Most of them wish their parents would get back together. This wish does not die when parents remarry. It often continues well beyond the time of the divorce and even after re-marriage, and stems from children's longing for life to return to the simpler way it was prior to the divorce.

I don't think the shock of divorce ever wears off children, which is one reason many of them cling to this dream long after it is clear to others that such an outcome is impossible. Because of this wish, children, including adult children, may unknowingly or knowingly interfere with parents who are trying to establish new relationships. Some children feel so strongly about this and act out such negative behavior against a parent's new partner that people actually forego remarriage.

It takes an extraordinary amount of tact and courage to deal with this situation. You do not want to alienate your children or create a hostile, intolerable environment that will end in another divorce, but at the same time you don't want to deny yourself a new, positive relationship and marriage. In some cases, children never come around, but a percentage of them accept, if not ultimately embrace, stepparents if they are provided with a happy, peaceful, and fulfilling environment. (I'll talk more about this later.)

It isn't easy to try to create new beginnings when your children must be your primary concern. Nothing about divorce is easy. Divorce when children are concerned can be hell.

Chapter 3

Custody Options: The Best Interest of the Child

Coming to terms with certain facts about divorce and its impact on you and your children is crucial if you are going to move through the custody process with any degree of levelheadedness and appropriate thinking.

By the time you find yourself dealing with custody issues, you will have addressed the initial questions about what life is apt to bring for you and your children in the immediate future and the things that are probably going to unfold in your home in the short term. Once your life stabilizes a bit (provided you are not dealing with radical concerns such as family violence, physical or sexual abuse, or alcohol or drug use), you will be confronted with the issue of where your children are going to live and who is going to be responsible for what happens in their daily lives, including such basic tasks as buying their clothes, taking them to the doctor, and attending school conferences.

More importantly, you will have to decide if they are going to live with one parent all the time and visit the other parent some of the time or if you are going to divide their time evenly between both of you. Initially, most parents take an emotional stand, wanting their children with them all the time. They might acknowledge that their ex-spouse has legal rights, but they still want the children to themselves. They also confuse custody and placement.

Many parents at this point in the divorce and custody process don't realize the difference between custody and placement. Custody generally refers to who has decision-making power over the children. It identifies who has legal rights, and not necessarily where the children will be living. Placement refers to the amount of time children will spend with each parent—or with whom they will live.

When deciding placement schedules, you must also realize that there are financial considerations. A primary placement parent generally will receive support from the other parent, and placement of the children may also determine who keeps the family homestead. These are decisions that can be made between parents, with the help of attorneys, through mediation, or, ultimately, by the court.

The process was more restrictive in the past. It was common practice in the 1800s for the father to be given custody of the children. Children were considered property and women were not allowed to own property. During the Industrial Revolution, people began recognizing the important nurturing bonds that develop between mothers and children, and the pendulum swung in the opposite direction. It was then widely believed that fathers did not have the capacity to be sensitive, or to nurture and care for children. The "tender years doctrine" was born and, for a number of years, mothers generally received placement of their children.

In the late 1960s and early 1970s, a new concept, known as "best interest," evolved, allowing children to be placed with the parent who represented their best interests. This meant that mothers and fathers theoretically were playing on a level field, with each having an equal chance of receiving placement of their children.

The Uniform Marriage and Divorce Act identified many factors that should be addressed when considering the best interests of children. Today, children are placed with their mothers in most cases after divorce and in more than half of the cases when there is a custody dispute. One reason for this is that fewer mothers than fathers work full-time, so mothers are usually more available to care for their children than are fathers. This is not to suggest that one gender is superior or inferior to the other regarding child-rearing skills.

Joint versus Sole Custody

You must decide if you want to ask the court for joint or sole custody of your children and which of you will have primary placement. Custody refers to who has decision making rights, while placement refers to how much time the child(ren) will spend with each parent. A number of factors should be kept in mind when considering this decision.

In joint custody situations, parents have joint legal rights. To make joint custody work, you and your spouse must be able to communicate well enough with one another to make joint decisions about such things as your children's education, nonemergency medical treatment, religious upbringing, marriage before the legal age, and early enlistment in the armed forces. Bear in mind as you work out this issue that visitation schedules, child support, and the overall mental health of all concerned are normally better in joint custody situations.

Helpful Hint

Joint custody is generally the better route to take because it reduces acrimony, increases contact with the children, and reduces future court conflicts.

However, if a divorce has been so messy that parents cannot work together, sole custody may be the better route. Under sole custody arrangements, major life decisions do not have to be cleared with the former spouse, although the parent who is assigned sole custody needs to be mindful of the child's need to have a relationship with the other parent. One of the problems that arises with sole custody is that it suggests ownership to the parent who has custody. When a custodial parent acts as if he or she owns the children, the other parent may feel excluded and stop visiting them or even stop making child support payments.

Because of this sense of ownership and the isolation of the other parent, courts and psychologists who evaluate children in divorce situations recommend joint custody most of the time. The thinking is that under such arrangements, parents are presumably more satisfied and children benefit from having regular input from both parents in decisions that affect their lives. For example, if children are going to change from parochial to public school, or if a child needs corrective surgery, parents should make these decisions together. As new situations arise in children's lives, it is usually better if both parents are involved in the decision making process. This involvement does not always happen in joint custody situations, but it is the goal.

A key issue to consider when deciding whether to pursue sole custody is that the custodial parent will be required to take on full responsibility for the children—there is no vacation from decision making, no partner, even if it is a former spouse, to share the burden. This task is an enormous one to shoulder alone, which is why joint custody is an attractive alternative for many parents.

Although parents usually have a choice about whether to seek joint or sole custody, some situations indicate the need for sole custody. You should definitely pursue sole custody if your current or former spouse:

- Is chronically mentally ill.
- Is an active alcoholic.
- Has a history of domestic violence or abuse.
- Has a history of physical abuse.
- Has a history of sexual abuse.
- Continually undermines the children's relationship with the other parent.
- Continually violates court orders.
- Refuses to communicate effectively with the other parent.
- Actively obstructs placement.
- Uses poor judgment in child care.
- Engages in behaviors dangerous to the children.

Chronic Mental Illness Leads to a Topsy-Turvy World

> **Helpful Hint**
>
> Being with a parent who is suffering from untreated or uncontrollable chronic mental illness wreaks havoc on children because it keeps them off balance, endangers their physical and mental well-being, and actually terrorizes them.

One case I've had involving mental illness was like a double-edged sword. The mother, a teacher whom I'll call Ellen, came from a dysfunctional family from which she was anxious to flee. She married a businessman, Robert, who she hoped would be her knight in shining armor and rescuer. The fantasy held up for about five years and they had four daughters. Robert became a senior executive and spent a lot of time traveling, so most of the responsibilities at home fell to Ellen.

Managing her home and children became a dreadful burden for her. As the magic began to fade from her marriage, Ellen started coming apart at the seams. She became unable to deal with Robert's absence and began losing her ability to handle even typical daily stress. Normal psychological defenses, such as crying and sleep, failed her, and Ellen developed a number of symptoms to distance herself from the situation at home, including abnormal anger with her husband and losing touch with reality. Ellen had to be admitted to a hospital, where she was given medication and told to go into therapy.

Robert eventually filed for divorce, and during the process it was discovered that he had a substance abuse problem. The children, who ranged in age from 6 to 13, found themselves dealing with the first two situations on the list of cautions mentioned earlier—Mom with the first and Dad with the second. The court said that because of Robert's substance abuse problems, Ellen should have the children. But Robert went into treatment under court supervision that included random urine screens, and he started recovering.

Ellen, because of her anger with Robert, would not let his substance abuse problems fade into the background. Even after their divorce, she continued telling everyone she knew about his drug abuse, including teachers at the school attended by their daughter Sandy, putting that child in an embarrassing and awkward position. Ellen, often still out of touch with reality, frequently called another daughter, Kelly, by Robert's girlfriend's name, ranting: "You're not Kelly, you're Laurie, and all you want is to get me out of the picture." When Kelly would ask her mother why she called her Laurie, Ellen would deny having done so, clearly unaware of her actions.

When the children were brought to me for counseling, they cried because they didn't understand what their mother was doing. They had no stability at home because from one minute to the next they couldn't predict if their mother was going to call them names, throw things at them, scream at them, or not recognize them. At one point, Ellen flew to Arizona, never telling Robert about the trip, and the children came home from school to an empty house. Mindy, the youngest of the girls, stood on the front stoop crying uncontrollably because she didn't know where her mother was and thought no one was home because the house was on fire.

As a result of what they were being subjected to by their mother, the children started losing touch with reality, behaving irrationally, and regressing, doing things too young for their years. Mindy, for example, would sit in my office chewing tissues, then sticking the wet paper on her body or spitting it on the floor. Jane, another daughter, would sit in my office staring at her hands as she made strange movements with them. Sandy would sit with tears streaming down her face, saying: "You've got to do something about this. When can I get out of there?"

Robert, who was deeply concerned about what was happening, won from the court an emergency transfer placement and moved his daughters to his home. The morning after the transfer took place, an angry Ellen telephoned the children, yelling at them, calling them names, and blaming the entire situation on them. "I don't know what you said," Ellen shouted into the phone, "but whatever you told everyone, you made this happen. It's all your fault." The children were devastated by what she said, and they became confused and anxious because they didn't understand what they had done wrong.

A short time after their transfer, however, the girls seemed very happy, and when they came to my office they gave me a spontaneous concert, singing songs they had been taught by their father and his wife. It's difficult to describe the joy I felt watching them as they sang. They were relaxed, teasing and poking fun at each other and chasing each other around the room. This was in complete contrast to how they acted around their mother, when they were always on their guard, waiting and wondering what was going to happen next.

Ellen had been granted supervised visitation, but after her disruptive phone calls, she dropped out of contact with the children. As this case illustrates, from a custody evaluation standpoint, children should be kept away from chronically mentally ill parents.

Active Alcoholism or Other Drug Abuse and Children Don't Mix

The problems experienced with alcoholics are in many ways similiar to what happens with parents who are chronically mentally ill. One of the major concerns is the lack of predictability, which leaves children off balance and always cautious and fearful, just as in Ellen and Robert's case. They wonder: "Is Dad (Mom) going to be drunk tonight, and if he (she) is drunk, is it going to be a happy drunk, a sad drunk, or a mad drunk?"

Alcoholics, like mentally ill persons such as Ellen, slip in and out of psychotic-like episodes and don't remember what they did when they were drunk. Many children who have been abused say their fathers, mothers, or both parents were abusive only when drunk. This is highly credible because alcohol reduces a person's ability to control his or her impulses.

Another problem for alcoholics is *denial*. They put so much energy into denying the existence of a problem that they can't recognize its seriousness. Alcoholics' denial systems are so strong that they don't realize when they are losing their marriages, children, or jobs. If they can't recognize something so involved and important, how are they going to tend to the day-to-day needs of their children? A recent national survey of more than 200 psychologists reports that the number one reason for granting sole custody to a parent was that the other parent was an active alcoholic.

Much research has been done in recent years about the effects of mental disorders on children of divorce. About a third of the children were resilient and did not have problems. However, approximately half of the adolescents had significant problems, especially when the mother was a substance abuser who had been hospitalized because of the mental disorders. In high stress families, children tended to have both psychiatric diagnoses and behavioral problems. It is suggested that when mentally ill parents are primary caregivers or significant secondary caregivers, community resources should be used as much as possible, including daycare and respite care and support groups.

The most acute problem with alcohol and other drugs is that they work, temporarily, to mask the emotional pain associated with the trauma of divorce. Children of active substance abusers tend to be more immature and impulsive, have lower IQ's, more school absences, and exhibit greater anxiety, depression, and behavioral problems. Children of divorce are more likely to abuse substances than children from intact families. Children of substance abusers are also more likely to be abused or neglected by the substance abusing parent.

Physical or Sexual Abuse: Confounding Dilemmas

The rule is the same for physical or sexual abuse: If you do this to your children, you forfeit the right to be involved in decisions that affect their lives. This is clearly for the protection of the children because people who have sexually abused youngsters may stop and not do it for years and then start all over again, and that's very scary. The notion that we no longer have to worry about an abuser who has been in therapy for a few years is not necessarily valid.

Sexual abuse is another confounding dilemma for children. If a child has been sexually abused by a parent, that doesn't mean the parent doesn't love the child and the child doesn't love the parent. It also doesn't mean that the parent hasn't taken the child to a zoo or a park or taught him or her to shoot baskets or ride a bike. Children like to capture good memories, such as outings or being taught fun things, and then try to resurrect the relationship with the parent(s) without the abusive component. The hope that this can be accomplished may make some children reluctant to report abuse. Another problem in dealing with abused children, and one reason why abuse may go unrecognized for a long time, is that children rarely tell the whole story at once. They usually send up a trial balloon to see how it is received. If it is received by an adult with an open mind, they tell more. If it is not, they generally don't. Once the abuse is known, however, a child cannot be left in that situation under any circumstances. (See Chapter 7 for a detailed discussion.)

Violating Orders, Communication Failure, Obstructing Visits

I consider parents who continually violate court orders, refuse to communicate with the other parent, and actively obstruct visitation, to be problem parents. By violating court orders or obstructing visits, they are undermining their children's relationship with the other parent. And by refusing to communicate effectively with the other parent, they are causing problems. I recommend couples therapy for parents who are getting divorced or who have gotten divorced probably as frequently as I do for married couples, because parents have to be able to communicate effectively with one another.

If you have a situation in which you continually try to get the other parent into therapy but he or she storms out or otherwise subverts the process, the basic message is that this parent does not want to make it as easy as possible for the children. The lack of communication will manifest itself in other areas and the children's relationship with the other parent will be undermined as one parent becomes more and more manipulative.

Many different actions can constitute a violation of court orders. Perhaps a mother is told by the court that she can visit her children but her boyfriend cannot be present because he has a criminal record, so she tries to include the boyfriend without anyone learning about it. Or a father keeps showing up for his assigned visitations but the mother isn't there with the children when she is supposed to be. Or a father is supposed to bring the children home to his former spouse at a particular time and day but he brings them back whenever he pleases. The parent who is willing to disregard judicial authority and do whatever he or she pleases is not going to listen to what another parent says.

Helpful Hint

Parents may not realize that by doing such spiteful things, they are negatively affecting their children.

Invariably at the holidays I get calls from parents who are supposed to start visitation at a particular time and place but the former spouse presents a conflict. I was involved with one family at Christmas time one year when the mother wanted to take her son to visit his grandparents in Florida. She asked her former husband if she could have the child the night before because the only flight she could get was especially early the next day. The father, who was a control freak, did not want to give the child to her the night before because it wasn't her visitation time. He promised to bring the child to the airport on time the next day.

The mother was at the airport when her ex-husband showed up, without the child, with the excuse that his mother had taken the child somewhere and he did not know where. We later learned that the child had been at home with Grandma all the while and the father was just harrassing his ex-wife. She lost their tickets and had to pay full price for another flight the next day, and the child was caught in the middle of a lie and manipulation told by his father. This situation is terrible for a child. Obstructing visits is another area in which parents can be so manipulative that children cannot predict their actions.

Endangering Your Children

This includes, for example, parents who take their children to bars. They don't want to find or pay for a babysitter so they take their youngsters to bars and stay out as late as they choose. In one case, a father put his five-year-old daughter on a table at a bar and had the child perform so he could get free drinks from other patrons. Also, parents who drink and drive with their children in the car are endangering their children.

Helpful Hint

Parents who use poor judgment in child care and whose behavior endangers their children are clearly incapable of making proper decisions for the children and should not share custody.

The problem is not only that these parents are endangering their children's physical well-being but also that children learn what they live. The basic message children learn from this type of behavior is that it is appropriate. These children are also more likely to grow up to be alcoholics than are other children. Such actions distort their value system and cheapen their dignity and sense of self-worth. What do these children learn from being taken to a meat-market-type bar where they can watch people grope each other or get staggering drunk? Worse yet, what do these children learn if one of the people being watched is their parent?

There's a long list of behaviors that are considered to be in poor judgment. For example, when is it appropriate to leave a child alone? Laws in some states say this is okay to do when a child is 11 or 12 years old, but does that mean every night? Does that mean all night? I had a case in which a five-year-old boy was proud to demonstrate in my office what his mother, who often left her children alone, had taught him to do to save his three-year-old sister if there was a fire in their house. Children are left alone thousands of times a day around the country and we hear about it only if a fire or some other catastrophe reveals that the children were left alone.

Ralph lives in Wisconsin and his ex-wife and children live in Minnesota. He has a cabin on a lake not far from a major city, which he allowed his 16-year-old daughter to use unsupervised for a party with her friends. The daughter asked him not to tell her mother about the party, and he didn't. No surprise to anyone, there was a considerable amount of alcohol consumed at the party, plus damage to the cabin and its contents. There were numerous driving-under-the-influence arrests after the party, and the father continued to agree with the daughter not to tell the mother anything about what had occurred. Not only did the father's behavior endanger his daughter, endanger other minors, violate the law, and expose him and his ex-wife to considerable liability, but also he was willing to engage in a deception with his daughter. At no time did he acknowledge the inappropriateness of his behavior, which resulted in a reduction of time he was allowed to spend with his children.

Separate Lives under One Roof, Then the Great Divide

When parents separate, or begin divorce proceedings and continue living under one roof, serious problems may arise stemming from anger, frustration, guilt, and loss. Add to this the subject of sole or joint custody and even couples who are making the best of a difficult situation can become outright hostile and aggressive. These actions are something children witness, soak up, and react to with behavior I've already outlined.

Parents living in the same house during separation give children false hope because they are saying one thing—that it's all over—but acting as if nothing has changed. That Dad sleeps on the sofa while Mom sleeps in the bedroom would be a cue to children that life isn't exactly like it used to be, but it may not be enough to make them understand how much life is really changing.

Keeping everyone under the same roof may lead to children being let down again. If Mom and Dad say they are getting divorced but then coast along for months living in the same house, their actions don't appear to children like parents getting divorced. For children, divorce starts the minute their parents separate. False hope is probably the most important consideration here. Imagine how devastating it can be for children if they develop a sense that their parents will change their minds and stay together and then, as you and your spouse pass through the various stages of divorce, they start hearing you talk about custody and whom they are going to live with!

As you move to that point, consider what your children are witnessing. They may hear you and your spouse calling each other names or see you throwing things at one another. Even if a relationship has not deteriorated to that level, children see the coldness between you. Once again, they learn what they live, and a cold war going on in the household can be very disconcerting to children.

Despite all that they witness, when asked, children will usually say that they would rather have their parents living in the same house. Frankly, life is easier when both parents are living in the same house.

When custody and placement become issues, life becomes even more difficult for children. They have to start following schedules, trying to keep track of which parent they are to be with on which day. They walk around mumbling, "Well, today is Thursday so I have to pack my suitcase to sleep at Mom's tonight." Calendars—some color-coded for younger children—have to be put on walls at home. Children look at them and read, "Yellow I'm at Mom's, blue is at Dad's and if both colors are on the same day, then I have to share the day with both of them." I've had children look at me in utter confusion, throw their arms in the air, and say, "I can't figure this out. I don't know where I'm supposed to be. Does Wednesday mean Mom's house or Dad's house?"

Under these circumstances, parents need to do all the things they did at the outset of the divorce:

Helpful Hints

- Don't argue in front of your children.
- Don't pull children into the middle of the custody and place- ment issue by discussing it in front of them or asking their opinions.
- Don't be abusive to each other in front of your children, and don't think you can get away with calling each other names and throwing things at each other while they are in their rooms supposedly asleep. They are most suspicious at that time because they expect these emotional explosions to occur when they are thought to be out of earshot.
- Communicate as effectively as you can with one another and with your children.

(continued)

Helpful Hints (Continued)

- Directly saying, "We're still getting divorced even though we're living together" is like putting salt in your children's wounds. Deal with it indirectly, occasionally saying things like, "When your dad and I get divorced ..." or "In a couple of months when your dad moves out ..." This reminds children that divorce is a process.

- Gradually introduce your children to the concept that their living situation may be changing, but that they should not worry because you will both continue to be active parts of their lives. You might explain: "When Dad and I get divorced, we might have to move to a new, smaller house (or apartment), but we'll make it wonderful together, and you'll be able to see Dad at his new place."

Giving Up Placement

As much as you want custody and placement to be worked out calmly and to the satisfaction of both of you and your children, you must proceed with these issues carefully and with good counsel. Do not act in haste or make such serious decisions under duress or while in the throes of emotional upheaval.

One classic mistake that a parent often makes at the time of separation or divorce is to say to the other, "You take the kids. I need time to adjust" or "I need time to finish school" or to reason, "You have the house and a better income, so you should take the children. When I adjust more (or finish school or have a more substantial living environment), I'll take them back."

Helpful Hint

Don't give up placement of your children on a "temporary" basis and expect to be able to get them back when you want.

Do not give up placement of your children on a temporary basis unless you understand and accept that you may never regain placement of them. It is not unusual, once the interim period has passed, for a parent to request the children's return, only to have the placement parent say, "No way."

Courts generally favor leaving children where they are if life is going smoothly. Therefore, the burden is on the nonplacement parent who wants the children back to prove they would be damaged by remaining where they are. You can't simply argue that you are offering a better environment for them, and that's why you want them back. The other parent generally doesn't have to prove anything.

Grandparents: Help or Hindrance

Grandparents can be invaluable in helping to resolve or mediate such critical decisions as custody and placement. They often see their grandchildren's position more clearly than do parents who are in the heat of the divorce and custody processes, and grandparents are frequently more sensitive and sympathetic to the way divorce affects children. Be aware, however, that grandparents can operate on two different levels.

I have had meetings in which I was trying to mediate with spouses and they just were not making any headway, so I would have them bring their respective sets of parents to the next meeting. Once I had the parents and grandparents in my office, I would tattle on the kids (the parents). I would say, "I just want you to know what's going on here. There's a tremendous amount of immaturity in these two people. They seem to think that fighting is more important than what's good for their child." Then I would look at the grandparents and say, "I need your help. You have a common grandchild here who is being destroyed by what his (her) parents are doing."

Grandparents who are willing to help in this way can be a marvelous resource. Whether we want to admit it or not, no matter how old we get we still want to please our parents. Putting parents into a situation where they must deal with their own parents can change the tone and outcome of mediation.

The other side is that grandparents can have a tremendous negative effect by causing more polarization than is necessary.

Because they are parents, they assume a protective position, saying things to their son or daughter such as, "You mean you're going to let that guy who had an affair on you have the kids?" or "How can you forgive her for being drunk all year?" So, we might have a parent trying to do what's best for his or her child, hoping to make custody and placement as easy as possible, but the grandparents are saying, "Don't let that slimeball near the kids."

Although you may want to be as amenable as possible with your former spouse for the good of the children as well as for your own peace of mind, you may find yourself being swayed by your own parents because you are beholden to them. Divorcing couples often turn to their parents for help with the financial burden of divorce (usually in the form of a loan) and sometimes with the upkeep of the children. Grandparents often think that because they are footing the bill, they have the right to have input into decisions. What we end up with, for example, is a dad who knows what's best for his children, but he has just gotten money from his father, who is saying, "Use this money wisely and make sure your wife doesn't get the kids." Dad finds himself in a true conflict position.

Helpful Hint

The only way grandparents will get custody is if both parents voluntarily allow it to occur or the court finds the parents unfit.

The custody and placement process is an exercise in balancing difficult choices and players, much like all other parts of the divorce process. Now that you have an understanding of custody and placement options, you probably have some ideas about what is right for your situation. Ideally, you and your spouse will be in agreement about what would work best for both of you and your children. However, such agreement is often not the case. In either event, you will need to work out the arrangements through the courts.

Navigating the Legal Waters

People caught in the heat of divorce and custody issues may look upon the legal process as nothing more than a quagmire, fraught with dangers waiting to suck them under. Some men and women allow themselves to become so overwhelmed by their emotions and by the enormous financial and child-rearing responsibilities that are thrust on them during this period that they can't see the proverbial forest for the trees. That's when they know it's time to seek the advice and security of an attorney.

Finding an Attorney

This can be one of the costliest moves you'll ever make in your life, but in some cases if you don't have a good attorney, the intangible and tangible costs to you and your children may be higher than you ever imagined. Attorneys' fees can be high, especially if you are embroiled in a drawn-out custody dispute. There are alternatives to litigation, however, including collaboration, arbitration, and mediation. As far as I'm concerned, mediation is one of the potential bright lights in this process and one very viable possibility for parents.

In mediation, parents try to work out agreements on divorce and custody issues with the help of an impartial, objective third party (mediator), who never tells them what to do, but who can make suggestions and try to keep the process moving forward. In arbitration, the third party (arbitrator) listens to you and your spouse, then he or she decides what you will do. Each of these approaches has pros and cons, which I will talk about later. With these approaches, an attorney can be your objective third party and offer you the benefit of his or her experience without the high cost of litigation.

Most people choose to have legal counsel represent them in divorce cases, particularly if child custody is an issue. Selecting an attorney in a divorce case is a much more important task than most people realize. Unfortunately, many people are willing to choose attorneys based on cost or whether they know the attorney from a previous setting, or for other less important reasons.

People often choose an attorney for a divorce action based on what happened in cases involving their friends or relatives. This information can be helpful. However, each case is different, and it can be difficult to generalize about how well someone represented an individual without knowing all the facts firsthand. You may think you know them, but your knowledge of what actually happened will be filtered through your friend's or relative's perceptions.

All too often, the results achieved in a case hinge on the competency of the attorney, and not the merits of the case itself. Competency is obviously an important issue. However, even the most competent attorneys cannot pull rabbits out of hats. The implication here is that, all things being equal, the more competent the attorney is, the more likely he or she is to get better results for clients.

You must ask several questions when considering hiring an attorney based on someone else's experience:

- Did the attorney identify all the issues?
- Was the divorce amicable?

- Was the attorney who represented your friend's spouse equal to, better than, or less competent than the one who represented your friend?

Recommendations from friends and family members can also be problematic because someone might think his or her attorney achieved good results when, in fact, the outcome could have been much better. Others may think the results were terrible, but their expectations may have been unrealistically high, and no one could have gotten what they wanted. Talking to a friend or relative may be helpful, but remember, their opinions are only one factor that should be considered.

Other factors should be kept in mind when choosing an attorney. First of all, remember that it is better to mediate, negotiate, or use collaboration for a divorce settlement than to go to court and fight it out. Consequently, your attorney should have strong negotiating skills. Although the barracuda approach might work well on television, it's usually best to keep the sharks out of the water when children are involved. However, if your spouse won't agree to mediate or mediation breaks down, you will need a lawyer with good courtroom skills.

In addition to good negotiation and courtroom skills, it is critical that your lawyer be experienced in divorce and custody cases. Another mistake people often make is hiring the attorney who handled their house closing, represented them in a minor automobile accident case, or negotiated their office lease. These generalist attorneys may not have the family law sophistication necessary to successfully represent your case. Family law is very complex and you have a lot at stake. You need an experienced family lawyer to lead you through this terrain. Look for an attorney who devotes at least half of his or her practice to family law.

Don't try to cut corners by hiring a friend or family member who happens to be a lawyer. If he or she knows both parents, the lawyer is put into the difficult position of having to take sides. In addition, people tend not to listen to the advice of their attorney friends as much as they would if a nonfriend attorney was representing them. In the end, this shortcut could not only hurt your case but also cost you a friendship.

Finally, don't be penny-wise and pound-foolish when selecting an attorney. Most family lawyers charge by the hour. I have seen a large number of cases in which individuals picked the lawyer with the cheapest rates and did not end up with the best results, particularly when their spouses had used more appropriate criteria in choosing an attorney. Utilizing a lower cost attorney may actually cost you more despite the lower hourly rate, especially if the lower rate is a function of inexperience.

Selecting an attorney based on his or her initial cost estimate may not save you the money you think it will. An inexperienced attorney with a lower hourly rate may take many more hours than an experienced attorney who can cut to the basic issues quickly and efficiently. You may also end up spending more money if a less-experienced attorney fails to initially address all the necessary issues in your case and you have to return to court.

To pick the attorney who is right for you, talk to friends who have been divorced and have been pleased with their representation, keeping in mind issues discussed in this chapter. Once you have a list of potential attorneys, narrow it down by meeting with them to determine the lawyer that you are most comfortable with and that you believe will best represent your interests. Many attorneys will not charge for an initial consultation of up to one hour and some charge a nominal fee for the first meeting, but ask about that when you make the appointment. The better attorneys will often charge less than their normal hourly rate, but will want to charge something as a way of the client getting some value for the dollar.

Many resources are available when you're looking for an attorney. A book called the *Martindale-Hubbell Law Directory* can be found in the reference sections of many large public libraries as well as in law libraries. This book lists attorneys by specialization, locale, and qualifications. *The Best Lawyers in America* is another good reference book. An attorney cannot buy his or her way into this book. Before a name is listed in this book, the attorney's background is investigated and he or she is included only if found to be highly qualified.

Another valuable source for finding family law attorneys is the American Academy of Matrimonial Lawyers. Furthermore, many attorneys and law firms have web sites today that identify the attorney's training, experience, publications, and/or speaking engagements. When the web site does not include the above types of experience, then you should question whether that attorney will be able to handle your case as well as you would like.

Local bar associations can also be helpful because they will provide names of attorneys according to specialization. This resource is valuable, however, only if the association requires members to be credentialed in some way. In some cases, an attorney need only submit his or her name to be included on a bar association list. Don't hesitate to ask what the association's criteria are for membership. Various states also have academies of family lawyers, whose members have undergone some form of screening for inclusion in the organization. Other professionals, such as accountants, therapists, and other lawyers, can also provide good referrals. Be willing to reach out to people you know and can trust.

Don't Be Attracted by Unrealistic Promises

Attorneys who say they will definitely get you custody of your children, who promise to "nail your spouse to the wall," or who lay out a plan that includes bringing experts into the case who they know will testify on your behalf, because they always testify the way the attorney wants, may be promising things they cannot deliver. You should be especially concerned if an attorney is promising things you previously lost in other court hearings or trials, or that other attorneys have indicated are not possible. A more realistic attorney will offer a good likelihood that he or she will be able to prevail on certain issues, but will offer no guarantee. You are in a vulnerable period of your life when you are getting divorced and seeking custody. Because of your heightened emotional state, you should be extra cautious about the people with whom you choose to work.

Helpful Hint

From the outset, be wary of any attorney who makes unrealistic promises or guarantees that he or she will get you everything you want.

Your attorney has an obligation to be realistic and not hold out false hope. Your attorney should also have the ability to listen and recognize that the decisions are yours and that it is your life without the attorney telling you what to do. Based on knowledge of the legal system, an attorney should tell you what you need to hear, not what you want to hear. You want someone who will represent you fully and present all arguments on your behalf outside the office, but who, in the office behind closed doors, will be completely honest with you about your chances.

Asking a potential attorney these questions during the initial meeting should help you make an informed and educated decision:

- What are your hourly and day rates?
- Can you give me an estimate of what the entire case will cost, including any custody dispute?
- How much of your work is spent dealing with divorces and custody issues? Do you consider this your area of expertise? What other kinds of law do you practice? (As I said earlier, you don't want your divorce and custody issues handled by someone who spends most of the time on house closings.)
- Are mediation, collaboration, or arbitration options in my case? Would you be comfortable operating in these settings on my behalf?
- Realistically, what are my chances of achieving what I want in this case? What are my chances of getting custody of my children? What are my options?
- How long do you think this case will run?
- Will you be available when I need you to represent me? (You do not want an attorney so overburdened that your case is handled "when he or she gets around to it," thereby creating postponements and delays, or hands it off to a less qualified attorney or a new associate.)

Avoid "Hired Guns" and "Dirty Tricks" Attorneys

Any time an attorney suggests actions that give you a sense of dirty tricks, a giant red flag should go up. Every community has its share of attorneys who are known for using dirty tricks in divorce cases. Although these lawyers may sound clever and promising and as if they are on your side, these attorneys are well-known by judges and often do not get the results in court that they have promised.

Dirty tricks attorneys who encourage you to participate in their schemes can lead you into a situation that will surely backfire. Once you start participating in these tricks, your children will become involved in the plotting and manipulating, which is something you want to avoid and that courts detest.

Children can't help getting involved in this behavior because it happens around them and they are sensitive to it, especially if they're young. Teenagers are apt to say, "You can play your silly games but leave me out of it." It's too risky for younger children to say something like that because such comments can lead to disciplinary action from the parent. Often, youngsters don't even recognize the motivation behind the actions of the parent and the dirty tricks lawyer.

On the same continuum with manipulation is lying, which can set children up for disappointment. Children who are enlisted into participating in dirty tricks may be led to expect some outcome in their favor. If the tricks fail, children are let down. From moral and ethical viewpoints, dirty tricks give children the wrong message.

Be forewarned that dirty tricks lawyers don't just play these tricks on the other side—they also play them on their clients. For example, two lawyers may have lunch to discuss a case and they spend about ten minutes during their meal talking about it. At the end of the lunch, the dirty tricks lawyer will say: "Just so our records are comparable, I'm going to bill my client for a two-hour conference with you." The other lawyer, if reputable, will say that he or she is only billing for the ten minutes. The rationale here is simple: A person who uses that kind of mentality in one aspect of the practice is going to use it in all aspects of the practice.

Parents involved in dirty tricks cases, have told me that they were afraid I would not recognize the manipulation on the part of their husbands or wives. And that is the most difficult thing for me to do as an evaluator because some people are artful manipulators. Let me illustrate how this can create more upheaval in a divorce case than might otherwise be expected. I recall a case in which the judge made an order nobody liked. The mother wanted to move to Arizona and was pleading the case that her daughter should move with her. After two and a half days of testimony, the judge became angry and said, "I don't want to listen to this anymore. I want to settle this case. Your daughter goes to Arizona with her mother for fifth grade, comes back to Milwaukee with her father for the sixth grade, goes back to Mom for the seventh grade, and returns to Dad for the eighth grade. Then we'll decide where she goes to high school for four years."

After that happened, the mother's attorney told me on the phone, "This case needs dirty tricks and that's why I brought another attorney into it." He was referring to someone who specialized in dirty tricks. The dirty tricks attorney came into the case and did such things as take the child's court-appointed guardian on a trip to Arizona. When the court heard about this, the child was ordered back into her father's custody, whether that was the most appropriate place for her to be or not. The dirty tricks back-fired and really upset the judge.

Utilization of a dirty tricks attorney can be compounded by using a hired gun expert. All communities have experts with reputations for testifying in the direction of the person who hires them. Hired guns are people who are described as authorities in various fields or professions and who are brought into cases as expert witnesses. As is true of the attorneys, the courts know who these people are and their testimony tends to carry less weight than the testimony of experts who are considered truly independent.

Reputable lawyers also know who the dirty tricks attorneys and hired gun experts are. If you approach a reputable lawyer after having used a dirty tricks lawyer or hired gun expert, he or she will probably tell you that overcoming the problems associated with having used such an individual will be more expensive than if you had used a reputable attorney from the outset.

Switching Attorneys

As the old adage says, don't switch horses in midstream. This advice also applies to switching attorneys. Once you have hired an attorney, try to stick with him or her. Using a series of attorneys over time may present problems in a divorce case. It is not in any way unreasonable for someone not to to mesh well with an attorney, necessitating finding a new one. If you believe that you have made the wrong first choice it is better to inverview other attorneys and make the switch as soon as possible. However, if you are into your fourth, fifth, or sixth attorney, people are going to ask why. You may feel you have legitimate reasons for switching that many times. However, the courts and other individuals involved in the process are going to wonder what prompted so many changes. If you find yourself often wanting to switch because of the advice attorneys are giving you, it may be that you are having difficulty accepting their advice, even though the advice may be reasonable and accurate for your case. If you are looking for someone to tell you what you want to hear, as opposed to what is realistic, and switch often enough, you are likely to eventually find an attorney who will support your position even if it may be unlikely that he or she will be able to deliver what you want.

When you switch attorneys, you are apt to incur additional expenses because the new attorney must take the time to become familiar with your case. Also, his or her predecessors may have done things that were not the best alternatives, but the new attorney is stuck with them and will need extra time to work out the best course of action to take under those circumstances.

It can be disconcerting to see your attorney interacting in a friendly manner in a courtroom or the halls of a courthouse with your spouse's attorney, especially when you may feel that you are at war with your spouse. It can be equally upsetting to see the attorneys make plans to go to lunch with one another or play golf after they have represented you in a bitterly contested case. Attorneys can be friendly with one another and still represent you fairly and fully. Since attorneys are bound by a professional code of ethics, you have a right to expect yours to represent you in a professional capacity.

Telling Your Story in Court

If your custody dispute ends up being tried in court, you will probably be required to testify. Direct examination is when your attorney questions you. You can expect him or her to spend a considerable amount of time preparing you for direct examination. It is more difficult, however, for your attorney to prepare you for questions that will be asked by your spouse's attorney, called cross-examination.

Cross-examination is typically a more uncomfortable experience than direct examination. Be as relaxed as possible and, as the oath requires, tell the truth. Remember that it is your spouse's attorney's job to ask you difficult questions to support his or her client's position. This does not mean your spouse's attorney dislikes or hates you or is out to get you. Listen to the question carefully, especially during cross examination, and answer only what is asked without volunteering additional information. Remember that this is testimony and you are not carrying on a conversation.

Acting as Your Own Attorney

An alternative to hiring an attorney is to represent yourself, which is called pro se (pronounced "pro say"). For people who can successfully negotiate placement and financial arrangements with their spouse, pro se is a wonderful approach. There is no reason why you should spend large sums of money for attorneys if you can adequately represent yourselves. Many communities have divorce pro se organizations that help people with the paperwork of divorce, explain the practicalities of the legal process, and offer advice for a relatively nominal fee.

Pro se, however, is not always the best approach to use. If your spouse has hired an attorney, you will be at a major disadvantage if you go pro se. Imagine being in a courtroom and representing yourself pro se when the attorney on the other side objects to a question citing specific legal cases to support the objection. You are not going to be in a position to adequately respond to those objections. Even if money is an obstacle, you owe it to yourself and your children to seek an equitable settlement regarding retirement funds, savings accounts, stocks, equity in the home, business valuations, and other forms of property and assets. Unfortunately, when you run out of money and the other side does not, pro se may be your only option.

Helpful Hint

Don't go the pro se route unless your spouse agrees to do the same.

Helpful Hint

Don't think that you can outsmart or out-lawyer the attorney on the other side.

Mediation as a First Step

Whether or not you hire any attorney, mediation is a good first step toward trying to reach a fair settlement. The best quote I have heard about why mediation should be used is "It is better to send your children to college than your attorney's children."

Many states require mediation before an individual is allowed to litigate a custody case, and mediation has become popular even where it is not required by law. If you choose to use mediation, you must select an individual who has appropriate credentials in this area. Many people call themselves mediators but have no specific training for it. The Academy of Family Mediators is an organization that accredits mediators. A divorce can be either fully or partially mediated, meaning certain issues are resolved in mediation while others must be settled in court if you cannot agree on them. Issues that can be resolved in mediation include custody and placement, financial terms, and division of property. Ordinarily, one person would mediate the divorce in a neutral capacity, although sometimes two mediators are used, one to represent the interests of each parent.

Mediation carries a number of advantages. The divorce can be resolved quickly and inexpensively. The mediation process generally costs a fraction of what litigation costs. It also leaves fewer scars on family members compared to going through the adversarial or litigation approach. Mediated cases are much less likely to be taken back to court than cases that were initially litigated. The mediation process takes into account each party's wishes and desires and tries to fashion a compromise solution. As I mentioned before, the mediator does not tell you what you should do or how you should do it. Instead, he or she tries to broker an arrangement acceptable to both parties. If you or your spouse are not happy with the final solution, you can simply walk away.

Choosing mediation does not mean that you cannot use an attorney. When I perform a mediation, I encourage the parties to take the mediated agreement to their respective attorneys to put it into legal language and draw up a stipulation that the parties can then sign and enter with their divorce decree. If an attorney objects to some of the language in the agreement, the parties can go back to mediation and rework some of the issues. This also holds true down the road if new issues arise.

Just as parents should not deal with the financial arrangements of a divorce in front of the children, likewise they should not discuss the process of getting a lawyer or what transpires in mediation in front of them. One problem created by allowing children to hear about these processes is that the parent is usually at such a high level of anxiety that it's difficult for the children not to be affected by that stress. Such discussions may indicate to the children (if they don't already know it) that the divorce process is going to be filled with anxiety and that they had better get ready for a rough ride. They may also hear Mom, for example, saying, "I've got to get the best attorney to fight for us." Children then get the additional message that a fight is likely to occur. A related point to consider is that children who see parents agonizing over their representation are given the impression that too much of the power over what is going to happen to them will fall to an attorney instead of to their parents.

One of the biggest advantages of mediation is that it gets the parents talking and puts them in a position where they must try to deal with each other in a reasonable way. This is crucial learning time for when they have to work with each other in the future about matters concerning their children, especially if they have been at each other's throats for a long time. I'm not talking about lip service mediation, meaning that you go once and the mediator writes a letter to the court saying this occurred, but that you've really had no meaningful dialogue or positive outcome. I'm talking about meaningful, hands-on, ongoing mediation, in which parents become aware of a more comfortable way to approach issues.

Mediation sets a very positive example for children, especially if they have seen you arguing a lot. Now they see you talking to each other and to them about what the ultimate plan is going to be, and children think maybe this isn't going to be as bad as they thought.

Mediation also indirectly affects children because good mediation costs about one tenth of what good lawyering costs. Parents, instead of spending an enormous amount of money going to trial, may spend $1,000 mediating a case, and they undergo less frustration and arguing and put less financial strain on the family.

The only negative that I see to mediation is when the process breaks down after children have been given hope. Some mediation cases break down because parents cannot come to terms with one another.

The mediation and arbitration approaches have many advantages. I've already said that mediation is less expensive, both psychologically and financially. Perhaps the most important advantage of mediation, however, is that you participate in decisions affecting you and your children instead of deferring to a stranger—a judge. Even if a judge is the best in the world, you run the risk of him or her reaching a decision that is different from what you or your spouse wants.

Although mediation is certainly a preferable approach to resolving problems, individuals can in no way mediate an agreement for a four-year-old child, for example, that is going to work for the next 14 years. Relationships change, children grow, school placements change, medical issues arise, and many other factors come into play between childhood and legal age adulthood. You must understand the likelihood that the initial mediation agreement will need modification as children get older. In most cases, when mediation is working well, parents can reach a modified agreement on their own. However, if mediation worked the first time, you should not be reluctant to go back and re-mediate the agreement when circumstances change.

I cannot emphasize enough how important it is to consider mediation to resolve differences in custody cases. Even if a mediated agreement requires difficult compromises, you and your children are spared the powerful negative effects of a court battle. Remember that if mediation does not work, litigation is always available to you. Hence, nothing is lost by first attempting mediation.

Collaboration

In recent years a new development has come on the scene in alternate methods of resolving divorce cases. This process is called collaboration. It is so new that there are a number of areas of the country that have not even begun to use the collaborative process, while there are other areas that have been using it for quite a while. The strongest feature of the collaborative process is that it allows everyone to work together toward the common goal of resolving the issues as quickly and easily as possible. Thus, the name "Collaboration."

In the collaborative process each party hires a trained collaborative lawyer and other collaborative professionals as needed to work together in an out-of-court, problem-solving, non-adversarial process. The lawyers and clients sign a written collaborative agreement before engaging in the process. The defining element of the process is that the parties and lawyers together stipulate in writing that the process will be terminated and the collaborative lawyers will be disqualified from continued representation of their respective clients if either party resorts to litigation. Many family law approaches to collaborative practice provide for mental health professionals as coaches or child specialists and financial specialists as part of the clients' divorce team. In these approaches, the clients have the option of starting their divorce with the professional with whom they have their initial contact or with whom they feel most comfortable. The clients and their initially retained professionals then choose the other professionals needed to help resolve the issues. The clients benefit throughout the collaborative process from the assistance and support of all of their professional team members.

The numerous and evolving approaches to collaborative practice share core elements, which are articulated in writing and explicitly agreed to between the clients and lawyers at the outset of the case. These elements always include:

- Negotiating mutually acceptable settlement without using court to decide any issues.
- Withdrawal of the collaborative professionals if either client chooses to go to court.

- Open communication and voluntary information sharing.
- A goal of creating solutions that take into account the interests of all parties.

In the collaborative process, as the clients engage their professionals, they sign written collaborative agreements to engage in the collaborative process and specifically agree that their lawyers cannot subsequently litigate any contested matter, and their mental health professionals or financial specialists cannot participate as individual witnesses or adversarial consultants in litigation. The integrity of the collaborative process is premised on the clients' safety within the container created by the process to honestly focus on interests and creative solutions in addressing their concerns without fear that such open communication will be used against them in a contested court process.

The process tools and hallmarks of the collaborative process endorsed by the clients and lawyers in the disqualification agreement typically include:

- A shared commitment to proceed honestly and respectfully without litigation or even threats of litigation.
- Active participation by the parties, including four-way settlement meetings to gather and share information, discuss options, and reach agreement on resolutions.
- An interest-based approach to negotiation, with the overarching goal of meeting the needs of both parties and their children.
- The ability to work with mental health and financial professionals in an interdisciplinary collaborative team to utilize the skills of each discipline to maximize the potential of positive emotional, financial, and legal outcomes for the family.
- Join retention of any experts needed in the process.
- Core element: disqualification of the collaborative lawyers and other team members from participation in any litigation between the parties.

In jurisdictions in which mediation is an adopted and recognized tool for dispute resolution, the communications during mediation are protected to facilitate the free flow of information and the ability to focus on interests. The collaborative disqualification agreement accomplishes the same kind of protection of the process for the parties by allowing the parties to proceed in a protected environment which facilitates open communication instead of gathering evidence. It assists in looking to the future rather than the past and transforms the focus of negotiation for both clients and lawyers by removing court as a constant backdrop. The disqualification agreement can also alleviate fears that hiring lawyers will foster disputes. Thus, pro se parties may consider the benefits of obtaining legal counsel and representation without the perceived risk of heightened conflict.

One of the great strengths of the collaborative process is the direct inclusion of mental health professionals. Roles for mental health professionals include coaches and child specialists. The collaborative coach (also referred to as a "divorce coach") is a mental health professional whose role is to prepare the client to participate effectively within the collaborative process. Though the collaborative coach is not functioning in the role of therapist, the coach does use therapeutic training and experience to assist the client in managing emotional and psychological issues that might otherwise impair the client's effective functioning and participation in the settlement process. The coach also communicates with other collaborative team members to provide insight and assistance to help facilitate the most effective and efficient process.

In individual meetings with the client, the collaborative coach helps the client understand and work through emotions and understand relationship and family patterns. The coach assists the clients in identifying and resolving emotionally charged issues, managing their anger, fear, or other overwhelming emotions, seeing the client's own role in communication and negotiation dynamics, and developing the coping and communication skills that will enable the client to participate productively in the collaborative process. The coach helps the client identify and prioritize concerns, interests, and long-term goals for themselves and their family. The coach may also help teach positive co-parenting skills, educate the client about ways to create a healthy divorce outcome for their children, assist in developing a parenting plan, and support, reinforce, and help the client communicate in a positive and productive way with their spouse. Finally, the collaborative coach's presence in the case provides an ongoing resource for the client to help in addressing emotional crises and parenting issues that may arise both during the case and after the legal component of the divorce has concluded.

In addition to individual coaching strategies, there are beneficial systemic interventions. Four-way meetings present an opportunity for coaches to reframe as needed and also model new and healthy ways of communicating. Coaches and clients can identify the triggers for each party and address them directly in the meeting or go back to individual coaching sessions to develop strategies to respond effectively and remain focused on interests and long-term goals. When parties experience success in respectfully reaching decisions in four-way meetings, it serves as a model and provides tools for the parties to utilize as future issues arise. Coaches also provide professional insight and advice to other team members, particularly the lawyers, to assist in understanding the emotional layers and needs of the clients and their interests in order to assist in communication and effective negotiation.

The child specialist is a mental health professional with specific training and expertise in child psychology and development and family systems, whose role is to assist parents in understanding and addressing their children's unique needs and interests. The child specialist also provides tools to parents and other team members to promote ongoing healthy relationships. The child specialist serves as a neutral advocate for the interest of the child and helps discern and share the child's feelings, needs, and preferences in the process. This professional provides a voice for the children throughout the process and helps the parents look at plans and actions through the eyes of their children, rather than just through their individual perspectives.

The child specialist assists the parents in their collaborative negotiations as they develop a parenting plan that addresses interests and concerns related to their children. That assistance may include: informing the parents about common reactions children have to divorce; discussing age related, developmental stages and pragmatic considerations bearing on parenting decisions and placement of the children; actively assisting the parents in their efforts to create realistic and thoughtful parenting plans that keep the interests of the children primary; and helping the parents anticipate and plan for future challenges they may face as they continue to co-parent after conclusion of the legal proceedings. The child specialist may also be a resource for the family after the legal process ends, when issues arise or life changes occur that necessitate a review of the original plan. This allows parents to obtain child-focused input, rather than using the court system to make decisions regarding their children.

The value of the process is dependent upon skilled, trained professionals as well as client commitment. The International Academy of Collaborative Professionals (IACP) is an interdisciplinary nonprofit organization that has developed standards for collaborative professionals and trainers from all disciplines as well as ethical guidelines. These standards and geographic listings of members are available at www.collaborativepractice.com.

Arbitration

Arbitration offers another way of reaching an agreement without going to court. With the success of the collaboration and mediation processes, arbitration is used much less frequently than it had been previously. It tends to be used more often in post-judgment (after the divorce is over) disputes than in resolution of the issues during the divorce itself. Arbitration exists in many forms, and it can be binding or nonbinding. Binding arbitration requires the parties to accept the arbitrator's recommendation. Nonbinding arbitration allows individuals to disagree with the arbitrator and attempt to find another solution. Unfortunately, nonbinding arbitration often has little effect because either party can disagree with the result and start the process over again.

Retired judges are often used as arbitrators. They have expertise in dispute resolution and have learned from years on the bench how to resolve problems. However, it is not unusual for attorneys and/or psychologists to serve as arbitrators in divorce cases.

Mediation and arbitration can be used in combination with one another. Arbitration can be an effective tool when the mediation process breaks down and leaves a number of minor issues to be resolved that don't require going to court. This process generally involves each of you telling your side of the story or stating your position and the arbitrator making a decision that supports one side or the other or is somewhere in the middle.

I know of a case, for example, in which the two principals, Mary and Jim, had mediated all aspects of their divorce. They were down to the last thousand dollars worth of personal property, which included a list of items several pages long. None of the items was worth more than $75. It was apparent that Jim and Mary were more interested in arguing with one another at that point than in reaching a resolution. The mediator scheduled three more sessions and said if they could not reach agreement after that, he would then serve as an arbitrator and divide the items. It was not too surprising that Mary and Jim were able to reach an agreement before those three sessions were up. If this combination approach is used, it is necessary for both parties to sign an agreement in advance that they understand the process and will not back out after the mediator/arbitrator has made a decision.

The Court Process

Temporary Orders

Whether you are mediating an agreement or litigating a case, at some time early in the process you will go to court either representing yourself or with an attorney to get temporary orders pertaining to placement of your children. Temporary orders are often issued by someone other than the judge who will hear your case. These individuals have such titles as "marital master" or "family court commissioner."

Helpful Hint

Don't be fooled by the term *temporary orders*.

Although these orders are intended to address placement, placement schedules, and support only for the period between the temporary order and the divorce, judges tend to resist change. Consequently, the parent who receives placement of a child through temporary orders will have an advantage when the case goes to court. Even though you can have it written into the temporary orders that they were made "without prejudice" to any of the parties, judges are still reluctant to make a change when it is not necessary.

The phrase *without prejudice* written into a temporary order suggests that when the trial occurs, these issues will be readdressed in court. Again, however, if children are placed with one parent as a result of temporary orders and life seems to be going well, a judge is not likely to upset the apple cart and require the children to change placement without knowing how they would react to another environment.

The period of time that temporary orders are in effect often serves as a trial period to see how things will go. If during this time the parent with placement exercises poor judgment, if problems arise in school or at home, if contact with the other parent is obstructed, or if similar problems arise, these factors will be held against that parent at the trial and may lead to a reversal of placement.

Temporary orders are needed, especially when the relationship between you and your former spouse is acrimonious enough for you to divorce. Under these circumstances, a custody dispute is likely to occur. It is foolish to think that you are angry enough to dissolve your marriage but pleasant enough to each other to say "let's sit down and work out a placement arrangement that is best for the kids" when the divorce has been filed. Temporary orders allow someone with a level head to review your case and make a decision about where the children will stay, at least temporarily. These orders also help prevent parents from interfering with visitation. If you are displeased with temporary orders, you can request a review by a judge.

Although it may be hard to believe, attorneys can be effective in resolving temporary issues without going to court. This is most likely to occur if the attorneys have worked together well in the past and know what is likely to happen under a temporary arrangement. Parents are often concerned that if the attorneys know each other well they won't fight for what they want. On the contrary, attorneys who know each other well usually work well together and lessen aggravation and cost.

Your Children's Worries

Children love to press their ears to doors to hear everything that is being discussed or argued about by their parents. Even if you are trying to keep them out of these discussions, children are apt to have an indication of what's being planned. One of the negative s of temporary orders is that they stretch out children's anxiety over how long a living arrangement will last, and children worry anew about where they are going to live and with whom. When you hear a child ask, "Where am I going to live?" you can understand how emotional this can be.

If your children are concerned about temporary placement, try to soothe and reassure them, but don't give them false hope or a message that's untrue because, as I said, the orders may become permanent. Instead of telling children that placement is temporary, you might say, "There are a lot of things happening now that might not be the way we'd like them to be. If we go to court, the judge will tell us the way it's going to be, but right now we'll just do the best we can."

Children can become very dramatic when a temporary order changes to a different permanent order that runs counter to what they want. A child may threaten to run away or even to kill himself or herself. Odds very strongly favor a child doing neither, but in some cases they do carry out their threats.

How do you know when children are being genuine about threats? It is sometimes difficult for parents to know, so I encourage them to get children into therapy as soon as even one such threat is made. Children who do run away can turn to organizations such as Pathfinders in Milwaukee, Wisconsin (many cities have organizations like this) for a safe haven and therapeutic care until they can go back home or are placed elsewhere.

One safeguard that can be taken if a child threatens to run away rather than live with a particular parent is to go to court and tell the judge that a placement recommendation is counter to what the child wants and that he or she has threatened to run away. Before the child learns that the placement order has been put into effect, the courts and mental health professionals have a chance to set up a safety net and get the child into therapy.

You don't have time to set up such an arrangement in a situation where a child has already been placed and says, "If you make me continue living with Dad (Mom) I'll kill myself." A child who is making a statement about where he or she *is*, not where he or she doesn't want to be, is raising a red flag. Parents facing this should immediately ask the courts, their attorneys, court-appointed guardians, and psychologists to take action, which can include putting a child into psychiatric treatment, changing placement, and therapy. One reason children make such statements is because they are impulsive by nature and don't think through the alternatives. Therapeutic intervention gives them an opportunity to consider all the options.

Custody Disputes

If you discover that custody issues aren't resolvable through a non-litigation process, the first thing you should do is put a support network in place. Make sure you have appropriate legal representation. Tell family and friends that you are involved in a custody dispute and that you are likely to need to lean on them for additional support. If you are a religious person, turn to clergy. It may also be the time for you to consider meeting with a therapist or counselor to make sure your approach to decision making is as objective as possible and in your children's best interests. Whereas friends, relatives, and clergy are likely to blindly support you, serving as advocate supporters and not as objective supporters, a therapist or counselor will provide objectivity, ensuring that you look at issues from many different viewpoints.

Many people choose to avoid custody disputes out of concern for the negative effects they will have on them and/or their children. Sometimes, however, custody disputes are unavoidable. The following information can help you understand what is likely to happen in a custody dispute.

The Guardian ad Litem

A guardian ad litem is appointed by the court to represent the best interests of the children. In most states, guardians ad litem are attorneys; however, courts in some states appoint nonattorneys as guardians ad litem.

In my experience, two types of attorneys become guardians ad litem. The first is the novice attorney, a recent law school graduate who looks at guardian ad litem appointments as a means of obtaining work and becoming known in the family law community. These individuals may not be adequately trained for guardian ad litem work or fully understand what is necessary to sufficiently fulfill the role of guardian ad litem. Many states require specialized training for attorneys before they can become guardians ad litem; however, some states require no training or pay only cursory attention to training.

The second type of person who becomes a guardian ad litem is the attorney who is truly devoted to understanding the needs of children and considers this a major part of his or her practice. These attorneys have been involved in family law for many years, in some instances decades, and they understand child development and are capable of communicating well with children. They also see objectively the needs of parents and children, and make recommendations that match their needs.

The two best guardians ad litem I have worked with were middle school teachers prior to becoming lawyers. By virtue of their teaching backgrounds, both had experience with children and understood their developmental needs.

Many experienced lawyers won't take guardian ad litem assignments because sometimes it's ugly work, and in some jurisdictions they have to accept the court's pay rate, which can be as low as $75 per hour. In cases involving parents who are financially secure, the courts appoint experienced attorneys to do guardian ad litem work and order that they be paid at their regular rate.

At the beginning of this process, parents usually don't know if a guardian ad litem will be appointed. However, if one is appointed, children literally get their own attorney, not to represent their wishes, but to represent what is in their best interest. Children have probably heard their parents talk about their attorneys and may have a jaded perception of what an attorney will or will not do for them. If parents have given the impression that attorneys fight for their clients, a child may think the guardian ad litem is a person who is going to fight for him or her, which may reduce a child's anxiety. On the other hand, if a parent has made negative comments about the other parent's attorney, a child may initially have little trust in the guardian ad litem.

Children have no way of gauging a guardian ad litem's competence, but they recognize if someone is caring and understanding and makes them feel comfortable and less anxious. Children tend to connect with a guardian ad litem who knows how to communicate with them and understands their needs. In some cases, however, children are saddled with guardians ad litem who are literally afraid to talk to the children because they don't know how. Children never connect with those people.

In very, very few cases is a guardian ad litem appointed at the beginning. A situation has to become extremely messy and ugly for this to be done. Even in cases that aren't that bad, however, many children see a considerable amount of ugliness as their parents move through the divorce and custody processes. In most cases, when a guardian ad litem is introduced, he or she is expected to raise a child's comfort level, and it may be very difficult for a child to respond positively because for so long nobody has been looking out for his or her interests.

Poisoning the Well

I was involved in one case in which the guardian ad litem for an eight-year-old girl named Michelle was not very good. Michelle needed a strong, competent, understanding guardian ad litem because she was at the center of an extremely difficult custody dispute. Michelle's mother had involved her in many of the things from which children should be excluded, such as manipulation and lying. For example, Michelle left a message for me one holiday at 10:35 p.m. on my office voice mail. She said hello and there followed a series of ums and uhs. I could hear her mother whispering in the background, but Michelle said nothing except ums for the entire length of the two-and-a-half-minute message. The next message was also from Michelle. She started out with ums and uhs, but then said, "I just wanted to tell you that I want to live with my mom. I don't like it with my dad." Then she hung up.

Her mother had become so desperate to gain placement of Michelle that she put this incredible pressure on the child by making her call on a holiday, past her bedtime, to deliver what appeared to be her mother's message. Courts, upon hearing about such behavior, are very reluctant to place a child with that parent. Such a parent is undermining his or her own efforts without realizing it.

Michelle trusted and loved both her parents, and she was not going to choose one over the other. She was being pushed into that position by her mother, who moved 30 miles away from her ex-spouse as part of her manipulation. Her argument for wanting custody was that she lived far away and it was difficult for her to visit Michelle because of the distance.

Michelle's mother convinced the child, who was living with her father, that she was going to be allowed to live with her mother. She told Michelle not to sign up for any activities at school because she would have to leave them when she went to a new school. Michelle's interpretation was that she didn't have to do homework, and asked, "Why do I have to work in this school when I'm going to end up in another school soon?"

Michelle ended up living with her father, after having gone through a year of school without accomplishing much. Because her mother had assured Michelle of living with her, Michelle was very disappointed when the decision favored her father. We started seeing the depression, regression, or acting out behavior that I talked about earlier in this book.

Michelle's mother poisoned the child against the guardian ad litem because he made temporary recommendations that were counter to her plan. As a result, Michelle would tell me that the guardian ad litem had lied to me, or that "I don't like him because he made me live with Dad and go to Dad's school." She was actually attending the same school she had attended before her parents divorced, which was the correct recommendation from the guardian ad litem. Because Michelle's mother didn't speak too highly of the guardian ad litem, who was Michelle going to believe and trust: a virtual stranger, who her mother said was bad, or her mom, who was making all sorts of promises to her? Michelle did not have a good relationship with her guardian ad litem, which was unfortunate because had he been more experienced and had her mother not talked about him so badly, he may have been able to help Michelle balance the confusion she felt about her situation and help keep her mother slightly more under control.

In the case of the four children that we discussed in Chapter 3, the guardian ad litem came into the picture four years after the case began. She was the second guardian ad litem in that case, because it had been closed and the first guardian ad litem dismissed. (Usually a guardian ad litem is dismissed after a trial or within six months after a trial. If a guardian ad litem is needed after that, sometimes a new one is appointed.)

In this case, a second guardian ad litem was appointed because the mother wanted to move to Florida, a considerable distance from where she and her children and her ex-spouse were living. This would have interfered with the father's visitation time. The guardian ad litem was called in to see if the move was necessary. These children were already having a difficult time when along came this stranger saying, "Trust me. I'm going to act in your best interests." These children had been through so much that they had no idea who to trust. But they were fortunate to get a very competent, caring guardian ad litem who earned their trust. They warmed up to her and started calling her by her first name. When crises arose, she came to my office to meet with the children and we talked to them together. It was easy to see the warm, trusting interaction between them, but that was based on the guardian ad litem's behavior, not on the children.

The mother in that case also tried to turn the children against the guardian ad litem. However, because the guardian ad litem was active with the children and they could see what she was doing for them, their mother was not successful. In Michelle's case, the poisoning worked because the guardian ad litem was not as involved.

The Custody Study

A guardian ad litem appointed in a case often recommends that a custody study be performed. This study may be done by a county-paid social worker who interviews the parents, makes home visits, and makes collateral contacts in the community before making a recommendation. Since the guardian ad litem and the person conducting the custody study are both court-appointed and are most likely paid by the court, the court will listen closely to their recommendations. Therefore, do not underestimate the importance of the input from the custody study and the guardian ad litem. When these people call to make an appointment as part of the divorce process, take their roles seriously, make yourself available, and be honest.

Custody Evaluation

A custody evaluation generally involves formalized testing along with interviews, contact with collateral sources, and meetings with attorneys. Custody evaluations are most frequently performed by doctoral-level psychologists with specialized training and experience in developmental psychology, family psychology, psychological assessment of adults and children, psychopathology of adults and children, the effects of divorce and custody arrangements on adults and children, relevant aspects of the legal system, research, theory, policy, and practice regarding divorce and child custody issues, and a working knowledge of the Ethical Principles and Code of Conduct for Psychologists.

I, along with many other researchers, have surveyed psychologists, family law judges, and family law attorneys throughout the country in a number of different studies. It is clear that psychologists performing custody evaluations, family law attorneys, and family law judges expect the following in evaluations: to observe children of all ages with their parents; a review of mental health records; a review of criminal records; a review of the children's school and medical records; contact with collateral sources (therapists, childcare givers, and so on); psychological testing to be performed on parents, children, and significant others; consultations with the guardian ad litem; interviews with the parents, children, and significant others; a report to be written, and the psychologist to testify in court. The majority of these individuals do not expect: the pleadings of the family law case to be reviewed; legal records to be reviewed; the parents' medical records to be reviewed; home visits; or consultations with the parties' attorneys.

A typical custody evaluation entails 4 to 10 hours of testing and interviewing per person, at an average cost of $1,000 to $1,500 per person. A psychologist is called into a case to perform a custody evaluation when the court, guardian ad litem, and/or either of the parents' attorneys feels that a person's mental health may adversely affect the children.

The American Psychological Association and the Association of Family and Conciliation Courts have developed guidelines for custody evaluations. As an informed consumer (whenever you hire a professional, you are acting as a consumer), you should know what to expect from the evaluation and the psychologist, and what the outcome is likely to be.

The main purpose of a custody evaluation is to determine what is in the best psychological interests of the children. Linking children's interests and well-being, the focus of the evaluation is on parenting capacity, the psychological and developmental needs of the children, and the resulting fit. The goal of the psychologist is not to assess whether the parents have any psychological or emotional problems, but to evaluate how they function on a day-to-day basis in their parental roles.

Helpful Hint

When you enter a custody evaluation setting, the most important factor to remember is to be honest.

Being honest may sometimes appear detrimental to your position, but if a psychologist learns that you were dishonest, it is likely to weigh heavily against you. You can also safely assume that the psychologist will find out about issues you are trying to hide, because in a custody dispute your spouse is interested in making you look as bad as possible and will gladly share such information with the psychologist.

Psychologists doing custody evaluations usually have access to records of arrests and other problems with the law, Child Protective Services reports, mental health records, school records, and alcohol and other drug abuse records. You can assume that the psychologist will check your rendition of what has occurred against official documents.

The frequency and recent nature of mental health problems and problems with the law are important issues. A parent who has been hospitalized in psychiatric units 10 times in the three years prior to the custody evaluation is much worse off than a parent who had one hospitalization 15 years earlier or as a teenager. Additionally, someone who has been involved in a number of crimes against persons, such as sexual assault, armed robbery, or assault and battery, is looked upon much more negatively than is a person who has been involved in misdemeanor crimes against property.

The psychologist will be interested in observing you with your children as part of the evaluation process. These observations can take place a number of ways and the approach depends on the psychologist's preference. The most effective way is for each parent to be observed alone with all the children together to determine how well he or she can handle them as a group.

Don't become too anxious about this observation period. It is likely to be short and rarely will it be the key element upon which a psychologist bases his or her recommendation. As much as possible, be yourself. Be relaxed and as natural as you can be.

A question often raised about observations is whether they should be allowed to occur between children and alleged abuse perpetrators, or between children and a parent when a restraining order is in place. One purpose of the psychological evaluation is to determine if abuse has occurred, if sufficient bonding between child and parent merits continued contacts, and/or if supervised or unsupervised visitation should be recommended.

Attorneys may strongly object to their client's children being in the company of a parent who has been accused of abuse or against whom a restraining order has been issued. However, psychologists have no other way to adequately evaluate interaction between parents and children. Courts recognize that the evaluator is a trained mental health professional who is obligated to act in the best interest of children. As a result, the evaluator will not allow the interaction to become psychologically or physically harmful.

Psychologists are obligated to take an impartial stance in custody evaluations. For this reason, the psychologist should be appointed by the court, the guardian ad litem, or agreed on by both parents' attorneys.

When a psychologist is called on to perform a second opinion evaluation, he or she is still required to remain objective and impartial. Therefore, don't assume that if you hire a psychologist to do a second opinion evaluation, the results will automatically favor you.

As I said earlier, a psychologist must have specialized competence to perform a custody evaluation. When a psychologist is asked to help determine whether sexual abuse has taken place, he or she must address many variables. The behavior of the child should be evaluated to see if it is similar to individuals who have been abused. The alleged perpetrator's behavior should be evaluated to determine if it is similar to that of sexual abusers. And, the behavior of the no perpetrating parent should also be evaluated for similarities with behavior of nonperpetrating parents. After all this, however, even the most competent psychologist may not be able to determine with any degree of certainty that abuse has occurred.

When a psychologist performs a custody evaluation, various questions will need to be answered, especially if one parent has made allegations of abuse against the other. These questions could be asked by the court, the guardian ad litem, either or both parents' attorneys, or the parents. Questions might include:

- Was the child sexually abused?
- Was the child physically abused?
- Will it be detrimental to the child to move to a different city?
- Do either of the parents' drug-related problems in the past present a threat to the child?
- Does the mental health of either parent pose a problem or threat to the child?

The psychologist should be made aware of these questions in advance so that the evaluation can be as thorough as possible.

To save time and money, psychologists are sometimes asked to perform a partial evaluation; that is, they are to evaluate only the parents, only the children, or one parent and the children without the other parent. Partial evaluations may save time and money, but they do not allow a psychologist to render a complete opinion. When a partial evaluation is performed, the psychologist should tell you and your attorney that limitations in his or her recommendations will be necessary. When only one parent is evaluated, the psychologist can state whether the parent is psychologically stable, but cannot make a custody or placement recommendation. Evaluating parents without the children makes it impossible for the evaluator to take children's developmental needs into consideration. Similarly, evaluating children without their parents does not allow a psychologist to consider parenting capabilities.

Informed Consent

It is important to obtain the informed consent of all participants before a psychologist performs a custody evaluation. This means that the psychologist should tell you the nature, purpose, and method of evaluation, who has requested it, and who will pay the fees. In most cases, either the court or the parents pay. When parents cannot afford it, courts may advance the funds and allow them to pay the court back over time. In most cases, courts will find a way of dividing the cost of evaluations between parents, based on ability to pay. However, in cases in which one parent brought the action, the courts may require that parent to bear the full cost.

As I mentioned, as part of the informed consent process, you should be made aware of what will take place during the evaluation. This will generally include a description of the psychological testing, what collateral contacts will be made, what additional documentation might be sought, and how the information will be reported. In most cases, psychologists will also want to meet with the guardian ad litem and/or both attorneys, and you should be told in advance if such a meeting is going to take place.

Clarifying financial arrangements is also part of informed consent. Many psychologists require you to sign a custody evaluation agreement that includes the areas discussed in informed consent and financial arrangements. Most experienced psychologists require the full cost of the evaluation to be paid in the form of a retainer, or at least be paid prior to issuing a report. Some psychologists charge a set fee per evaluation while others have an hourly rate. This must be disclosed in the informed consent.

You should expect no surprises regarding costs. A psychologist is required to identify at the outset any additional services that are not included in the cost of the evaluation. Most psychologists, for example, do not include in the evaluation fee the cost of testifying in court or at a deposition. You can expect a psychologist to require payment in advance for testimony. And if a court date is canceled without warning, they generally charge for the time that had been reserved for the court appearance because it cannot be used.

Confidentiality

Mental health professionals adhere to confidentiality, which suggests that information will be kept private and not shared with anyone.

Helpful Hint

In custody situations, however, confidentiality is not likely to be upheld.

The limitations on confidentiality should be disclosed to you prior to the evaluation or at least at the beginning of it. As part of my approach to evaluations, I have each parent sign a statement indicating they understand that the results of the evaluation will *not* be confidential and will be shared with the court, attorneys, and other pertinent individuals in the evaluation process.

Parents involved in individual psychotherapy prior to the evaluation may want the content of those therapy sessions kept out of the divorce process. In such a case, you are allowed to protect your confidentiality by "invoking privilege." This means you feel the content of the therapy sessions is privileged communication and you will not sign a release for that information. Some states uphold privilege in a custody fight, others do not, and others have special rules and exceptions. You need to find out from your attorney how your state deals with the issue of privilege.

If you take this approach, the other side is likely to wonder what you are trying to hide. Some courts do not allow privilege to be invoked when a parent's mental health is called into question as part of a custody dispute. In those cases, the court may order the parent to sign a release for the information.

You must also realize that invoking privilege is generally an all or nothing situation. You cannot release the information to one person and then refuse to release it to another. For communication to be truly privileged, it must never be released to anyone.

As I said before, mental health and criminal history will also be evaluated. The extent of the history, frequency of problems, and how recently they occurred are taken into consideration. In one case, Peter, a stepfather, was being evaluated as part of a custody evaluation. It was found that he had a 14-year criminal history that included felony convictions for crimes against property and person. He had been convicted twice for sexual assault, twice for armed robbery, and had served eight years in prison. The ultimate recommendation was that the children be allowed to visit with their mother, but Peter could not be present. Furthermore, because Peter's sexual assaults had been against minors, if he ever had contact with the children, visitations with their mother would be terminated.

Psychologists view the use of collateral information in different ways. I prefer to get as much collateral information as possible to avoid surprises during court testimony. Some psychologists, however, prefer to perform the evaluation without collateral information and may or may not review it later on.

To Supervise or Not to Supervise

After weighing the data from the psychological and personality tests and interviews, a psychologist is required to render opinions based on what is in the best interest of the children. As part of this process, supervision of parental visits may be necessary. Supervision is often required in cases of substantiated abuse, severe alienation, active drug or alcohol abuse, or if one parent is mentally ill. The process of moving from supervised visits to unsupervised visits generally follows these steps:

1. Therapeutic supervised visits. These visits take place in the confines of a therapeutic session with a psychotherapist. Initially, these contacts would only occur in the therapist's office. Prior to moving to the next step, the therapist may take visits outside the office into the community. Parks, restaurants, and shopping malls are possible locations for these visits. At the end of the visit, the therapist provides feedback to the participants to address problem areas. The therapist can also facilitate the reintroduction of family members to one another. The therapist is also permitted to terminate or suspend a given session when a problem arises and to discuss that problem with the various family members. Once a sufficient comfort level has been achieved, the parties are ready for the next step of supervision.

2. Supervised visits by a disinterested third party. This disinterested third party would be an individual who does not have a relationship with either of the parties and who is generally paid for the service of providing supervision. This supervision can take place on-site or in a neutral location. Many jurisdictions have public and private agencies for this purpose.

3. Supervised visits by an interested third party. An interested third party would be described as someone who has

a relationship with one or both parties. This individual must be approved by the parents, the guardian ad litem, and/or the court-appointed evaluator. The interested and disinterested supervisors should have the power to terminate the visit at any time that it is felt that inappropriate interaction is taking place between the parent and the child(ren). Furthermore, those supervisors should report back to the guardian ad litem and/or court appointed psychologist as soon as possible to discuss the concerns that were generated during the visit.

4. Monitored visits. An unsupervised monitored visit is one in which the parties are continuing to meet with an outside individual, for example, a therapist, to evaluate the effectiveness of the visits, with the individual having power to report back to the guardian ad litem and/or the court-appointed psychologist. The parent and the child(ren) would meet with the therapist just prior to the contact to discuss what will occur and immediately following the contact for the purpose of debriefing and discussing any issues that may arise.

5. Loosely monitored visits. Loosely monitored visits follow the same format as monitored visits. However, in loosely monitored visits the therapist, parent, and child(ren) meet on a weekly basis to discuss how the contacts during the previous week have gone and to make suggestions for contacts for the next week.

6. Completely unsupervised, unmonitored daytime visits.

7. Completely unsupervised, unmonitored overnight visits. In making this recommendation, the evaluator must be aware that finding supervisors in these cases is often not easy.

Completing all of these steps can take as little as several months or as long as several years. The younger the children at the beginning of supervision, and the more severe the infractions that result in supervision, the longer this process takes. Conversely, the older the children are or the less severe the infractions, the more likely it is that this process could be completed in a couple of months.

The psychologist's recommendations should also note whether therapy should be part of the process following divorce.

This may include individual therapy for either or both parents and/or family therapy to deal with extended family issues. Parents often complain that extended therapy will be very costly; however, this expense is the price to be paid for being unable to come to terms without getting involved in a custody dispute.

You may want a copy of the report that is generated by the evaluation.

Helpful Hint

Most psychologists are reluctant to give parents a copy of the completed report for fear it will be misunderstood or misused in the divorce action.

Unfortunately, some parents take these reports and disseminate the information to friends and relatives as a way of trying to demonstrate the correctness of their position. Because of this potential for misuse, many psychologists instead write a summary letter for the parents.

The conclusions and recommendations of the psychological evaluation should include:

- Whether there should be joint or sole custody.
- Who should be the primary placement parent.
- What type of placement time the nonprimary placement parent should get.
- Whether the visits should be supervised.
- What type of therapeutic intervention, if any, is needed.
- Statements about any special circumstances in the case.

Regardless of whether you use arbitration, mediation, or litigation to resolve a custody dispute, the third party making the decision will weigh the needs of the children, the wishes of the parents, and the results of the evaluation. This information will be used to decide the best placement for the children.

Relocation Cases

Although abuse constitutes a major area of concern in custody disputes, it is not the only problem that can arise. Imagine, for example, that you have been divorced for four years and, except for some minor glitches, the placement schedule developed by you and your ex-spouse has worked well. Then, all of a sudden, you receive a phone call, letter, or formal notice that your ex-partner is moving out of town and wants to take the children along.

Let's assume that this move is for a legitimate purpose, such as a job transfer. What should you do? Should you fight the move? Let them go?

Whenever a move like this takes place, the children lose. A child who has had reasonable access to both parents and suddenly finds himself or herself in a position in which the other parent is going to be almost entirely excluded from his or her life is not going to be a happy child.

If an issue like this is taken to court, a judge will decide if the children move or stay. An ensuing court battle will be financially and psychologically costly, and the court will take a dim view of the parent who wants to move away with no real necessity. It becomes more difficult to convince the court that a child should move away when he or she will be leaving not only friends but extended family on both sides, a school in which he or she is performing adequately, and a neighborhood in which the child has enjoyed some stability. In such situations, the court is likely to allow children to remain behind with the nonmoving parent. In circumstances in which a move is essential and both you and your ex-spouse are excellent parents, the judge has a tough call to make, and very often small details—such as a child being able to have a pet in a new location or having to give one up—lead to a decision.

Several factors should be considered when you are deciding to take this issue to court. The first is whether the parent who is moving away will continue to allow you reasonable access to your children or if he or she will use the move to cut off your relationship. In situations that have been characterized by a lot of anger, lack of cooperation, difficulty obtaining compliance with court orders, and so on, your ex-spouse will more likely use moving away as an opportunity to cut you off from your children. And generally once the move is made, even if things do not go well, you will have difficulty getting the children back.

A second area that you need to evaluate is whether you can afford ongoing access. A court may order that you be allowed to visit your children, but suppose you can't afford it or you can't get the time off from work?

You also need to take into account the financial and psychological cost of fighting the move. Tens of thousands of dollars could be spent waging this battle over the course of a year or two, and that's money that could be used to visit your children in the other city. Psychologically, a court battle at this juncture could take a relationship that has been relatively cooperative and turn it topsy-turvy, and you are not likely to achieve the same level of cooperation afterwards.

This situation takes on another dimension when the move is being orchestrated for a marriage or new relationship. How does this affect children? To answer that question, I'll tell you about Tammy, who wanted to move from Wisconsin to Colorado with her children to marry a man she had known for three months. Her ex-husband was concerned about the planned move and went to court. In the interim, the guardian ad litem ordered a background check on the new significant other and found that he had an arrest record that included 17 convictions and a number of prison terms over ten years. The convictions included two for felonious armed robbery and two for felonious sexual assault.

The court ordered that Tammy could move to Colorado but the children were not to have contact with that man. In the ruling, Tammy was also told that if she intended to marry him, she would not receive placement and her children would not be allowed to move with her.

What kind of influence would Tammy's new man have had on her children? Whose best interests was she looking after? What would have happened if her ex-husband had not intervened and the guardian ad litem had not stepped in to help resolve the matter? You must do your homework, be alert, and not let anything adversely affect your children. If you decide to allow your children to move with your ex-spouse, make sure a court order is entered or an agreement is signed allowing you significant access during nonschool time, similar to schedules outlined in Chapter 5.

When the parent and the children end up in different cities, a schedule can be developed to maximize time between the children and the parent left behind. The left behind parent should receive summer placement (defined as one week after school is out until two weeks before school starts), have the right of first refusal for all long weekends during the school year (such as teachers' conferences, teachers' convention, President's weekend), and two-thirds of the school vacations days allotted for Thanksgiving, Christmas/winter break, and Easter/spring break. Furthermore, the left behind parent should have the option of going to the city where the children reside and having placement of the children for up to four one-week blocks of time in that city. They could stay with friends or relatives of the left behind parent if there are any in that city, or the left behind parent could stay at a "Residence Inn" type of place for the week. The parent would be responsible for getting the children to school and activities, helping with homework, and any other activities that a parent would ordinarily engage in. If this type of schedule is implemented, the parent who is left behind will end up with substantial periods of placement for at least 10 out of the 12 months of the year. I have had parents say to me that they actually have better quality time with their children under these circumstances because the focus is exclusively on spending time with the children and not engaging in other activities.

Since one parent has chosen to leave, it is not unusual and should be expected that the court may require that parent to pay more than half of the transportation costs for the parent left behind. A two-thirds/one-third split is not unusual.

Going Back to Court

People who need to return to court after a divorce are said to be dealing with "post judgment" concerns, meaning additional action is taking place after the original divorce judgment was entered.

One of the main reasons people return to court is because of a change of circumstance between the time a divorce was filed and the time they go to court to argue their case. A change of circumstance may include:

- A change in physical or mental health of a parent that reduces his or her capacity for carrying out parental abilities.
- A change in financial circumstances that makes it less feasible to adequately care for a child.

- Introduction of a new person into the children's lives who may be a negative influence (such as Tammy's significant other).
- Discovery of physical or sexual abuse.
- Repeated instances of bad judgment, such as sleeping with school-age children, taking children to bars, showing them R- or X-rated movies, problems with internet pornography abuse, or giving them illegal drugs.
- The onset of or return to alcohol or other drug abuse.
- An attempt to alienate the other parent.
- Lack of cooperation with court orders.
- Obstructing visits.

Change of circumstance can also involve one parent relocating and wanting to take the children with him or her. The presumption of the court is that children are better off when they don't have to change their residence, so, once again, the parent who is attempting to change must prove the necessity. In cases where the relocation seems unnecessary, the court is not likely to even entertain the notion. If a child's environment is not ideal, a parent may need to relocate to improve the child's living conditions. In such a case, the positive reason for the move would outweigh the negative impact on a child who has to change settings.

If a court battle ensues over a change of circumstance, it is likely that psychologists, social workers, and other professionals will be brought in to look into the concerns generated by the change or proposed change. As in all other instances, you must carefully weighh the financial and psychological cost of going back to court along with the cost of not fighting.

Contempt of Court

It is unlikely, unless the infraction is extremely serious, that you would be found in contempt the first time you violate a court order. However, if more violations occur, a judge is likely to find you in contempt and give you a fine, jail time, or rescind your placement privileges.

> **Helpful Hints**
>
> A judge can find you in contempt of court for not following his or her orders.

One of the most common reasons for finding a parent in contempt is failure to pay child support. Many parents have been jailed for this. Removing a child from the state without notifying the other parent can also result in a contempt or more serious findings.

Appeals

Television and movies have led us to believe that every court decision that someone doesn't like is appealed. In reality, very few divorce cases are appealed. When an appeal is filed, the appellate court is likely to refer the case back to the court and judge who made the original decision and ask him or her to reconsider it. In most cases, when an appeal is made, the appellate court upholds the original decision. This doesn't mean that you should not appeal a decision with which you are dissatisfied. It just means that you have to consider the circumstances, what you and your children stand to gain or lose, and the financial and psychological costs of appealing a case. Generally, psychological wounds created by the divorce will remain open during the appeal process, prolonging your recovery and that of your children.

Child Support

It should not be used to redecorate the home, take vacations, or for other inappropriate things. Child support consistently misused can represent a change of circumstance and a judge might consider changing placement of the children.

> **Helpful Hints**
>
> The sole purpose of child support is to support your children.

Most states have guidelines or laws to accurately determine how much money is needed to support a child. Although support used to be determined on a percentage basis, most states do not follow that standard and instead use other formulas to determine support. Some states have support payments automatically deducted from the paying parent's payroll check. The money is sent to the court, which then sends it to the primary placement parent. If the person paying support loses his or her job, support payments are likely to be temporarily suspended.

Kidnapping

You may entertain the fantasy of running away with your children if divorce and custody battles become really bad. Just be sober about this and remember that it's a terrible idea. In the vast majority of parental kidnapping cases, the parent is located and many are convicted of the crime and jailed. Apart from the criminal implications and ramifications, if you take your children and you are found, you will probably never be able to spend unsupervised time with them again. To compound matters, the very person you are trying to keep your children from will probably be awarded placement while you are in jail and, most likely, permanently.

Parents sometimes think they can flee to a foreign country where they will never be found. This is not true. Any country that belongs to the Hague Convention will help find children and will return them to the country from which they were taken. Depending on the laws of the country in which the children are found, the parent who absconded with them will either be jailed there or returned to the country from which the children were snatched. Many countries have kidnapping laws that are stricter than those in the United States.

The Hague Convention on International Child Abduction

The Hague Convention was adopted for a number of reasons, not the least of which was to deal with the difficulty of locating children in foreign countries. It also serves to facilitate problems locating attorneys in countries to which a child has been abducted and to reduce difficulty having a custody order recognized in a foreign country. In the past, parents who abducted their children would often go to court in a foreign country to get a court order for their custody, thereby legitimizing the abduction. The situation would contain two conflicting court orders, which made it even more difficult to have children returned home.

The Hague Convention attempts to facilitate the prompt return of children to the country from which they were kidnapped and to ensure the custody rights and laws of the country. Under the Convention, a judge must order the return of children under the age of 16 when they have been wrongfully taken from a country. Exceptions allowed for not returning children under the Convention include a great risk of physical or psychological harm, an objection by the child to being returned when he or she is old enough to make that objection, or a violation of human rights principles if the child were returned.

As of 2007, countries subscribing to the Hague Convention include: Argentina, Australia, Austria, Bahamas, Belarus, Belgium, Belize, Bosnia and Herzegovina, Brazil, Bulgaria, Burkina Faso, Canada, Chile, China, People's Republic of Croatia, Cyprus, Czech Republic, Denmark, Estonia, Finland, France, Georgia, Germany, Greece, Honduras, Hungary, Iceland, Ireland, Israel, Italy, Latvia, Lithuania, Luxembourg, Macedonia, Malta, Mexico, Monaco, Montenegro, Netherlands, New Zealand, Norway, Panama, Paraguay, Peru, Poland, Portugal, Romania, Serbia, Slovakia, Slovenia, South Africa, Spain, Sri Lanka, Sweden, Switzerland, Turkey, Ukraine, United Kingdom of Great Britain and Northern Ireland, United States of America, Uruguay, Venezuela, and Zimbabwe. This list changes on a regular basis. The reader is cautioned to search and check Hague Convention on International Child Abduction.com for revisions.

Chapter

5

Two of Everything? Dealing with the Practicalities of Placement and Custody

In most custody cases, one parent is designated for primary placement of the children, although a shared placement arrangement can be made, under which children would usually spend equal time or close to equal time with each parent. Different states have different terms that apply to time spent with the noncustodial parent. Terms like visitation, placement, access, accompaniment, and companionship are used in various states. For the purpose of this book, I will always use the term placement to represent any of these terms. Because primary placement is the norm, however, the amount of time a child should spend with the other parent needs to be determined through alternate placement schedules.

Although primary placement may be the norm, more and more states are using terms like "substantially equal placement" to identify the amount of time that the children spend with each parent. Substantially equal placement does not mean exactly the same number of days with each parent. The consensus among mental health professionals is that substantially equal placement can range anywhere from 60/40 in one direction to 40/60 in the other direction and still allow for substantially equal time with each parent. For parents to argue about anything that falls between 60/40 and 40/60 is more a function of arguing about quantity than quality of time with the children. Unfortunately, these decisions are all too often driven by financial concerns.

Guidelines for determining the most appropriate placement patterns should keep in mind how much time you would like to spend with your children and how much time you would like the other parent to spend with them. They include:

- Consider your child's developmental level in terms of what he or she needs to grow in a healthy, well-rounded manner.

- If you have used a placement pattern that might seem to be developmentally inappropriate but has been successful for some time, your child is very adaptable. Check anyway for symptoms or problems that you may have overlooked or ignored, such as difficulty at transfer, unusual dependency, and unusual detachment or spaciness. If your child exhibits no symptoms, you might be able to continue the pattern.

- If a child shows signs of attachment problems, such as difficulty separating from parents and difficulty moving from one situation to another (called transitions), consider having him or her evaluated by a mental health professional.

- If a child develops symptoms when making a transition from one parent to another, such as clinging behavior or refusing to go on a visit to a parent or grandparent, or shows symptoms in situations other than visitation, such as refusing to go to school, consider (a) that visitation problems may exist (such as abuse, neglect, conflict); (b) that the child may be attempting to please the parent who is being left behind; and (c) that the child may find leaving the parent less painful if he or she makes everyone upset and angry; and (d) has a difficult temperament and finds any change difficult.

- If a child is going on a parental placement with an older sibling with whom he or she has a good relationship, consider allowing longer placements.

- If the conflict between parents continues to be a problem, consider neutral transfer points for placement, reduced frequency of transfers, and/or the possibility of sole custody.
- If the nonprimary placement parent is mentally unstable, consider reducing placement frequency and duration. Also, consider supervision or termination of parent access.
- If the nonprimary placement parent is an abuser, consider supervision or termination of placement.
- If a child has a difficult temperament, consider increasing stability by changing the location of the placement to a neutral setting such as a park or a grandparent's home, assuming she or he is neutral. You might also consider longer visitation times and fewer changes for added stability.
- If a child is severely alienated from a parent, consider very brief placements (30 minutes to an hour) with or without supervision.
- If parents are separated by a great geographic distance, consider frequent placements for young children if you can afford it. The primary placement parent should take the child to the nonprimary placement parent for at least half the visits, with nightly return to the primary placement parent. The rest of the time, the nonprimary placement parent should travel to the city of the primary placement parent. Also, avoid long visits with very young children. Children older than seven tolerate longer placements better.
- If a long time has passed since a child has seen a parent, but you or your child want to renew contact, consider phasing in a schedule to allow the child to get used to the other parent and rebuild trust. If neither the child nor the primary placement parent trusts the other parent, consider supervised phase-in placements.
- If the custodial parent spends a lot of time doing chores and driving car pools, is under stress, has few friends or relatives to share child care, and has a low income, he or she may benefit from some help with child care responsibilities from the noncustodial parent. Consider increased placement times.
- If a child has an easy temperament and adjusts well to changes, and you want to change the placement schedule,

consider how it will affect the child before you make the change. Too often, parents create and change placement schedules based on what is convenient for them rather than on a child's welfare. What's more, a parent is more likely to overlook how a change will affect an easygoing child.

Whether a case is tried in court or mediated, or whether an agreement is reached through stipulation or collaboration, a placement schedule must be developed. One of the most common and time-tested placement schedules is every other weekend with the noncustodial parent.

The amount of time each child physically spends with his or her parents can vary. The traditional arrangement allows for an 11/3 split—the nonprimary placement parent has the children on alternate weekends and one day during the off week, or 3 out of every 14 days. Placement schedules can be made on an 11/3, 10/4, 9/5, 8/6, or 7/7 basis.

Whenever possible, keep these decisions between you and your ex-spouse because unfortunately, when left to a judge's discretion, the best possible solution may not always occur. Although judges may be well-meaning, some of them don't understand child development enough to avoid making orders that are detrimental to children.

Placement of Young Children

The placement of young children can be a thorny issue. Young children (below three years of age) generally develop attachment relationships with one or both of the parents. When both parents have been truly equally involved in all aspects of childrearing, it is likely that both of the parents will be come primary attachment figures. However, when one parent has provided most of the childcare, that parent is likely to be a primary attachment figure and the other is not.

Research tells us that when a child becomes stressed, the child looks for the primary attachment figure to reduce the stress. When that person is not available, the stress increases. When a child reaches approximately four years of age, children are able to carry with them the notion of the primary attachment figure and reduce their own stress.

Helpful Hint

As a result, the common wisdom is that there should be no regularly scheduled overnight placements with children under one year of age with a nonprimary attachment figure.

Instead, there should be frequent contacts of short duration. This translates into four to five contacts a week approximately two to three hours long each. These contacts should be arranged at different times of the day so that the nonplacement parent can feed the child, bathe the child, play with the child, bed the child down, and engage in other activities with the child. It is certainly recognized that it can be inconvenient to implement a plan of this nature. However, it is important to remember that it is only temporary and is clearly in the child's best interest to provide a feeling of stability and trust in the environment. Not to do so could potentially lead to lifelong problems with trust, relationships, and feelings of security.

For children beyond two years of age, there generally is no reason why overnight placements should not be scheduled starting with one per week and gradually periodically adding an additional overnight as tolerated. What happens with children between one and two years of age is largely dependent upon a number of factors. The well adjusted child with parents who do not fight, who does not show signs of tension or anxiety, where the parents live geographically close to one another, can likely tolerate overnight placements between one and two years of age. However, with an anxious child who has parents who still fight, a child who has difficulty with transitions, and parents who live geographically distant from one another, overnight placements for children one to two years of age may be ill-advised. It can be very helpful during these years to have a mental health professional as a consultant to determine when overnight placements are appropriate for your child and when an increase in the number of overnights is appropriate.

The Ackerman Plan

As a general rule, I am not in favor of alternating plans because they tend to be confusing and disruptive for parents and children. For example, a parent might have a child on Monday, Wednesday and Friday, and the other parent has him or her on Tuesday, Thursday, and Saturday, or one parent might have a child from Sunday to Wednesday and the other parent gets him or her from Wednesday to the following Sunday. You as an adult would have difficulty moving this often, so think of what it does to your children.

I recommend schedules that allow a child to have a sense of home and permanency. If parents want to work out a schedule that gives each parent equal time, they should let the child spend half the year with the primary placement parent and the next six months with the other parent on a primary placement basis.

Both parents have something valuable to offer their children. The traditional visitation schedule puts parents in the position of having to make one of them a "real" parent and the other a visitor. To give both parents parenting time, I developed an alternative plan that seems to have worked quite well over the years.

The plan (see Table 5.1) is an extension of the traditional visitation schedule of alternating weekends. Instead of the weekend being from Friday night to Sunday afternoon or evening, I extended it to four days, from Thursday after school or work until Monday morning when school begins. With this long weekend, a parent has to help with homework, take children to sporting and other school activities, and provide discipline. The nonprimary placement parent also has an additional contact day on the off week. This part of the schedule is called the 9/5 plan.

During nonschool time, the alternate placement parent has the child 10 out of 14 days, and the primary placement parent has

	Sun	Mon	Tues	Wed	Thurs	Fri	Sat
Week 1	Y	Y	Y	Y	X	X	X
Week 2	X	Y	Y	Y	X	Y	Y

X = overnight at father's home
Y = overnight at mother's home

Table 5.1 9/5 Plan

him or her from the end of the day Friday until Monday morning, with one contact day during the alternate week. This plan was originally called the 9/5–10/4 flip-flop arrangement; however, Judge Patrick Madden in Milwaukee County Circuit Court labeled it the Ackerman Plan.

The Ackerman Plan gives one parent primary placement during school time (September 1 to June 1) on a 9/5 basis as described above. The other parent has primary placement of the child on a 10/4 basis during nonschool time (June 1 to September 1, Thanksgiving week, two weeks at Christmas, and one week at Easter). Using this plan, the 10/4 parent would have the children 10 out of 14 days for four months a year, and the 9/5 parent would have the child nine out of 14 days for eight months a year. The 9/5 parent actually has the children approximately 20 days per year more than the 10/4 parent.

Some people have argued that this plan gives children to the 10/4 parent for all holidays. But the 9/5 parent actually has the children for four days during the two weeks at Christmas and for two days at Thanksgiving and Easter.

When deciding which parent will have primary placement during school time and which parent will have primary placement during nonschool time, several factors should be considered. Generally, the parent who is better able to support children academically and is more available to help with homework should have primary placement.

The Ackerman Plan is only one example of a placement schedule. There are many variations, any one of which may be better suited to your lifestyle and capabilities (see Table 5.2 for other plans). Whatever plan you and your spouse decide on, you'll need to be flexible and work together.

The Ackerman Plan is an expansion of the traditional alternating weekend schedule that allows for substantially equal placement. In cases where equal placement has been ordered, a 2/2/5/5 schedule (as shown in Table 5.2) can be preferably to a 7/7 schedule. In the 2/2/5/5 schedule, one parent has every Monday and Tuesday, while the other parent has every Wednesday and Thursday, with Friday, Saturday and Sunday being alternated. In setting up a schedule of this nature, each parent can count on having the same days every week, which would allow that parent to put the child in an extracurricular activity on their night without fear of whether the other parent would cooperate during the

4/3/3/4

	Sun	Mon	Tues	Wed	Thurs	Fri	Sat
Every	X	X	X	X	Y	Y	Y
Week	X	X	X	Y	Y	Y	Y

X = represents days spent at the father's home
Y = represents days spent at the mother's home

2/2/5/5

	Sun	Mon	Tues	Wed	Thurs	Fri	Sat
Week I	X	Y	Y	X	X	Y	Y
Week II	Y	Y	Y	X	X	X	X

X = represents days spent at the father's home
Y = represents days spent at the mother's home

Table 5.2 Other Schedules

off week, since they will have that child on that given day every week. In addition, it helps parents with flexible work schedules to count on at least the same two days every week that they can work late and the same two days every week that they would need to be home earlier for the sake of the children.

In the event a 7/7 schedule (week-on/week-off) is selected, there should be a midweek contact for dinner with the other parent. For example, every Wednesday the children would have dinner with the parent that did not have the children that week. Especially with younger children, it can be difficult for the children to go a whole seven days without seeing the other parent.

Bad Schedules

Unfortunately one of the favorite schedules that people employ is having the children with one parent every Monday and Wednesday, the other parent every Tuesday and Thursday and alternating Friday, Saturday, and Sundays. This turns out to be a 1/1/1/1/4/1/1/4 schedule, which requires 9 changes in a 14 day period of time (see Table 5.3). I am not sure that there are many adults who could tolerate that many changes on a regular basis and maintain their stability.

Judges have been known to implement 3/3 schedules, rotating the children every three days to prevent too much time from passing without seeing each parent. Unfortunately, the calendar

1/1/1/1/4/1/1/4	Sun	Mon	Tues	Wed	Thurs	Fri	Sat
WEEK 1	Y	X	Y	X	Y	X	X
WEEK 2	X	X	Y	X	Y	Y	Y

3/3	Sun	Mon	Tues	Wed	Thurs	Fri	Sat
WEEK 1	X	X	X	Y	Y	Y	X
WEEK 2	X	X	Y	Y	Y	X	X
WEEK 3	X	Y	Y	Y	X	X	X
WEEK 4	Y	Y	Y	X	X	X	Y
WEEK 5	Y	Y	X	X	X	Y	Y
WEEK 6	Y	X	X	X	Y	Y	Y

Table 5.3 Bad Schedules

is set up on a seven-day basis and not a six-day basis. The 3/3 schedule requires a six week rotation before returning to what happened in week one. There is virtually no stability in a schedule of this nature.

General Rules

Parents have many factors to consider when planning visitation and holiday schedules. Following are several rules of thumb.

Holiday Placement

Because holiday placement supercedes regular placement schedules, you are required to be extremely flexible to avoid problems and confusion. For example, if your weekend to have the children falls on Christmas and the other parent has holiday placement, the other parent will get the children. Holidays are a big issue in divorce situations. Emotions run higher than usual, and your children are filled with a combination of exhilaration over anticipated celebrations and anxiety about how you will handle them. Once again, their feelings must be given precedence over your own. Every time a holiday comes around, I am inundated with calls from parents with placement questions and problems (remember the mother and child whose plans to go to Florida were foiled by a manipulative and spiteful ex-spouse). Children are highly sensitized to even subtle changes in your moods and to what you say about holiday plans. Work these things out ahead of time to avoid last-minute chaos and tears.

In the past visitation schedules traditionally allowed for holidays to be alternated. My preference, however, is for families to share holidays as much as possible instead of alternating them. This does not mean that the parents sit down together for a holiday meal, but that the children split the day between the parents. Sharing, of course, assumes the parents live in the same city. When holidays are alternated, children lose the chance to spend holiday time with half of their extended family. Not only do they miss out on visiting with one of their parents, but also with the aunts, uncles, cousins, and grandparents on that side of the family. Most of us have fond memories of extended families getting together during holidays. When holidays are shared, children have the opportunity to develop their own fond memories of both sides of the family. Here are some suggestions that may help in your planning:

> ***Thanksgiving*** One family can have Thanksgiving dinner earlier in the day, while the other can have dinner later in the day. Children can have Thanksgiving dinner with one family and dessert with the other.
>
> ***Christmas*** Christmas can be divided into Christmas Eve and Christmas Day. Children can spend Christmas Eve with one parent and Christmas Day with the other. However, if both parents want to have Christmas Eve or Christmas Day, then the Christmas Eve/Christmas Day placement can be rotated on a yearly basis.
>
> When children reach school age, Christmas visits generally include a school vacation. At this time parents may want to take a vacation with their children but be unable to do so because of the restrictions of the visitation schedule. Winter break can be shared. For example, in odd-numbered years, the mother could have the children from beginning of vacation through Christmas Eve and the father could have them from Christmas Day until school recommences. As a

result, each year one parent has the children during the majority of the break. In even-numbered years the situation would reverse.

Easter Easter can be shared by having the children spend Easter morning and Easter brunch with one family and Easter dinner with the other family.

Fourth of July Many activities take place on this holiday, including parades, picnics, fairs, and fireworks displays. The day could be divided so that some activities occur with one family and other activities are shared with the other.

Jewish Holidays Jewish holidays can be divided the same way. One parent could have Erev Rosh Hashanah, the other parent could have Rosh Hashanah day. The same plan can be used for Yom Kippur. If both parents want the same day, it could be alternated from year to year. With Passover, one parent could have the first seder and the other the second seder. This could remain constant from year to year or alternated. Chanukah is a long holiday that can be easily shared.

Religious Events First communions, confirmations, and bar and bat mitzvahs are important events that should be shared by both families. Generally, religious facilities are large enough that both families could attend without having to sit with one another. Parents certainly should put their differences aside long enough to participate in these important religious events with their children.

Other Holidays Children should spend Mother's Day with their mother and Father's Day with their father. Each parent should be allowed to have contact with children on his or her own birthday. Children's birthdays are seldom celebrated on the actual birth-date. One parent can arrange for a birthday party on the weekend before the actual birthdate and the other parent on the following weekend. The child will enjoy two birthday celebrations. Memorial Day and Labor Day are considered minor holidays and can either be alternated or shared depending on the parents' wishes. Many parents look at Labor Day and Memorial Day as three-day holidays, which allows for a three-day visit.

School Events

School events include graduations, school plays, athletic events, teacher conferences, concerts, and similar activities. It would be hoped that the parents would be able to set aside their negative feelings as much as possible to attend the events together. If not, the areas are certainly large enough that one parent could be in one area and the other parent in another. It is unfortunate when this process has to be relegated to parents having to choose whose turn it is to attend a particular school event.

Who Will Feed the Children

Whoever has the children at 6 P.M. is responsible for feeding them. Remember that, especially with young children, mealtime decisions are a basic concern. Don't let them hear you squabbling with your former spouse about who has to make dinner. It makes children feel unwanted, heightens their anxiety, and can trigger arguments between you and your former spouse—the last thing children want to see or need to experience any time, but especially during holidays.

Transportation

The receiving parent transports the children, so you have to make arrangements in advance for them to be picked up and dropped off at a designated place. This procedure reduces the amount of conflict that can arise over transporting children. Don't allow yourself to give into any temptations to play dirty tricks, such as showing up late or not being home at the appointed time.

Be Flexible

I can't emphasize enough the need for flexibility. Don't expect to make up time that is lost to the other parent for holiday visits. Over the course of your children's childhood, this time will even out.

Make Decisions for Your Children

Don't allow children to manipulate visitation schedules. Make decisions for the children and abide by those decisions. Encourage children to have a good time with the other parent and to share their experiences with you in a healthy, positive way when they return. Don't let the tail wag the dog.

The Right of First Refusal

The other parent should have the right of first refusal for alternate placement. If it is your time for placement and you will be out of town or otherwise unavailable to take your children, before taking them anyway and then hiring a babysitter, ask the other parent if she or he wants to have them. Don't be upset, however, if the other parent has already made other plans.

Parents need to decide when the right of first refusal takes effect. If the time frame is three or four hours or less, it may be impractical to implement the right of first refusal. However, if the time frame is five or six hours or more, it is generally better to implement the right of refusal. There have been a number of cases where we have had to withdraw the right of first refusal because either or both of the parents abused the process, manipulated it, or were generally uncooperative. Parents must remember that a process like the right of first refusal is for the benefit of the children and should not be interfered with by the parent's inappropriate behavior. Right of first refusal does not work with parents who are still fighting. It just gives them one more thing to fight about.

Separating Children

Parents often feel that children can be separated so that each parent has an opportunity to have a child of his or her own, so to

> ### Helpful Hint
>
> It is generally not a good idea, when establishing placement schedules, to separate children.

		Sun	Mon	Tues	Wed	Thurs	Fri	Sat
					Splitting Children			
Week I	Child I	Y	X	X	Y	Y	X	X
	Child 2	Y	X	X	X	Y	X	X
Week 2	Child I	X	X	X	Y	Y	Y	Y
	Child 2	X	X	X	X	Y	Y	Y

One child 9/5 with one parent
The other child 50/50 with the other parent

Table 5.4

speak. However, when children don't live with one another, they don't experience sibling rivalry, and they lose the experience of learning to share and becoming aware of someone else's needs. Even though parents don't like to be exposed to their children's sibling rivalry, it serves as a training ground for interpersonal relationships during adulthood.

Another important consideration in establishing a placement schedule is making sure that children have adequate contact with the same gender parent during adolescence. As I mentioned earlier, children ordinarily, through a natural process, gravitate to the same gender parent during adolescence. When a placement schedule does not allow for adequate contact time with that parent, certain developmental experiences are lost or reduced.

When children are split, for whatever reason, it is important for the time with each parent to overlap as much as possible. For example, if one child is with one parent most of the time and the other child with the other parent most of the time, the schedule should be developed in a way that the children can spend as much time together as possible. See Table 5.4.

Uninterrupted Time

Children in shared or alternating placements spend the entire year moving from one parent to the other. Because of this constant shuttling, each parent should have up to two weeks of uninterrupted time during the year, one week at a time, which would take precedence over regular visitations, but should not be used to manipulate the schedule. This way, one or both parents can plan vacation time without worrying about the visitation schedule.

Blocks of uninterrupted time should be planned well in advance to avoid conflict. Sixty days notice is an accepted practice.

Different Cities: Creating a Placement Road Map

Most of the suggestions already mentioned apply to situations where parents live relatively close to one another. These suggestions can hold up when they live in different cities, provided the cities are not too far apart. However, a considerable distance between the locations creates a greater likelihood for conflict. Parents living in different cities can use variations of placement schedules to maximize the amount of contact between parents and children.

Unfortunately, parents living a great distance apart find it virtually impossible to share placement time during the school year. School schedules are such, however, that much contact time is available during the year. Teacher conferences, teacher planning days, teachers' conventions, President's weekend, midwinter and spring breaks, and traditional holiday times allow for flexibility and visitation. Any four-day weekend during the school year should be made available to the out-of-town nonprimary placement on a right of first refusal basis.

The nonprimary placement parent should be allowed to travel to the city of the primary placement parent for up to four weeks of placement time, one week at a time, during the school year. Of course, travel expenses can be a major issue. To save money, you might try to arrange to stay with a friend or relative.

You should also give the nonprimary placement parent the lion's share of summertime. It's best if you allow that parent to have the children from one week after the last child is out of school until two weeks before the first child returns to school. This arrangement allows a decompression period after school is out. In addition, it allows the children to spend a couple of weeks with the primary placement parent to get ready for school, possibly go on vacation, and decompress from their summer visit with the other parent.

These approaches allow the nonprimary placement parent living in a different city to have face-to-face contact with the children almost every month of the year if his or her personal finances and time permit. People who are self-employed or have professional careers may be in a better position to use this approach.

Transporting children from one city to another has changed dramatically since 9/11. Many more flights are delayed, cancelled, or missed because of scheduling concerns. When children travel from one area of the country to another it may require that they transfer planes in a given city. Even assuming that the airline personnel are as competent and supportive as necessary, no parent is going to want their eight- and ten-year old children staying overnight in a hotel, unsupervised, hundreds or thousands of miles away from home. As a result, as inconvenient as it may be, it is now necessary for a responsible adult to be at both ends of all flights. For example, when flying from Milwaukee to San Francisco, it is often necessary to transfer planes in Denver. In this situation, one parent could accompany the children from Milwaukee to Denver and put them on a plane to San Francisco, and the other parent would pick up the children in San Francisco. Or, the Milwaukee parent could send the children to Denver, with the San Francisco parent meeting them in Denver and accompanying them to San Francisco. However, should there be a responsible adult living in Denver who is known to both the children and the parents, this person could meet the children and take care of them in the event of a cancellation, missed flight, or other problem. In that case it would not be necessary for a parent to fly to Denver or from San Francisco to meet the children in Denver.

Spending Additional Time with Your Children

The nonprimary placement parent naturally wants to spend as much additional time with his or her children as possible. Time can be increased in a number of ways without changing placement or visitation schedules. A parent can be a den mother or scout leader, a team coach or car pooler. Attending athletic events, practices, recitals, and performances also provides additional contact. Being available to take children when the other parent cannot gives you more time together. And, when the nonprimary placement parent's work schedule differs from the other parent's schedule, the nonprimary placement parent can act as a resource instead of children being placed in day care or with babysitters or relatives.

Making Things Work under New Rules

By now, you realize that what I said earlier is true: If you have children, your relationship with your ex-spouse doesn't end after the divorce, the rules just change. Although the situation can be tough if the divorce was not amicable, you and your ex-spouse will need to develop a new way of communicating with one another under this new set of rules.

When parents continue to fight after the divorce, their children experience significant mental health problems, including severe acting out behavior or depression. If you can't put aside your anger for your own well-being, at least put it aside for the well-being of your children.

Helpful Hint

Don't send messages to each other via your children.

Although asking children to pass along messages about visitation schedules, child support, and other matters might seem simplest or easiest, such requests put children in an impossible "monkey in the middle" situation, pressuring them and directly involving them in matters that are your province. Children actually become happier, more relaxed, and feel better when they see their parents communicating with one another and know they won't have to be messengers.

If children are to be kept out of such a negative position, you and your ex-spouse must understand and follow the rules that come into play in separation and divorce as well as the new behaviors that come with them. This adherence is crucial if you are going to make placement and visitation schedules work.

The Master Schedule

Once you have explained to the children about your divorce and reassured them that it is not their fault and that you both still love them, it is time to bring some semblance of normality back to the household.

This point is absolutely crucial and brings to mind a five-year-old boy named Jimmy, who came to my office one day crying because he couldn't figure out where he was supposed to be, when he was supposed to be with which parent, and how he was going to finally understand it all. Thus, the title of this book: "Does Wednesday Mean Mom's House or Dad's?."

I sat with each of his parents and Jimmy and helped develop a master schedule that Jimmy could understand. We did this by creating a calendar for him to use. Different colors represented each parent, and each day of the week was colored in with the color of the parent whose house Jimmy would be sleeping at that night. This removed much of the anxiety from his schedule because he was able to start seeing some order in his life.

It is essential to bring as much structure and organization to children's lives as possible soon after a separation has taken place. The use of a master plan or schedule is one way to do this. When the schedule or plan is created, each parent and each child should be given a copy of it for reference until it becomes automatic. As best you can in the beginning, adhere strictly to this schedule, making as few exceptions as is realistically possible. Once children become familiar with it, variations can be introduced and the children will handle adjustments with greater ease.

A general calendar can be used for the master plan. One approach is the one we used with Jimmy—shade in various days with the color assigned to each parent, and use both colors on a day when a transition is scheduled. If your calendar looks like a dish of rainbow sherbet, you know you have planned too many transitions for your child. Any schedule should minimize transition time and maximize time spent with each parent.

A lot of tugging, pushing, bartering, and I suppose, some manipulating take place on both sides when creating master schedules, but children love them for a number of reasons. Little children like the colors and glitziness, but all children like them because the schedule is easily accessible and they don't have to repeatedly ask Mom or Dad for information about where, when, and with whom. The calendar isn't going to yell or snarl at them or get angry with them for asking. It's there and they can deal with it.

Once the two of you separate, it is important to maintain as many household routines and rules as possible. Stability will increase a child's feelings of security and reduce the number of new rules he or she has to learn. Don't develop temporary new rules that will only be in place for a short time, thus requiring children to learn another new set of rules later on. Changing routines and rules at this time, with all the other changes that are occurring in the family, increases the level of disruption for children.

The Parenting Plan

Parents develop a parenting plan as part of the divorce or separation process. Many states require, by law, that a parenting plan be submitted to the other parent, and/or the court, and/or the guardian ad litem prior to going to court.

Dr. Genevieve Clapp suggests many different issues that should be addressed in that plan, including:

- How will communication be handled (mail, phone, or meetings)?
- What decisions will be shared? How will they be made?
- Will you both agree to the other parent's autonomy when he or she is with the children?
- When will the children be with each parent? What will be the logistics of transferring each child? Be specific. What time? Who will transport? Will children have eaten first? Who will oversee homework? What things are expected to return with them?
- What will be done if a scheduled visit cannot take place?
- How will each holiday and school vacation be divided? Be specific about times.
- When will the child and nonresident parent talk on the phone?
- How long can each parent take the children away on vacation? How much notice should be given the other parent? Should the vacationing parent provide an itinerary and emergency phone numbers?

- Try to agree on some basic rules for both homes, for example, about bedtime, discipline, homework, and television viewing.
- How will children continue the relationship with the non-custodial parent's family? Who will go to teacher conferences, and how will information about school progress be shared?
- What activities will children continue? Dance and other lessons, summer camp? Who will pay for them?
- How will children be supported?
- How will medical, dental, child care, and college bills be paid? How will future disputes be resolved?

These questions and many others need to be answered prior to the divorce taking place. If you cannot easily sit down with each other and answer them, you must use a third party, such as a counselor, mediator, or therapist.

Attorneys often like to have parents sign a parenting agreement as a way of indicating that they agree to follow it. This means that if the plan is signed and one parent doesn't follow it, this action could be used in future court proceedings as an indication of that parent's lack of cooperation, contempt, or lack of regard for the children's needs. As always, before you sign anything, make sure you understand the ramifications.

As part of your parenting plan, you need to determine not only what areas you will agree on, but also those areas on which you will disagree. I remember a little boy named Ricky who climbed on the hood of his mother's car, using the bumper as a step. He walked across the hood, up the front windshield, over the top of the car, down the back windshield, across the trunk and then jumped off. When his mother confronted Ricky about it, he claimed that his father allowed him to do this on his car when he visited him. Ricky's mom quietly explained that his father may allow him to do that at his house, but the rules were different at her house.

Two important messages come out of this example. One message is that children need to understand that different places have different rules. This is a concept they probably have already learned. For example, children know that different rules apply when eating at a fast food outlet than when eating at a fine restaurant. One reason parents get divorced is because they don't always see eye-to-eye on all situations, and we can assume that they won't always agree on discipline or child-rearing rules. When rules are different in different places, you should be aware of the differences and teach your children that what may be acceptable in one household might not be acceptable in the other. However, don't try to convince children that you are right and the other parent is wrong.

Helpful Hint
CHECK IT OUT!!!

The other important message is **CHECK IT OUT**. Ricky said his father allowed him to engage in such behavior, and this angered his mother. However, before letting anger get the best of her, she called Ricky's father, who said that Ricky had seen a neighborhood child do that and the father had warned Ricky, "Don't you ever try that on my car." If Ricky's mother had not checked with his father, she would have never known that Ricky had lied and that his father actually disapproved of such behavior. By looking into it, she prevented Ricky from manipulating his parents and playing one against the other. It also gave Ricky the message that he would not be able to get away with this kind of manipulation in the future because his parents were communicating with one another.

Children feed into how their parents interact with one another. Whether in an intact family or not, children try to play one parent against the other. In a nonintact family in which the parents are not communicating, when something comes up and Mom says no and the child then asks Dad and he says yes, Mom may never know what Dad said, or she may find out and become very upset with him for undermining her authority with the child. When I tell you that parents need to communicate about their children, I realize that I'm asking you to do something outside the marriage that you may not have been able to do inside it, but this communication is critical for the benefit of your children. **CHECK IT OUT!!!.**

Visits and Flexibility Work Hand in Hand

Jockeying schedules can be a nightmare if you allow it to be. Here's a classic illustration of this. Bill called his ex-wife, Sally, to tell her that the following Wednesday was the father/son soccer banquet, marking the end of the soccer season, and that he wanted to take their son Chuck to the banquet. Bill wanted to trade his scheduled Thursday visit with Chuck for Wednesday so they could attend the dinner. Sally said, "No way. You're always trying to change the schedule. We went to court and the judge ordered the schedule and that's the way it's going to be." Sadly, Chuck became a victim of his mother's anger.

Parents must understand that a visitation/placement schedule is a general guideline with a general set of rules. However, as I said before, flexibility is one of the main concepts that must be incorporated into any schedule. Chuck's mother was not punishing her ex-husband by her actions, she was punishing Chuck by forcing him to miss the banquet. This situation illustrates how one parent's anger toward the other parent overcomes concern for the child. The appropriate response from Sally would have been, "Sure. You can take Chuck to the soccer banquet and you don't have to worry about making up the day. It will all even out in the long run."

Helpful Hint

The hardest part of parenting is seeing your children hurt and knowing there's nothing you can do about it.

This happens most frequently in divorce, which is why it's so important that you try not to contribute to it. One of the biggest sources of hurt for children of divorce is disappointment, and when they are disappointed you may look for a way to compensate, such as finding something else to do. Sometimes you can't fill the void. Your children hurt and you can't do anything about it. It's true that sometimes life isn't fair.

In another situation, Tom and Beth came to me for mediation. As is true in any mediation I perform, I asked each of them what their agenda was. Tom said, "Before we can mediate anything, Beth needs to give me three days of visitation that she owes me." Beth looked at Tom in disbelief and said, "I have no recollection of ever having the children for three days that you were supposed to have them."

Tom pulled out a notebook in which he had recorded time spent with the children over the past three years. He said, "On February 2, you were 10 minutes late in bringing the children back. On March 3, you asked to have the children for an extra hour because your parents were in town." There were several pages of entries. Tom flipped to the last page and said, "All of these times over the last three years add up to 72 hours and 18 minutes that I should have gotten but I didn't."

I told Tom, "I can't believe you expended the energy necessary to keep these records when it could have been spent more productively in other ways." Beth said she was sure if she had kept a similar record, the amount of time Tom had the children when he should not have would have exceeded 72 hours. The point was well taken.

Actions like Tom's are destructive and nonproductive. Tom was still angry with Beth for several reasons, but he had better ways to express that anger than by keeping those records. He had nothing to gain by this action. Instead, he looked foolish to the attorneys, the guardian ad litem, the court, and the mediator.

Transition Times Made Easier

The most difficult part of a visitation is the transition time, when a child moves from one parent's setting to that of the other parent. Children might resist leaving one parent's home or going to the other parent, not because they don't want to visit or return home but because they don't like the transition. Many children don't like transitions of any sort. Parents can mistakenly assume that a child's crying at the time of a transition means he or she does not want to go with the other parent. Before coming to this conclusion, consider if the child has difficulty with transitions in general and that the crying is his or her way of demonstrating that difficulty.

You have many ways in which to make transitions easier for children. You should decide in advance where the transition will take place. As I said earlier, I favor the general rule that the receiving parent will pick up and drop off the children. However, parents who live some distance away from one another may have to meet each other halfway. Some parents object to driving a long way to pick up children, driving home for the visit, and then repeating the journey to take them back to the other parent. They don't realize that the driving time extends visitation time. Many of the best conversations I've had with our children occurred when I was taking them from one place to another. Children are generally relaxed when they are traveling and conversation is casual. They are not pressed to complete a conversation in a short time like they are, for example, during a telephone call. Traveling time also gives parents an opportunity to eavesdrop on their children when they talk among themselves about unimportant things that might not otherwise be discussed.

Anger Gets in the Way

Unfortunately, in some situations parents don't get along with one another well enough to prevent anger from interfering with transition times. In such situations, transition may need to take place at a neutral site. For example, one parent could drop the children off with a friend or relative 15 minutes before the other parent is to pick them up, thus avoiding a conflict. I have seen cases where the courts have had to order transitions to take place at police stations because parents could not find an effective way to transfer children without getting into an argument. Imagine how disruptive, unnatural, and possibly fear inducing, it is for a child to have to be taken to a police station several times a month to make the transition from one parent to the other.

Overcoming Resistance

Children can directly resist transition, and parents have often asked me what they should do when they have difficulty getting a child to begin or end a visit. They ask, "Should I physically pick the child up and put him or her, kicking and screaming, into the car?"

If you experience such difficulties with transition from time to time, don't worry about them. Sometimes children just don't want to visit Dad or Mom and it has nothing to do with whether they like or love the parent, but with the physical space that parent has to offer at that time. A parent might try to manipulate the schedule based on her or his perception of a child's wishes when it's really a reflection of the child not wanting to leave the familiar environment at that time. It's more a question of what the child doesn't want to leave than what the child doesn't want to do.

I don't think children should be allowed to choose whether they want to visit a parent. If difficulties persist, consider counseling or therapy for your child to help him or her work out these problems. Don't empower young children by allowing them to make a decision about visitation. It isn't their choice. Both of you are parents and presumably you both love your children. If a child doesn't want to visit with one parent, the other should say, "I understand that you don't want to do this, but the issue is not whether you go or not, the issue is what can we do to make it better, because you are going." Once children become teenagers, however, you will have more difficulty forcing them into going somewhere they really don't want to go. Be prepared to do a lot more talking and reasoning with teenagers.

Helpful Hint

Children don't get to choose whether they go to school or not or take their medication or not, so they shouldn't get to choose whether they visit or not.

During these periods, the parent who is leaving the child must make the child feel more comfortable instead of shouting and blaming the disruption on the other parent. I have been involved in cases in which parents were each pulling one arm of the child in opposite directions. The child was literally caught in the middle of an ugly situation between the parents.

The greatest resistance to transition often occurs when a change in schedule is sprung on a child and he or she has no time to think and psychologically and physically plan for it. This includes canceling placements. Never, except in extreme emergencies, cancel visits at the last minute. One child, Julie, is in individual therapy as part of the whole conflict resolution between her parents regarding their divorce. One of the biggest problems Julie has is that her mother cancels Julie's placements with her father at the last minute. Over two months, seven placements out of eight were canceled this way. This behavior makes it difficult for Julie to visit not only her father but also the rest of her siblings, who live with him. Whether her mother's last-minute cancellations stemmed from anger toward Julie's father, disorganization, lack of cooperation, or another issue, she didn't understand how it was affecting Julie.

The thinking has changed significantly in recent years about forcing older adolescents to visit with a parent with whom they don't want to visit. This issue now is looked at more from a developmental perspective than merely looking at the child's age. One of the developmental milestones that 15-, 16-, and 17-year-olds are encouraged to go through by their parents is to be independent thinkers. Yet, when we witness them engaging in independent thinking about whether they want to visit the other parent or not, we tell them they don't have the right to do that. The current thinking is that considerable weight should be given to what the 15-, 16-, and 17-year-olds are saying about not wanting to visit with the other parent if those reasons are logical, can be supported by facts, and represent mature thinking. On the other hand, if the reasons are superficial, hollow, and are not logical, then little if any weight should be given to these statements.

Discipline is another area that can affect visitation placement. You should not withhold time with the other parent as a form of punishment for your children. This is not fair to them or to the other parent. Parents should also not expect punishments or discipline to be extended to each other's homes without mutual agreement. For example, if a child has been restricted to the bedroom as a punishment, you cannot expect that when the child goes to visit the other parent, the visit will start off with the child being restricted to the bedroom, thereby finishing the punishment you doled out before the transition. However, if a child is to be punished because of a major rule infraction, such as violating curfew, shoplifting, being caught with alcohol, or starting a fire in the trash, you should discuss appropriate punishment with your ex-spouse. The two of you should decide if the punishment will be in effect at both households or just the household in which it occurred or in which the child was staying at the time.

As we saw in Ricky's case, children are less likely to try to manipulate parents when they recognize that the parents are communicating. The easiest way for parents to encourage acting out behavior and manipulation on the part of their children is not to communicate with one another. How surprised children are when they discover that their parents are talking to one another and are aware that they have been manipulated.

Dividing Property with an Eye on Details

When parents separate, they usually divide their furnishings to allow each of them to have a reasonable household for the children. However, small details are often overlooked during the division process. Remember that you are getting divorced from your spouse, not the children. Many photographs and momentos are just as important to your children as they are to both of you. Because of this, family photos should be divided between both parents. If you encounter a photograph that both parents want, have it copied. When children travel to and from parents' homes, they should be allowed to bring a picture with them. It may be a photo of a parent, pet, bedroom, or grandparents—whatever makes them feel comfortable. Compiling a small album for a child to travel with is a good way to increase his or her comfort level and help make transitions easier.

One little girl named Jenny told me that when she visited her father at Christmastime, he gave her "all sorts of neat presents." But he told her that she couldn't take them home with her; she would have to play with them only at his house. She said, "I cried when he told me that, but there wasn't anything I could do."

When you give someone a gift, it belongs to that person, not you. Giving a gift to a child and then taking it away by saying he or she can't have it all the time is destructive. The child may want to take the gift home to show the other parent out of pride, to be able to play with it and enjoy it, or to share it with friends. One of parents' common fears is that if they send a gift home with a child, he or she won't be able to bring it back on the next visit. This, too, can be a problem. If your child brings home a gift and wants to take it back during the next visit, he or she should be allowed to do so. You can give very young children a tote bag or suitcase to fill with toys to be transported between households.

Helpful Hint

A gift is a gift. The child gets to choose where the gifts stays, not the parent.

Toys help children master certain developmental skills. Parents should not have to invest in separate sets of toys for both households. When parents live a great distance from one another, separate sets of toys may be unavoidable. Some toys cannot easily be transported back and forth on a regular basis, such as bicycles. However, in most circumstances, duplication should not be necessary. Don't punish your children by not permitting them to take toys back and forth just because you are angry with your ex-spouse.

This same rule applies to sending clothes back and forth. It is difficult enough to make ends meet when maintaining two households. I was involved in one case in which the mother would go to school in the middle of the day to retrieve her children's winter jackets so they couldn't wear the jackets to their father's home. In another case, the father made his children take their new tennis shoes off before they went home to their mother. Such actions turn parents' problems into children's problems, and they are usually carried out with little regard for how they affect children. Unfortunately, they may require court action.

Don't Move Like a Thief in the Night

Parents move when they separate and divorce. If you are planning a move, the most important factor to keep in mind is to notify your ex-spouse as soon as possible of your new address and phone number. If a move is going to take place, your children will want to talk about it with your former partner. Don't swear them to secrecy about a proposed move because this puts too much pressure on them. A move can be a family event for children if it is handled properly. This would not apply in abuse situations.

If the move that is being considered is the actual separation at the beginning of the divorce process, avoid making it on a holiday or a birthday. Otherwise, from that point forward your children will always associate that holiday or birthday with "the day my parents got divorced" or "the day Mom (Dad) left." You should not intentionally give children a lifelong negative association.

Children should be allowed to see the parent's new home as soon as possible. Even better, encourage them to help with the move. One of the biggest mistakes parents make is moving while the children are away. How destructive it is for children to go to school, only to come home and find that Dad (Mom) has moved out of the house. One research study showed that in 40 percent of cases, parents separated and moved apart without notifying the children in advance. How will children be able to trust their parents about the future when such an important event is handled this way?

Children want to feel useful and helpful during the moving process. They can load and carry boxes, and can help with unpacking and putting things away. Remember, also, that when moving day comes and furniture is divided, it should be done according to children's needs, not just your own. For example, Mom may be sufficiently angry with Dad to allow him to take only one chair, one table, and one bed. However, she must remember that her children will also be in that environment, not just her former partner.

Parents' Rights

Parents have a number of rights by virtue of being parents. They also have rights that have been mandated by laws, generally covering such areas as their children's education, medical treatment, and religious upbringing. While you are trying to come to terms with these issues, observe one cardinal rule: don't make your problems your children's problems.

Helpful Hint

Don't turn your problems into your children's problems.

School Conferences

Ben and Pam, who had never found a way to effectively communicate with one another, attended Amy's kindergarten conference. The kindergarten teacher happened to be sensitive to issues surrounding divorce, so she sat between Ben and Pam. When the teacher began discussing Amy's progress, she brought out the school schedule for the parents to see. She only had one copy, which she handed to Pam. Ben grabbed it from Pam. An argument ensued, and it wasn't long before Ben and Pam were hitting each other in front of the teacher. How was that teacher ever again going to be able to interact with Amy without remembering this scene? How were school authorities ever going to be able to view either of the parents without having a negative picture of the way the parents interacted? This behavior turns the parents' problems into the school's problems.

Many schools refuse to allow divorced parents to attend the same conference because of the possibility of this kind of behavior. They ask parents to designate which of them will attend conferences, and some schools allow two separate conferences to give each parent access to information about their children.

A related question that is often raised is whether stepparents should be allowed to attend school conferences. Imagine how uncomfortable it can be for a teacher to have to address two parents and two stepparents at a conference, especially if the two sides disagree about something. As a general rule, only parents should attend school conferences. However, if the couples get along with one another, it can be advantageous to include stepparents, since they may have homework or other school-related responsibilities toward the children. It is certainly important for children to recognize that parents can put their differences aside long enough to sit together at a school conference because they care about the children's best interests.

No Time Out When School Events Are on the Calendar

Your children are likely to take part in school plays, conferences, athletic events, graduations, school dinners, and other special events as part of their normal development and growth process.

It is crucial for both parents to take an avid interest in school activities and to make every effort for one or both of them to attend as many functions as possible. This has a tremendous impact on children. For example, I saw a young girl named Sherry as part of an updated custody evaluation, and she was obviously deeply depressed.

Sherry's parents had been divorced for a number of years but still had not found a way to get along with one another. Even though this animosity troubled Sherry, she became accomplished in athletics and was on the school basketball and soccer teams. Both of her parents attended athletic events, but they sat on opposite sides of the field or court. However, as problems between her parents escalated, Sherry had to ask her father to stop coming to the events because she was afraid they would get into an all-out fight and embarrass her in front of her friends and teammates.

As is true in many of the cases I cite in this book, because of the disagreements between her parents, Sherry was forced into the terrible position of choosing one parent over the other. The gym, concert hall, playing field, and dining room are all large enough for parents to be able to attend school events and avoid each other or avoid conflict for the sake of their children. Even better, let the children see both parents sitting together peaceably.

When a child is made to feel that he or she has to pick one parent over the other, the relationship between the selected parent and the child is artificially improved and the relationship with the nonselected parent artificially deteriorates. It's not a real improvement based on anything concrete. As time passes and the child grows older, the artificial improvement begins to peel away because it doesn't have a solid foundation, and the once-favored parent may lose favor with the child.

A child who witnesses escalating anger between parents—to the point where they become verbally or physically abusive, engaging in pushing, calling each other names, and throwing things at one another—not only becomes very upset but may also become fearful of the parent who instigates the violence. If the child perceives both parents as instigators, the relationship between them and the child will deteriorate.

Lying to your children or involving them in lies is also a way to undermine your relationship with them. For example, in Michelle's case (see Chapter 4), her mother (who was trying to keep custody away from her ex-husband) panicked before a trial date because things were not looking very good for her, and she reported to police that Michelle's father was physically abusing the child. When the police spoke with eight-year-old Michelle, she told them that she had no idea what her mother was talking about, and that she had never said any such thing. This undermined the relationship between Michelle and her mother because even a child of Michelle's age can figure out what her mother was doing. Michelle had been a strong ally of her mother, but she had trouble understanding why her mom would do something like that.

The attachments between parents and their children can go through a polarization process, during which the parents' relationships with their children change as their own relationship changes. Michelle's relationship with her father deteriorated as her mother became more angry with him. Michelle had decided that she was safer being on her mother's side because her mother assured Michelle that she would win custody of her. When relationships change, sometimes they are salvageable and sometimes they are not.

Children often tell me that Dad says one thing and Mom says another and they don't know whom to believe. I never tell them to believe one or the other. I tell them to look at the behavior of both parents. Children can believe parents who do what they say they are going to do. Children just watch their parents' behavior, and over time they recognize which parent is more honest and more even tempered. Even if children are not instructed to do this, they eventually figure it out.

Records

You can very easily tell a doctor or the school that you are divorced and that two copies of each record or report should be made and one sent to each parent. Don't create animosity by trying to have important records withheld from your ex-spouse. He or she has a

---

Helpful Hint

I can think of no circumstance in which school or medical records should be legitimately withheld from either parent unless your state law allows it under certain conditions.

right to know how children are performing in school and if they are healthy.

Both of you should know about children's illnesses. From time to time, emergencies may arise and it may not be possible to notify the other parent immediately. A parent may also find it necessary to make emergency decisions before the other parent can be notified; however, such circumstances are rare. Remember that in a time of medical emergency, children can be soothed by the presence of both parents, so you should try to reach each other as soon as possible.

Parents may disagree about whether a child should undergo a particular medical treatment. In my experience, this occurs most often with illnesses such as Attention Deficit Hyperactive Disorder (ADHD), allergies, and asthma, for which medications or treatments may have uncertain or questionable results or in which the illness itself is vague or easily misunderstood. One parent may favor using medication while the other will disclaim the illness and refuse to administer medication. Such situations can go so far that each parent has a separate doctor to support his or her position.

In the meantime, you may be exposing your child to repeated testing and examinations and perhaps even different types of medication. I have known children who were subjected to duplicate eye examinations, dental examinations, and physicals. I have seen parents throw away eyeglasses purchased by former spouses. I have even seen parents take children for a repeat of a complete psychological evaluation because they were afraid to trust the results of an evaluation obtained by the other parent. Your child is much better off if you and your former spouse can find common ground, agree to disagree if that is the case, and reach some resolution rather than subject your child to duplicate medical services.

College Education

As I said earlier, stipulated agreements or court orders that are signed at the time of a divorce often do not include provisions for college education. I have been involved in cases in which as much as $1,000,000 has been spent unnecessarily on attorney's fees for protracted custody battles. In some of those cases, the children's opportunity to go to college was seriously jeopardized because of the amount of money spent on the legal process.

It is deeply saddening when children finally are ready for college and they discover there is no money for tuition. Financial assistance and scholarships are available, but if parents' credit has been sufficiently damaged in the divorce process, those monies might not be accessible to their children. This problem can be avoided in many cases by making some provisions for college savings at the time of the divorce. For example, support payments can be reduced and the difference put into a trust or escrow account for college, or all or part of the money netted from selling the family home can be put into a college fund.

Religious Training

Numerous conflicts arise between parents over religious training for children. These arguments tend to escalate when parents have different religious backgrounds and did not stipulate prior to the divorce and/or separation what form the religious training should take. You are being unfair to your children when each of you takes them to different places of worship and you argue about which is most appropriate.

In one case, John grew up in a household in which his father was Jewish and his mother was Catholic. After they divorced, his father took him to synagogue on Saturday mornings and his mother took him to mass on Sundays. As John grew, he resented this so much that he rejected religion. When he reached adulthood, he embraced no religious affiliation. In another case, Christine refused to visit her father because he would not take her to confirmation class, which fell during his placement time.

How unfortunate that a disagreement between you and your former partner may result in your children having no religious affiliation or may prevent them from realizing religious milestones. Regardless of your convictions, you must remember that much of the moral and ethical education that children receive comes from religious school and worship experiences. One or both of you refusing to cooperate in this process puts additional strain on your relationship with each other and with your children.

Phone Calls

Telephone calls between children and the nonprimary placement parent are very important. However, they must be handled in a reasonable and responsible way. I have been involved in cases in which parents called their children 5 to 10 times a day; cases in which parents insisted their children talk on the telephone for 30 to 45 minutes; cases in which parents refused to allow children to take calls from ex-spouses, saying the children were busy, playing, or doing homework.

Phone contact must be accomplished under appropriate guidelines. Except in emergencies, you do not need to speak with your child by phone more than once a day. Even when you are only calling once a day, you may encounter times when your children, especially the younger ones, simply aren't interested in speaking on the phone.

Denying children phone contact with the other parent on a regular basis can be detrimental because children need to know that Dad or Mom is just a phone call away, and that they can speak with that parent anytime they need to, especially if parents live a great distance apart. Occasionally, children will want to speak with their parent during nonscheduled phone times. As long as they are not using this as a means of avoiding responsibilities, they should have this access. Speed dial can be taught to very young children who are incapable of remembering or dialing a series of numbers.

One approach to dealing with children's need for phone time with the nonprimary placement parent is having a second telephone line for that purpose. If that phone rings and the children are not home, an answering machine can take messages for them. If children want to call the other parent, they can do so without fear of reprimand. The responsibility of making sure that this is not abused falls to both parents.

Phone calls between you and your ex-spouse should not be used as a weapon or a means of playing dirty tricks. One example of this was in an ongoing custody dispute case involving a couple named Lee and Sheila. Several times Sheila had made it difficult for Lee to have contact with their children. At one point, Sheila wanted to ask Lee to change placement times but she was certain he would not agree to it. She called him, put him on the speakerphone in front of all the children, and then asked him for a change in the schedule. This stunt was a blatant misuse of phone communication, and it put Lee in a lose/lose situation.

Helpful Hint

Phone calls should not be put on speakerphones, should not be recorded without instructions from attorneys or courts, and should not be interrupted by extraneous behavior, such as distracting children by asking them questions or having them perform unimportant tasks.

Sheila had done this to Lee, repeatedly interrupting his calls to their children by giving them things to do, having discussions with them, and reminding them of chores.

In this case, for a number of reasons, placement was transferred from Sheila to Lee, and she continued to misuse telephone calls. For example, she would allow the children to call her between one and two o'clock in the morning and spend a considerable amount of time talking, using the excuse, "If my children need me, I will talk to them." It would have been just as appropriate for her to say, "I understand you would like to talk to me, but we must do this during normal waking hours." On one occasion, she stayed on a call with her children for six hours, claiming they needed to talk to her that long. Sheila did not recognize that it was actually she who needed the contact for that duration.

All of this resulted in the court ordering one telephone contact per day, not to exceed 30 minutes, if the call was made by the children and three phone contacts per week if the calls were made by Sheila. As I have said before, parental actions like Sheila's often backfire, and the parents end up with less contact with their children than they might have had if they had controlled themselves.

The electronic age has dramatically changed the form of communication that can take place between parents and children. E-mails, cell phones, text messaging, video computers, and the like are readily available and should be utilized whenever practical. It certainly makes a child feel closer to the absent parent when there is considerable geographic distance between them if a video camera method can be used. With the advent of the internet and other forms of electronic communication, it may be more difficult to monitor the contact between parent and children, especially when the court has placed restrictions on such contact. Most of these electronic devices have the capacity to block certain incoming and outgoing communications. It is clear that as each year progresses, these forms of electronic communication will become more and more sophisticated and will require more and more monitoring on the part of parents.

Presents

Children usually enjoy giving presents to their parents on birthdays, Mother's Day and Father's Day, holidays, or for anniversaries. Even if they can't give gifts, they should be allowed to send cards. You need to remind your children of these occasions for the other parent and help them select and send cards and/or presents. Although you may still be angry with your ex spouse, your children aren't; this is another time when you have to set that anger aside for their sake. Remember, if you cooperate in helping children obtain these things for the other parent, that parent is more likely to cooperate in helping them do the same for you.

Vacations

Vacations involving parents and very young children should be kept to no more than five days, because when young children start missing home they become anxious and irritable, and soon the experience may become unpleasant for you and them. As children grow older, they can handle vacations of two weeks or more.

Vacations should be planned in advance, with plenty of communication between parents about when they will occur and other details. As children grow, you must consider summertime activities when planning vacations. Don't fall into the trap of planning so many activities that it's impossible for the other parent to have any vacation time with the children. Children may come to resent your interfering with their time with their other parent. In addition, if the issue ever went to court, the court is likely to hold this against you. Just as you should allow children to cart toys and clothes between your households, you should also allow them to take a few photographs, stuffed animals, and other comforting mementos on vacation with you.

Finances

The two things parents argue about most after separation and divorce are finances and time with the children. Many states have statutory requirements regulating the amount of support that should be provided for children. In those cases, parents have no choice about how much they pay. Remember, you are supporting your children, not the other parent. One of the most difficult aspects of these controversies is when children are brought into them. I cannot begin to count the number of children who have told me, as part of a custody evaluation, how much their parents earn, how much support is being paid, who gets the deductions, how much in arrears one parent might be, and other financial facts.

Children may want to know this information but they do not need to be told it. Allowing children to have access to such information is destructive and unwarranted because it elevates the children more to the level of an adult, puts additional burdens on them, and may even draw them into arguments with their parents. Often when custody recommendations are being made, parents who provide such information to their children are viewed negatively by the custody evaluator, guardian ad litem, and/or the court.

When children ask questions about this information, you should merely say, "I understand your interest in money, but this is an adult issue. Your mother (father) and I will do whatever is best for you and you don't have to worry about it." Initially, children will worry about these issues anyway. However, as time passes and new history is made, they recognize that they have no need to worry because their parents are handling the financial concerns.

Parents Working after a Divorce

When a parent has not had to work prior to a divorce and is required to work after one, children will have greater adjustment problems than if both parents were working prior to the divorce. Psychologically, children can feel like they have lost a second parent. Divorce may necessitate a parent working part-time after never having worked before, or going from part-time to full-time employment to support or help support the household.

Work schedules should be considered when determining placement schedules. A situation in which one parent must get a child up at 4:30 or 5:00 a.m. to prepare the child for preschool, day care, or school and then go to work, but the other parent would not have to get the child up until 6:30 or 7:00 a.m., is taken into consideration in the decision-making process. However, this situation is not a major item and will not outweigh more serious concerns.

None of this is easy and if this is the first time you are getting divorced and dealing with custody and placement issues, it can be terrifying new ground to cover. However, learning to efficiently deal with this myriad of scheduling and placement concerns will actually benefit you as you move through the divorce and custody processes because you will be better able to handle some of the other pitfalls that lie ahead.

How to Parent Apart

Parenting in an intact family can be exhausting and exasperating at times, so imagine how challenging parenting apart can be, especially if your children are adolescents or teenagers and you have been parenting as a couple for a long time. Even if your ex-spouse wasn't an especially active parenting partner, at least he or she lived under the same roof and may have occasionally shared in decisions, discipline, homework, and other responsibilities that parents have toward their children.

As with many other facets of separation and divorce, parenting apart has its own set of rules, adjustment period, and characteristic problems, centering on maintaining two separate households with two distinct adult schedules and I hope, by now, a master schedule for the children.

You must be as flexible and communicative when parenting apart as I have asked you to be in other aspects of life during and after the divorce process. Being as preemptive as possible and nipping problems in the bud can put you in a much better position to develop a positive attitude toward parenting apart and to avoid the aggravation and emotional upheaval associated with dealing with full-blown problems.

Don't be afraid to share the responsibilities of parenting with your ex-partner simply because he or she no longer lives under the same roof. You may feel as if you are losing an element of control because not all parenting will be done under your watchful eyes, but if you are vigilant and keep lines of communication open (as did Ricky's parents), you and your former spouse should be able to find common ground for parenting even though you are apart.

Parenting apart has some plus sides, which can be especially welcome during this stressful time in your life. Both of you will come to value time you have alone without your children. Even parents living together in an intact family often ask each other to occupy the children from time to time so that tasks can be performed, errands can be run, or some quiet time can be enjoyed. This is also true when parents are separated or divorced.

During this time, it is important for parents to provide children with an environment that allows them to continue to express their love for both of you and to spend private time with each of you. You should tell your children, as many times as is necessary, that you love them and will continue loving them, regardless of what is happening between you and their other parent. These initial stages of divorce are fraught with doubts on the part of children, wondering if the love that has been present in the past will continue in the future. It is much better for you to err in the direction of telling your children too often that you love them instead of erring in the direction of not telling them enough.

The Family Conference: Increasing Avenues of Communication

Because it is inevitable that conflicts will arise within the family structure, with or without the other parent, the family conference approach is valuable to deal with all areas of concern. It opens lines of communication, gives you both a forum in which to share ideas and discuss problems, and allows children to see that you are actively dealing with issues that concern them. I recommend that family conferences take place at least once a week with participation by all members of the family who live together. Each week a different family member is designated as the recording secretary to take notes about what is discussed. These notes provide future reference if any questions arise about what was discussed or what decisions were made during conferences. Obviously, very young children should be excluded from note-taking responsibilities.

A number of rules apply to family conferences. Name-calling, shouting, and derogatory statements are not allowed. Anything a child discloses during one of these conferences should not be held against him or her in the future. Family conferences are opportunities for children to express concerns without having to worry about reprisal at a later time. If an issue arises during a family conference that involves the parent who is not present, you should communicate that information to that parent, or he or she should be invited to a future family conference to discuss the matter.

A United Front

When dealing with problems, either in a family conference or another setting, parents should, as much as possible, try to present a united front. As I said before, you don't want to leave room for a child to manipulate a situation and get away with unacceptable behavior. Bear in mind, also, that reasonable people sometimes disagree and you may end up with different rules in different settings for the same set of circumstances. If this happens, make sure your children know the different rules so they have reasonable expectations and can respond reasonably.

Making Placements Better

It is not unusual for children to complain to one parent that they don't like visiting the other because it is "boring." You can expect to hear complaints such as, "All Dad does is sit and watch sports on television," or "All Mom does is talk on the telephone to her friends." It is not unusual for the parent who has moved out of the family home to have an inferior or less desirable household, which may be a turnoff to children. One home may not offer as much space or as many opportunities for entertainment or as much furniture as the other home does. Children can be very critical of this, even to the point of hurting your feelings, although often not deliberately.

When trying to deal with a situation in which one dwelling is less desirable than the other, do not try to compensate by becoming a "Disneyland parent." The Disneyland parent always tries to make life very attractive for the children by taking them places, buying things for them, or giving them privileges that may not otherwise be available. Not only can this become financially costly, but it can cost children in terms of what they expect from you as well as give them an unrealistic perception of the world. In addition, when you become a Disneyland parent, you either neglect or have less time for necessary parenting activities such as disciplining, running errands, and doing homework. As time progresses, the cost of being a Disneyland parent becomes prohibitive.

Placements can be made more desirable to children without becoming this kind of parent:

- Allow children to invite friends or younger relatives, such as cousins, to spend the entire placement time, or at least part of it, with you.
- Let children be actively involved in planning placements. Talk to them about what will be done, where it will be done, who will be there, and how long the placements will last.
- Remember that in most placements your children will be with you for a relatively short time. Pay attention to them and their desires, even if this means giving up television or telephone time. Make that sacrifice for their sake.

Prior to the mid 1980s people talked about loyalty issues when children feel that they need to be loyal to one parent or the other. Unfortunately, situations evolve that result in children believing that they cannot have fun with one parent without being disloyal to the other parent. For example, if mother cooks the meals, does laundry, takes the children to practices, helps with homework, and listens to problems, it is much safer to be loyal to the mother than it is to the father.

In the mid 1980s a psychiatrist named Richard Gardner identified a phenomenon called Parental Alienation Syndrome (PAS). Over the next fifteen years there was considerable disagreement among the professional community as to whether Parental Alienation Syndrome actually exists. After Richard Gardner's death in the early 2000s, the concept of Parental Alienation Syndrome has basically been shelved. A second generation of thinking about alienation has been well published and well accepted. Professionals who are touting Parental Alienation Syndrome in any divorce case are not aware of the current literature and are dealing with an archaic concept.

This is not to suggest that alienation does not occur. However, alienation as described by Richard Gardner is no longer accepted as an accurate portrayal. When we look at alienation today we look at if from the perspective of there being three separate components. There is the aligned parent, the rejected parent, and the children. When the aligned parent engages in behavior that is designed to program the children against the other parent in a seemingly unrelenting campaign, this is called alienation. When the rejected parent engages in behaviors that are causing the children not to want to be with that parent, such as abuse, alcoholism, or other emotionally damaging concerns, this is referred to as estrangement. The children are estranged from the rejected parent, not because of what the aligned parent is doing, but because of the negative things that the estranged parent is doing. The third component is the behavior of the child(ren).

Helpful Hint

The current thinking about alienation is that everyone contributes to the alienation.

When assessing alienation, it is essential to evaluate the child's characteristics, the aligned parent's characteristics, and the rejected parent's characteristics. When the professionals have identified which of these characteristics are at play in a particular case, they should be dealt with through a therapeutic environment outside of the court setting.

The aligning (alienating) parent generally has a deep mistrust and fear of the other parent and is convinced that the other parent is irrelevant and/or an evil influence on the children.

The rejected parent's attempts to visit are considered harassment. The aligned parent often does not pass along letters or phone messages, supports the children's right to make their own decision about visiting, and makes the child feel that the other parent is not worthy of the child's attention. The rejected parent is denigrated in the child's presence, while the child is encouraged to point out that parent's faults. The aligned parent will go so far as to convince the children that the other parent does not love them, never loved them nor cared for them. Lastly, the aligned parent believes that the other parent is dangerous to the child.

The rejected (alienated) parent is often passive and withdrawing in the face of the conflict. He or she will often deal with the rejection of the child by counter rejecting the child as a way of saying, "Well if you don't want to be with me, I don't want to be with you." The parenting style is often harsh and rigid. The rejected parent is self-centered, immature, critical, and demanding. Lastly, the rejected parent finds it difficult to have empathy for the aligned child. They will personalize by saying, "How can you do this to me" as opposed to saying, "Look what this is doing to the children."

The children contribute to the alienation process in a number of different ways. They often feel abandoned by the rejected parent. Younger children with lower cognitive ability are less likely to understand the dynamics of what is occurring in alienation. Children with an uneven temperament who are vulnerable are also unlikely to understand the dynamics. The child is also more likely to engage in alienating behavior if there is a lack of an external support system to help the child throughout the process.

The final stage of this alienation process is very interesting—in most cases, children turn away from the alienating (loved) parent and toward the alienated (hated) parent. Children eventually become angrier with the alienating parent than they ever were with the alienated parent for pressuring them into hating the other parent for no good reason. For example, during a visit to my office, Gary told me that his son, Curt, who was 11 years old, didn't want to visit him. His son called him names, said he hated Gary, and misinterpreted everything Gary said and did. The court-appointed psychologist in the case suspected that Curt's mother was alienating him from his father. I told Gary that nothing much could be done if the court was not willing to take action. However, I also told him that as Curt grew older, at about 15 or 16 years of age, the likelihood was great that he would reverse his feelings and become angry with his mother. Gary accepted this, but lamented that he would miss having a relationship with his son during some of Curt's developmental years.

When Curt turned 16, he recognized that his mother had alienated him from his father. He ran away from his mother's home several times and eventually moved in with his father permanently. Now in his early 20s, Curt has a much closer relationship with his father than he does with his mother.

Power to the Children

A classic example of this can be seen in Susan, who came to me after having been ordered by the court to undergo therapy because she had allowed her five-year-old son to decide whether he visited his father.

Children do not start developing the ability for abstract thinking until they are about 11 years old, and they do not completely develop this ability until they are about 15. As a result, directly incorporating children under 11 in the placement decision-making process is grossly inappropriate. You can listen to the wishes of children between the ages of 11 and 15, but placement decisions should not be made solely on the basis of what they want. One of the dangers of giving a child this much power at such an early age is what occurs during adolescence. Because these children are already accustomed to making decisions that they should not ordinarily make, they expect to do the same thing during adolescence, making decisions you may not want them to make about sexual activity, alcohol consumption, and leaving home.

A judge is not likely to order a child aged 16 or 17 to have visitation or placement that is opposed to his or her wishes.

Helpful Hint

Parents can make a big mistake by empowering children in areas where children should not have much say because of their age and inability to understand abstract issues.

Exceptions would be made under extraordinary circumstances such as unacceptable and/or harmful behavior like alcohol or drug abuse.

Children as Coequals

Your partner has moved out. You have relied on him or her for years to help make important and minor decisions. In this scenario, you may unknowingly find relief in relying on your children to fill that same comfortable role that had been filled by your ex-spouse. Children become overburdened when they are used as confidants about financial matters, relationships, or work-related problems. Even if your child volunteers to fill that role, wanting to talk about such crucial matters, you must realize that it is better not to familiarize him or her with details of adult problems. When children ask about these issues, just say, "That is an adult matter and you do not need to be concerned about it."

Children have told me that their parents have asked them such questions as:

- Should I go to bed with my new friend?
- Should I take your mother or father to court for back support?
- Should I quit my job?
- Should I accept my friend's proposal?

Asking a child to respond to these concerns leads to pseudo-maturity, which then leads to the same kinds of problems associated with giving a child too much power too early.

Children weathering the divorce process can also become overburdened when they feel too responsible for their own upbringing. Children who have to cook their own meals, do their laundry, care for younger siblings, and do household chores before they are physically or emotionally ready to do so can feel overwhelmed and terribly overburdened. This can cause deep mood swings, can alter performance in school if children are extremely tired from responsibilities at home, and can increase their anxiety and frustration.

Helpful Hint

Children should not sleep with their parents, and they should not be allowed to start sleeping with them after separation or divorce as a way of providing extra nurturance or support or because you feel sorry for them.

Sleeping Arrangements

Allowing a child to start sleeping with you after the other parent has moved out can be psychologically dangerous. This behavior sends a mixed message to children and could lead to them becoming more insecure than separation or divorce would normally make them. You can also create feelings of rejection if you allow them to sleep with you for a while and then suddenly try to rescind permission. In extreme situations, this behavior can cause children to fantasize that they are able to replace the absent parent in the parental bed. Although such an extreme response is unusual, it can occur and so this behavior should be avoided.

As is true in intact families, children can be allowed to sleep in your bed under special circumstances (something has frightened them, such as a thunderstorm or nightmare, and they come to you seeking comfort). However, when this occurs you should explain to your child that this is an exception, not a rule, and that when the exception has ended, the child will go back to sleeping in his or her own bed. If a child expresses fear about sleeping alone after separation or divorce, you should soothe your child in his or her own bedroom. Lights can be left on, radios or tapes can be softly played, or you can comfort him or her by reading stories in the child's bedroom.

Children in the Middle

Mike and Judy came to my office to have me mediate differences between them involving their child, Emily, who was two-and-a-half years old. During one of our meetings, both parents were enraged over an incident that had occurred the day before. Mike said that he had returned Emily with an ice cream cone at three o'clock in the afternoon. He said Judy became so angry because he had given Emily ice cream at that time that she grabbed the cone and crushed it on Mike's chest. Judy said that wasn't what had happened, and in her version of the incident Mike became so angry when she suggested the ice cream might ruin Emily's dinner that he grabbed the cone from the child's hand and crushed it on Judy's chest. Mike and Judy spent 30 minutes in my office arguing about which version was correct. They invited me to speak with Emily, with neighbors who had witnessed it, and with a friend who was sitting in Mike's car at the time.

I said it didn't matter who had crushed the ice cream cone—what was of greater concern was that Emily had been caught in the middle and had witnessed her parents acting this way. But my comments were lost on Mike and Judy and they continued arguing until I finally asked them to leave.

Another way that parents put their children between them, which I have already mentioned, is by requiring them to carry written or oral messages back and forth. Parents' anger toward each other can become so intense that they don't recognize when they are putting their children in the middle and what detrimental effects this can have on the children.

French Fries versus Mashed Potatoes

In one of my cases, an 11-year-old named Tara told me that she was making decisions about where she was going to eat based on what each parent was serving. The night before our meeting, for example, she had spoken with her mother, who was serving meat with mashed potatoes. Tara's father was serving meat with french fries. Since she liked french fries better than mashed potatoes, Tara decided to eat at his house, which he allowed. She said that her parents competed with one another over who was going to serve the more desirable meal in an effort to woo Tara to each of their homes.

We should not be surprised that Tara ended up with a perverted sense of judgment. What her parents did amounted to bribery. It is certainly all right for children to move freely from one parent's house to the other; however, the motivation for the movement is important. Two different levels of emotion were at play in Tara's situation: Her parents allowed her to manipulate them, and she was given such decision-making power that it extended to every other facet of her life, including whether she went to school, what clothes were bought for her, and who she was going to be friends with. This child insisted on having such total control over her own life that she would get into screaming matches with her mother in front of their home over french fries. Her mother would warn, "If you go to your father's house, you're never coming back," and Tara would scream back, "You hate me!" and so on. Tara would go to her father's house and he would let her do anything she wanted because he didn't want to argue with her.

If you are in the process of creating a monster like this, you have to get back to one of the main rules of thumb: *Winning is never more important than what is best for your child.* The best way of stopping this process is for both parents to start working together for the good of their child. If, for example, Tara's father would take a stand, saying, "You can come over here, but you're not getting dinner because you're supposed to be eating at your mother's house," Tara would start backing off. However, as long as her parents remain at odds and continue battling each other and Tara for her attention and time, Tara will continue to act out of control. The best solution is for you to hold your ground and let the child see that the parents can communicate effectively with one another.

Sadly, Tara succumbed to the ongoing 15-year acrimony between her parents by the time she reached her middle twenties. She died from either an accidental or a suicidal overdose of drugs. She is one of five children I have been involved with who committed suicide in their late teens or early twenties following years of arguing between their parents in divorce cases.

Another french fries or mashed potatoes situation can occur when children learn that one parent is more permissive than the other. As I mentioned before, virtually all parents in intact families have experienced children playing one parent against the other. Why assume that anything different will occur in nonintact families? Children who learn that one parent is more permissive while the other is more restrictive will seek out the permissive parent whenever they want something. Children get away with this behavior repeatedly because you and your ex-partner are not communicating adequately with one another, and the children know it.

Eleven-year-old Tracy was competing in a national amateur athletic event for children. She was signed up to participate in two events. An extremely gifted child, Tracy excelled academically, artistically, athletically, and interpersonally. She was in Phoenix for the national event and decided that she did not want to participate in the second of two events that she was signed up for. Her mother stated that she must participate because that's why they were there and it was her obligation, while her father stated that, since she already participated in one event and succeeded, if she was tired and did not want to participate in the other event she did not have to. The disagreement between the mother and the father escalated in front of Tracy, resulting in a physical altercation in front of Tracy, and ended up involving the authorities. The parents came to me separately, trying to convince me that the other parent caused all the problems. The point lost by the parents was that it did not matter who was right or wrong; what mattered was that the child was subjected to fighting between the parents. Tracy went on to participate in the event, finished second last, which was her worst showing ever, and reported that all she could think about during the event was the fighting between her parents.

A Different Sort of Communication

Parents in the throes of divorce often ask their children about what's happening in the other household. Unless you have good reason for concern, this is another taboo.

> ### Helpful Hint
> Don't pump your children for information about the other household.

One case I recall involved an eight-year-old named Todd, who came to my office complaining that he did not like to visit his father. When I asked why, Todd blurted out, "Because he asks me so many questions. He asks me if the house is clean enough. He asks if we eat enough. He wants to know if my mother is dating. He asks me what her boyfriend's name is. He asks if her boyfriend stays over. He wants to know what time I go to sleep. He asks me what movies I watch...," and he went on and on.

You will find out over time what happens in each other's households just by listening to your children and having normal conversations with them. Children generally share information if we have patience. They may not do it as quickly as we would like or when we would like, but they will talk if you give them the opportunity through personal and phone contact.

If you have more than one child and your visitation time is limited, you may occasionally find it necessary to visit with each child alone to give him or her time to talk. These private conversations provide a special kind of quality time, allow a child to confide in you beyond the earshot of siblings, and can be a special problem-solving time.

When speaking with your children, you can ask general things about their visits with the other parent, such as what they did or where they went and if they had a good time. However, don't expect them to grind out every small detail. Tell your children that if they want to discuss any of what happened during the visit, they should feel free to do so, then drop the subject until they bring it up.

Another element of communication involves how you speak to your children—the terminology you use and how you explain what's happening in the family. For example, one of my clients was an eight-year-old boy who came into my office wanting to discuss "primary placement." This term is not part of an eight-year-old's vocabulary. But when parents are telling children too much or are communicating with them on an adult level, children speak like junior adults. They catch onto the lingo very quickly and will want to talk about stipulations and status conferences, only because one or both parents are giving them too much information. Communication like this is a form of overburdening your children by making them deal with adult issues.

Fighting in Front of the Children

When I perform a custody evaluation, I have found that one wish children most frequently share with me is for their parents to stop fighting with one another. They also often say that fighting between their parents is what makes them sad or mad. Children whose parents continue to argue up to five years after the divorce are much more likely to have significant psychological problems.

If you must argue with each other, do it without the children being present and where they can't hear you. And, as I said before, don't express your anger for one another through your children by actions such as withholding phone contact, interfering with visitations, or preventing children from accepting gifts.

Check It Out

CHECK IT OUT!

CHECK IT OUT!

CHECK IT OUT!

I cannot say often enough that you need to verify the things children say and do by checking them out with one another. This reminds me of a high school principal who said at open house, "I promise not to believe all the things your children say about your home, if you promise not to believe all they say about our school."

Children have active imaginations. They fill in blanks with fantasy when they have partial information. They distort and exaggerate facts and will take advantage of opportunities to manipulate adults. Any time your child tells you a story about something that has happened at the other household, before you believe it, check it out. To get you to approve a particular behavior or action, children will attempt to convince you that the other parent allows it, when that may not be the case. You will find this behavior especially in situations involving discipline issues, television, computer use, and movie viewing, what children are allowed to eat, what their bedtime is, and who they are allowed to associate with.

Checking things out lets children know that they cannot make statements and assume you will not verify them with each other. Checking it out reduces manipulation, lying, and anger between parents.

Secrecy

This is one of the pitfalls of parenting apart that I've already mentioned, but it is worth repeating.

The biggest part of the secrecy issue is that it puts so much pressure on the child. If you tell a secret to a three-year-old, he or she quickly tells somebody else, because at that age a child does

> **Helpful Hint**
>
> Asking children to keep secrets from parents puts them in a difficult position and heightens their anxiety and stress.

not know that *secret* means not telling anybody. But older children who understand the concept of secrecy feel tremendous pressure. Secrets entrusted to children often include, "We're moving," "I have a boyfriend," "I took you to the doctor," "You're changing schools," followed by "Don't tell Mom" or "Don't tell Dad." Not only does a child have to worry about the consequences of telling the other parent, but now he or she must also keep track of what can and can't be spoken about.

Parents wonder why their children don't do well in school while the parents are advancing through the divorce process. Imagine a second grader sitting in class trying to remember what it was that she was supposed to tell Dad and what she couldn't tell him, instead of listening to the teacher explain the number system.

Older children get sucked into the same thing but they become coconspirators. They learn that keeping secrets and lying by withholding information are part of the rules of being in a divorce situation and they try to invoke the rules themselves. For example, a teenager might say to a parent, "Why don't you let me go to the dance tonight and we won't tell Dad," or "You can let me sleep over at my friend's house but we don't have to tell Mom because she doesn't like my friend."

Where to Live

Separated and divorced parents should live as close to each other as is reasonably possible. This doesn't mean you have to live next door or across the street, but you should think in terms of blocks and not miles. The advantages of living close to one another far outweigh the disadvantages. This is another potential bright light for children, and one of those opportunities for parents to soften the hard times associated with divorce, if they can deal with it effectively. This arrangement gives children easier access to both of you and gives both of you easier access to each other. It makes life simpler and often removes some of the anxiety and frustration associated with visitation transition times, transportation, emergencies, and communication.

Older children can actually walk or ride a bike or bus between your homes when you live within a reasonable distance of each other. This easier access also applies to schoolwork and special projects. When parents tell me that they could not possibly live that close after separating or divorcing because they don't want to see each other all the time, I ask them, "How many neighbors do you know who live three blocks from you?"

Problems with the Other Parent

Ellen came to my office wondering what she should do about her ex-spouse, Harry, who had a pattern of disappearing and then reappearing again in her life. He had left home when their son was born, was gone for three years, then reappeared and had regular contact with the child until he was five. Harry then disappeared again. Three-and-a-half years later he came back on the scene and Ellen did not know if she should reinstitute regular contact between him and their son.

Ellen's son remembered nothing about his father except that he kept going away. He couldn't recall anything they had done together or what the man looked like. He had even told some of his friends that his father was dead.

A number of parents follow this here-one-day-gone-the-next pattern and in those cases the question is always asked: Should they be allowed to reenter a child's life? If we could be guaranteed that a parent would reenter a child's life and keep in contact throughout childhood, we wouldn't need to ask this question. However, this constant disappearing/reappearing act may continue throughout a child's life and does not provide the kind of stability and security children need for appropriate development.

The basic message to parents is this: If you want to be part of your child's life you must be consistently available, not just when it is convenient for you. In some cases, parents have lost the right to have contact with their children because of the inconsistency of moving in and out of the children's lives.

Parents Who Won't Visit

Parents cannot be forced to visit their children. This neglect can be very damaging and frustrating for a child who longs to spend time with a mother or father who has become disinterested.

This is a difficult situation for the primary placement parent. How can you convince children that Mom or Dad still loves them when they don't send birthday cards or attend school concerts? On the other hand, how do you tell children that maybe the other parent doesn't love them anymore? You can't do that. But these children pick up that feeling and a shroud of sadness covers them all the time. It really is sadness. You can see it in them and feel it when you are in their presence. They are communicating, "I just don't get it." And, of course, many of them wonder what they did wrong to turn the other parent against them and what they can do to fix it.

This reminds me of a case in which the parents had their children on alternating full weekends and the father came to see me for mediation because he wanted to spend less time with his children. He wanted them only every other Saturday afternoon, but his ex-wife was pleading with him to spend more time with them and be a parental influence. The children, in the meantime, wanted to know what was wrong with their father, why he didn't call them anymore, and why he only wanted to see them for a few hours every couple of weeks. The father shared the short time that he spent with his children with his girlfriend, and the children began believing that he cared more about her than he did about them. They may have been correct.

When this sort of thing happens, you must explain to your children that you wish the other parent would spend more time with them, but, unfortunately, it is not within your control. Be as supportive as you can and reassure them of your love and dedication, but do not offer false hope that the other parent may some-day increase visitation. He or she may never do that, and such failed expectations can be devastating for a child. Simply tell your children that you hope their other parent will eventually spend more time with them, but you can't make any promises. You can also try to find substitutes for your children to spend time with, such as relatives of the same gender as the parent who doesn't want to visit, or volunteers such as Big Sisters and Big Brothers.

Lack of Cooperation

I cannot begin to recount from the two thousand-plus divorce-related cases with which I have been involved how many times a parent came to my office frustrated, demoralized, and reduced to tears because he or she could not obtain the cooperation of the other parent in matters pertaining to their children. I have seen cases in which parents have tried to share necessary information only to be spurned by their former partners and cases in which courts repeatedly, but to no avail, warned parents of the negative effects of lack of cooperation, undermining relationships, and acting against the best interests of their children. In spite of warnings, some parents insist on remaining uncooperative, taking a case to court a dozen times in three years, arguing, manipulating, and being more concerned about being angry with their ex-partner than doing what is best for their children.

When ex-spouses engage in this behavior, you must simply try to make the best of it. Some parents have attempted to terminate parental rights of the uncooperative parent, but courts agree to that only in rare instances when parents are guilty of dangerous or abusive behavior involving their children.

The Mentally Ill Parent The less time a child spends with a mentally ill parent, the better off that child will be. If, during a custody evaluation, I see a parent who appears to be significantly mentally unstable, it weighs heavily against that parent.

One of the most important factors in child rearing is that the environment be predictable, stable, and safe. When living with a person who is severely mentally ill, the environment will be unpredictable, insecure, and perhaps even unsafe. It is extraordinarily difficult for children to grow up in a setting in which a particular behavior is rewarded one day, punished the next, and ignored the third. Children grow up feeling insecure, not trusting their environment, and having considerable difficulty with interpersonal or close relationships. Add to this uncertainty the typical issues for a child whose parents are divorcing, such as what school he or she will attend and if basic necessities are going to be met regularly, and it can be mayhem.

The truly mentally ill parent does not communicate in a way a child can understand. In some cases, such parents are speaking languages adults can't even understand—a kind of jibberish that accompanies chronic mental illness. Children not only have difficulty communicating verbally with such parents, they are also kept off balance because they never know what mood the parent is going to be in on any given day: happy and content, aggressive and yelling, hitting and screaming, or sad and crying. At this point, the child's insecurity reaches an emotional level instead of staying on a concrete level, and that is even more devastating to a child because it is embedded in unpredictability.

In situations like this, children's whole lives are chaotic. They can't count on anything. They never feel grounded. They don't feel confident enough to raise their hands in a classroom and take the risk of answering a question, knowing it might be wrong. They withdraw and become passive, which is reflected in their school grades.

Some of these parents get into therapy with positive results. But different kinds of psychological problems exist. If someone's psychological problem, such as depression, is caused by a bodily chemical imbalance and medication can fix it, that solution is workable while the parent continues to take the medication as long as necessary. This solution is different than for a parent who has a character disorder. Parents with severe character disorders are likely to teach their children that character disorder behavior and the children have no way of understanding its consequences.

As I mentioned earlier, alcohol and drug abuse provide a similarly unstable environment in which it is equally difficult to raise children. Parents who have a history of substance abuse but are currently clean and sober find it difficult to understand the effects that their drug- or alcohol-induced behavior had on their children. They often don't remember anything they said or did, and they must rely on their children and the other parent to accurately recount their behavior, something very painful for everyone. When parents have engaged in prolonged substance abuse, visitation time should be made contingent on random, clean drug screens. If drug screens reveal renewed abuse, visitation should be supervised or suspended until the problem is once again under control.

Living with a mentally ill parent or one who abuses drugs, alcohol, or both becomes a tremendous burden on children. If the children are old enough to understand that the parent is in trouble, they tend to feel responsible for that parent as well as for themselves and their siblings. Some children end up in role reversal, providing for the psychological stability of the parent and becoming the parent's therapist, confidant, and supporter. As soon as it is discovered that a child is in this situation, it must be rectified as quickly as possible.

The longer this type of overburdening continues, the more likely children are to develop significant depression, personal relationship problems, and/or retaliatory acting out behavior in an attempt to rebel and fight back against the burden and the parents who have allowed it. An environment like this in which children must learn to cope with the most extreme conditions simply to survive is emotionally abusive because the children are being beaten up psychologically every day of their lives.

Chapter

7

Maltreatment

The word maltreatment is used to describe any type of abusive behavior that can occur within a family, including physical, sexual, and psychological abuse, neglect, and domestic violence.

Since the first edition of this book, no other area in divorce cases has been more widely researched or raised more awareness than maltreatment.

From the mid-1970s until the mid-1990s, there was a dramatic increase annually in the reporting of maltreatment of children in the United States as the country became more aware of the incidence of maltreatment and encouraged reporting suspected maltreatment. Reports also increased as health care specialists and schools were required to report suspected cases of maltreatment of children and as a result became more aware of the physical and psychological signs of maltreatment.

In the last decade, these reports have leveled off and in some areas decreased. It is thought that one reason for this may be that the number of cases being reported as awareness increased has maxed out and by now has leveled off. It is also thought that it may be decreasing because of an awareness of the consequences of maltreatment.

The most recent statistics from the U.S. Department of Health and Human Services show that about three million referrals affecting five million children were made to child protective service agencies throughout the United States in the most recent year reported. About two-thirds of those referrals were reviewed for further investigation.

> More than three quarters of the children... had been abused by a parent or parents.... In almost half of those cases it was their mother.

Half the children who had been maltreated were White, a quarter were African-American, and 15 percent were Hispanic. Women accounted for 59 percent of the people who had maltreated children. More than three-quarters of the children who were the subjects of reports of maltreatment—84 percent—had been abused by a parent or parents and in 41 percent of those cases it was their mother. Nineteen percent had been maltreated by their mother and father.

Trends show that above half of maltreated children are neglected, one-quarter are physically abused, and one-tenth are sexually abused.

Many of the children involved in cases of alleged physical or sexual abuse are four years old or younger. It is very difficult to have a coherent conversation about abuse or neglect with a child that young, which is one of the overriding problems encountered when dealing with such accusations.

Research shows that children under the age of four are unreliable reporters. They have poor memories. They are highly susceptible to suggestions (people telling them what to say or do) and often do not have the language skills to adequately describe what has happened to them. Their age can also cause them to misinterpret something that has happened and, depending upon the nature and/or extent of the abuse, they may not recognize an adult's actions as being wrong.

> Many of the reported instances of physical and sexual abuse of children go unpunished because of the age of the victims.

Physical Abuse

It is generally understood that not all cases of abuse are reported. One reason for this is the difficulty in defining what constitutes physical abuse. For example, many forms of physical punishment that were widely considered acceptable over the past 100 years, including spanking, are now considered abusive. Punishments involving the use of wooden spoons, rulers, paddles, switches, or belts that leave bruises, welts, and other marks are today considered physical abuse.

Who Will Be the Abusers?

Research shows that certain characteristics are common among abusers. For example, parents are more likely to maltreat their children if the parents:

- Use drugs or alcohol. Compared to nonalcoholic parents, mothers are three times more likely to abuse or neglect their children and alcoholic fathers are eight times more likely to do so.
- Are isolated, with no family or friends upon whom they can depend.
- Were emotionally deprived, abused, or neglected when they were children.
- Feel worthless and have never been loved or cared about.
- Are in poor health.

The U.S. Department of Health and Human Services notes in its Children Abuse Prevention Treatment Act that many abusive and neglectful parents do not intend to harm their children and often feel remorse when they mistreat their children. Despite feelings of guilt or remorse, parents' own problems may prevent them from stopping their harmful behavior and may cause them to resist outside intervention. Therapy may help parents overcome that resistance and help them change their abusive and neglectful behavior.

Children are more likely to be at risk of maltreatment if they are unwanted, resemble someone the parents dislike, or have physical or behavioral traits that make them different or especially difficult to care for. A child's age is also a factor in maltreatment. Research has shown that many children who are abused are very young—the weakest and least able to defend themselves.

Environmental factors such as changes in one's financial situation, employment, or family structure can also increase the likelihood of a person becoming an abuser.

Several general characteristics have been found in physical abusers:

- It is likely they were physically abused as children.
- They have a lower tolerance level for and a more intense reaction to the negative things children do.
- They display more physical symptoms of generally poor health.
- More of them have mental illnesses such as personality disorders, which can so deeply affect their behavior as to make it difficult for them to function in an acceptable manner at home, at work, and in social settings.
- They have lower strength of ego than nonabusing parents, which contributes to their using physical strength and/or the threat of it against those less able to defend themselves.
- They have low self-esteem and a poor self image.
- They have difficulty controlling their behavior and look for an external means of control, such as alcohol or drugs.
- They have greater expectations for appropriate behavior from their children and hold their children to standards far exceeding what would generally be considered the norm for children in their age group(s).
- They experience greater stress, even over minor events, and have a higher incidence of depression.

- They have greater levels of anxiety than nonabusing parents.
- They tend to feel socially isolated.
- They have less interaction with their children than nonabusing parents.
- They rely on power as a form of discipline.

Proving Abuse

In any situation, when a person is accused of a misdeed, evidence and witnesses are needed to prove innocence or guilt, and so it is with accusations of physical or sexual abuse against children. Evidence and witnesses are particularly vital in abuse cases because so many of the victims are too young and challenged to adequately and accurately describe what has happened to them.

Relatives and neighbors often witness abuse or have seen evidence of it in the form of bruises or broken bones or in a child's behavior. When there are no witnesses, or none are willing to come forward, physical evidence becomes a primary source of information to substantiate abuse. This is one reason why health care professionals, teachers, school nurses, and other care givers outside the family circle are trained to be attentive to physical signs of abuse on children and radical changes in their personalities and behavior.

Despite greater awareness of the maltreatment of children, the number of cases in which claims of abuse are substantiated is declining instead of increasing. This is partly due to a lack of adequate funding for social service agencies, which investigate charges of abuse. We have all read in newspapers about instances of child abuse and maltreatment that "fell through the cracks" because an agency responsible for following up on a report was understaffed or otherwise poorly staffed and could not properly manage its load of cases. It is important for reports of abuse to be followed up quickly because bruises and marks can be gone in a few days.

Even if abuse is proven and the child victim is removed from the abuser and the dangerous environment, the effects of abuse can be long lasting. We know this not only from treating and tracking abused children over a number of years, but because so many abusers were abused children.

Consequences of Childhood Physical Abuse

Psychologists Robin Malinosky-Rummell and Davis Hansen published a paper in 1993 about the long-term consequences of childhood physical abuse. In their research, they found that adolescents who were aggressive and violent were more apt to have been physically maltreated as children than the general population. Boys in residential treatment centers and children in mental health treatment facilities were also more likely to have been physically abused than children in other groups. Prison inmates were more likely to have been physically abused as children than the general population, and they were more likely to have engaged in abuse, showing that abuse begets abuse.

Perhaps the most startling finding of Malinosky-Rummell and Hansen was that one-third of individuals who were physically abused or neglected as children ended up abusing their own children.

This spills over into areas of life and relationships. The researchers found that 5 percent of adults who had been abused as children inflicted some form of violence on their dates. And when they married, adults who had been physically abused as children were also more likely to be violent toward their spouses.

This presents an important consideration for married couples whether they have children or not: When your partner is abusive, you must decide if you want to stay in that relationship or escape for your own good and the good of your children or any children you may have if you stay together.

Once again I will remind you that children learn what they live. They are sponges soaking up everything they hear and see from their parents, other adult caregivers, and even other children. When a victim of spousal abuse stays in an abusive relationship he or she is teaching the children that it is okay to beat a partner or to be beaten by one. This is one way that being a victim and a victimizer can be passed from generation to generation, becoming like a family legacy.

Physically abused children manifest what they learn from you—their own abuse plus yours if you are an abused parent. These children tend to be more unruly than nonabused children, and they display more acting out behavior and disorders. There is a direct correlation between the amount and severity of physical abuse that a child endures between the ages of 2 and 12 and the amount and severity of acting out behavior that child exhibits during adolescence.

> People who were physically abused as children are more likely to kill or injure.

The basic message is clear: The more you physically abuse a child, the more he or she will act out that punishment as an adolescent, including turning to drugs and alcohol. Thirty percent of children who have been sexually and physically abused become substance abusers during adolescence.

The effects of abuse are so pervasive that people who were physically abused as children are more likely to kill or injure. They have more emotional problems than nonabused children, including anxiety and depression, and more psychologically based physical problems, such as hostility, paranoia, and psychosis characterized by hallucinations, delusions, disorientation, and disorganized thinking. It is also more difficult for them to build and maintain personal relationships, and they have more academic and vocational difficulties than the general population.

The most recent research shows that about one-half of the concerns about neglect and abuse in families involved in custody disputes are likely to have some basis in fact. This suggests that reports of abuse and maltreatment of children made during a custody dispute need to be addressed and should not be dismissed as merely the result of a high conflict divorce. There could very well be a serious problem.

Helpful Hint

The overall message that springs from the research is simple:

DON'T ABUSE YOUR CHILDREN and DON'T ALLOW YOUR CHILDREN TO BE ABUSED.

Almost every aspect of a child's life is negatively impacted by physical abuse, so everything humanly possible must be done to avoid exposing children to this abuse. If you are an abuser or afraid that you will become one, get psychological help. If your spouse or partner is an abuser, get out of the relationship.

Family/Domestic Violence

More attention has been given to the issue of family or domestic violence in the past decade than to any other form of maltreatment because of heightened awareness. The media have paid more attention to it and the courts even now have family violence centers to which they refer fathers who are abusers and mothers who are the victims. I also think that sensational cases involving public figures have raised public awareness. Popular writing has also changed the degree to which the public is aware of family violence. There are things people are willing to put into print now that they were not willing to write about 10 to 20 years ago.

We used to think of domestic violence as relating only to one parent *hitting* another parent. We now know that domestic violence or domestic abuse encompasses a number of components, many of which are psychological.

These are some important basic facts about domestic violence:

- The American Medical Association says that 25 percent of the women in the United States, or 12 million women, will be abused by a current or former partner during their lifetime.

- There are an estimated 4 million cases of domestic violence in the United States each year or about one assault every 15 seconds.

- Women in the United States are more likely to be victimized by a current or former male partner than by all other assailants combined. More than 50 percent of all women who are murdered are killed by male partners, and 12 percent of murdered men are killed by female partners.

- More than half the people accused of murdering their spouses had been drinking alcohol at the time of the killing. And, almost half of the victims of spousal abuse murder had been drinking alcohol at the time of the killing—about the same proportion as victims of nonfamily murder. People accused of killing people to whom they were not related were even more likely to have been drinking.

- Circumstances associated with domestic violence include miscarriages, alcohol and other drug abuse, attempted suicide and other forms of mental illness, low birth weight babies, pain, injuries, and permanent physical impairment.

- Forty-seven percent of men who beat their wives do so three or more times a year.

- Battering may start or become worse during pregnancy. More than 23 percent of pregnant women are abused during pregnancy.

- Twenty-one percent of all women who use hospital emergency and surgical services are battered.

- One in four married couples experiences one or more incidents of domestic violence, and repeated severe episodes occur in one marriage out of every four.

- The amount of social support, negative life events, and maternal history of child abuse affect a mother's ability to parent her children.

- Women who feel they have active social support networks are less depressed and traumatized and can feel less overwhelmed by child care and issues at home.

One of the leading researchers of domestic violence and domestic abuse is Lenore Walker. Although she as been controversial in some areas, Walker has heightened awareness about the issue of domestic violence. She reported:

- Fifteen percent of batterers were reported as unemployed while in the relationship in which they beat their partner.

- The violence escalated in frequency and severity over time.

- Battered women had attitudes about women's roles that were more liberal than those of most of the population.

- Battering took place in the childhood homes of two-thirds of battered women.

- Battering took places in four-fifths of the childhood homes of batterers and one-quarter of the nonbatterer's homes.
- One-half of battered women reported being sexually molested or abused as children.
- There was a high rate of arrest and conviction of batterers for offenses other than family violence.
- Sex was used by the batterer as a weapon to dominate women in the same manner that physical violence was used.
- Women who were battered said batterers were unreasonably jealous.
- Battered women believed their batterer would kill them.
- Children in homes where the parents had a battering relationship were at high risk for physical abuse and almost all were psychologically abused by living in the violent atmosphere.
- Battered women reported experiencing more anger when living with a batterer than with a nonbatterer.
- Eight times as many women reported using physical discipline on their children when living with batterers than when living alone or in a nonbattering relationship.
- Battered women were more socially and financially isolated when living with a batterer.
- Use of weapons during incidents in a battering relationship increased over time.
- There was more alcohol abuse than drug abuse in battering relationships.
- Batterers who abused alcohol tended to be from homes of a lower socioeconomic status.
- Battered women ranked high on indices that measure depression.

Domestic Violence and Custody

Many states have enacted laws in the past decade that require domestic violence issues to be addressed as part of any custody evaluation. But researchers are still worried that many child custody evaluators do not understand or are not familiar with the accepted models used to make such evaluations and to determine the effects of domestic violence on children. If a custody evaluation is being done in your case, and there is any concern about whether or not domestic violence has occurred, it is important to make sure the evaluator understands the dynamics of assessing domestic violence related issues.

This is important because children who are resilient develop ways of coping with domestic violence and can escape many of its psychological effects, but the development of children who are not resilient is sabotaged by domestic violence. A custody evaluator must be able to assess if there is any domestic violence in a family, how it is affecting each child, and who the batterer or batterers are because this should influence the placement of children and conditions of parental visitation.

Issues that need to be examined in assessing an abusive environment include:

1. Criminal conduct (copies of any complaints to police should be obtained by the evaluator).
2. Substance or alcohol use.
3. Power and control issues.
4. The psychological components of abuse.
5. The cycle of abuse.

A widely used model developed by prominent researchers of domestic violence Bancroft and Silverman to address these issues looks at the psychological as well as the physical components of abuse. People guilty of domestic abuse engage in activities that have a psychological impact on their victims, including:

Control

Abusers use criticism, verbal abuse, financial control, isolation and cruelty against their victims. They try to control the checkbook, credit cards, phone calls, social activities, and access to important people, including relatives such as grandparents or aunts and uncles who might try to intervene if they discover an abusive situation.

Sense of Entitlement

They believe they have special rights and privileges in relationships that no one else may have, and that this entitlement gives them the right to use physical violence and psychological control. They also believe they are superior to others, especially their victims. They demonstrate this by showing contempt for their partners, and a belief that they should educate and improve their victims.

Possessiveness

Abusers and batterers often view their partners and children as property or objects that they own. Hence, they believe they can do with them whatever they choose, and take from them, even by force, whatever they want.

Fear of Abandonment

Though not widely recognized, batterers often have a strong fear of abandonment, and their desire to control is a way of preventing themselves from feeling or being abandoned.

Confusing Love and Abuse

Some abusers will say: "I only do this because I love you." They experience anger expressed through violence, then justify the violence as an expression of love.

Manipulation

Batterers have developed a wide range of manipulative behaviors that they use in domestic violence. These behaviors include manipulating situations to create an excuse for violent behavior and to cover up acts of family violence.

Externalization of Responsibility

Batterers generally do not take responsibility for their actions and instead blame them on others, usually the objects of their abuse. They blame their abusive behavior on their partners, often saying things like: "She knows how to push my buttons," or "He deserves what he got." By blaming others, the abuser is using denial to shift responsibility for his or her actions and minimize the extent of the abuse.

Parenting Style

Batterers use an authoritarian parenting style. In so doing they may be underinvolved and neglectful and in the process put responsibility for parenting on the partner. They show less physical affection and consider child rearing to be the domain of the women. They often show a lack of knowledge of their children's lives including education, medical care, friends, after-school activities, and child development. In spite of the fact that they leave child rearing to the mother, they will often undermine the mother's authority by doing things that are contrary to discipline the mother has imposed or by criticizing her to the children to convince them that the mother doesn't know what she is doing.

One of the most disconcerting aspects of the batterer is his or her ability to perform well under observation. They present themselves well, make a good first impression, and others cannot conceive of their being anything but model individuals. One psychologist dubbed this kind of behavior "the sick but slick syndrome."

To Stay or Not to Stay: Is That Your Quandary?

Whether or not a person should remain in an abusive relationship often arises in discussions with victims, especially in therapy. One way of answering this question is to look at something we have already mentioned in this book—the effect of an abusive relationship on children. Two prominent researchers of domestic violence, Leslie Drozd and Nancy Olesen, note that batterers serve as models for their children, teaching them that:

- The victim is always to blame for almost everything.
- The use of violence is justified as a way of imposing one's will or resolving problems.
- Boys and men should be in control and girls and women should submit.

- Abusers do not experience consequences for their actions.
- Women are weak, incompetent, or stupid.
- Fathers are better parents for teenage boys than mothers, and teenage boys need to escape the influence of their mothers.
- Anger causes violence.

To sum it up quite simply, if this is what you want your children to learn, remain in an abusive relationship. If this is *not* what you want your children to learn, *leave!!!*

Emotional/Psychological Abuse

The U.S. Department of Health and Human Services says:

> A child is considered to be emotionally or psychologically abused when he or she is the subject of acts or omissions by parents or other persons responsible for the child's care that have caused, or could cause, a serious behavioral, cognitive, emotional, or mental disorder. In some cases of emotional/psychological abuse, the acts of the parents or other takers, alone, without any harm to the child's behavior or condition, are sufficient to warrant Child Protective Services intervention. An example would be if the parents/caretakers use extreme or bizarre forms of punishment such as torture or confinement of the child in a dark closet. For less severe acts, such as habitual scapegoating, belittling, or rejecting treatment, demonstrable harm to the child is often required for Child Protective Services to intervene.

An example of emotional or psychological abuse is if a parent restricts a child to his or her room any time the child is not in school as a way of not allowing contact with other children. Neglect also includes failure to provide appropriate medical treatment, permission for drug or alcohol use by a child, or failure to provide needed psychological or medical care. Any behavior in which a parent engages that interferes with a child's ability to develop appropriate self-esteem, social competence, and positive interpersonal relationships is an aspect of psychological maltreatment.

Parents may, at times, say things in jest to their children that might be construed as offensive or emotionally abusive. If something is said or threatened often enough, a child may believe that it is true or that it will occur and t hat belief makes the comment psychologically or emotionally abusive. Here are some things parents say that are abusive:

- Saying to a young child: "If you don't stop acting that way I'm going to leave you alone and never come back."
- Coming from a father who believes a child is not his own: "You're not mine. Get out of my sight. I don't want to have anything to do with you."
- Threatening to send a child to a foster home or detention center or threatening to pack a child's bags and make him or her leave.
- Repeatedly calling a child "dummy" or "slob" or other even less flattering names.
- Telling a child that he or she is useless and will never amount to anything in life.
- Telling a child that you wish he or she had never been born.

A parent is guilty of maltreatment when he or she is consistently unavailable to respond to children's needs or ignores or rejects the children. Maltreatment includes not meeting physical needs, failing to feed children, failing to keep them clean, and even dressing them inappropriately. Another form of maltreatment is called infantilization, which occurs when a parent insists that a child engage in infant-like behavior or behaviors that are typical of children many years younger than the child.

In general, infants tend to be psychologically maltreated through rejection, unavailability, malnourishment, or inconsistency. Children are usually maltreated through behaviors that suggest they are unloved, unwanted, inferior, or inadequate, and through removal from their home. Adolescents tend to be mistreated in the same manner as children, but the patterns are often stronger and more elaborate.

Psychological or emotional abuse can also take the form of dominance or dependence.

The U.S. Department of Health and Human Services says that abusers:

> Use the children to maintain power and control over their partners. For example, they belittle or degrade the children as a means of harassing the victim. Abusers may frighten their victims by using looks, actions, gestures, or loud voices; by smashing things; by destroying the victim's property. Abusers may threaten to take the children away from their spouse, to harm the children, or [to] commit suicide. Men who [use their form of] abuse may control their partner's activities, companions, or whereabouts. [They] often control what their victims do, whom they see, and where they go. Many abusers feel threatened by anyone with whom their victims have contact.

Sexual Abuse

As in cases of physical abuse of a child, one of the difficulties that arises in dealing with child sexual abuse cases is the inability of people to accurately define what constitutes sexual abuse.

For example, there is disagreement over whether a child catching a glimpse of an exhibitionist is sexual abuse. Most people would not consider it abuse if a child was shown *Playboy* magazine by an older friend with whom he or she plays, but what if a child was shown hard-core pornography? Does a other sleeping with her child constitute sexual abuse in the absence of sexual touching? What if the child is a teenager who becomes aroused by this? Many people would agree that a 19-year-old woman who has sexual contact with a 6-year-old boy has committed sexual abuse, but not if the boy is 16. But what if the boy is 14? What if a 14-year-old boy initiates the experience with the woman and later views it as positive?

The U.S. Department of Health and Human Services defines sexual abuse to include "fondling a child's genitals, intercourse, incest, rape, sodomy, exhibitionism, and sexual exploitation." To be considered child abuse, these have to be committed by a person responsible for the care of a child (for example a parent, babysitter, or daycare provider). If a stranger commits these acts, it would be considered sexual assault and handled by the police and criminal courts.

Although the number of reported sexual abuse cases has increased over the years, there has been a 40 percent decline in substantiated sexual abuse cases. It is not known if this decrease reflects disagreement over what constitutes sexual abuse, a decline in actual cases of sexual abuse, or if there has been a change in the way people report such incidents, a change in the way such cases are investigated, or changes in policies or programs within child protection agencies.

Who Are the Sexual Abusers?

As a result of research pertaining to sexual abusers, researcher David Finkelhor theorized that:

- Some groups of abusers have an unusual need for power and domination.
- Most groups of offenders who have been tested using psychological monitors show unusual levels of deviant sexual arousal to children.
- Many offenders were themselves victims of sexual abuse.
- Alcohol is connected to acts of sexual abuse in a larger number of incidents.

Finkelhor also noted that children are at higher risk of abuse if:

- A child is living without one of his or her biological parents.
- A child's mother is unavailable either because of work outside the home, disability, or illness.
- A child reports having a poor relationship with his or her parents or is being subjected to extreme punitive discipline or child abuse.

One of the most frequently asked questions in child sexual abuse allegation cases is whether the perpetrator is likely to sexually abuse again. This is called recidivism. The greatest risk for repeat offending occurs in the first 5 to 10 years after the original offense. One study showed that 42 percent of the sexual abusers included in the survey were reconvicted of child abuse at some time. Of those repeat offenders, 23 percent were reconvicted more than 10 years after they were released from prison.

Evaluating Sexual Abuse

There are a number of myths relating to the evaluation of child sexual abuse allegations that have been identified by one of the world's leading experts in this area, Kathryn Kuehnle.

Myth: Reliable estimates exist on the incidence of child sexual abuse in the United States.

Fact: The actual number of sexual abuse victims may never be known.

Myth: Only a minority of children do not tell when they have been sexually abused.

Fact: Two-thirds of adults who claim to have been sexually abused as children did not tell anyone about the abuse at the time it happened.

Myth: Coercion/threats and fear of being harmed decreased the likelihood of a child telling that he or she was sexually abused.

Fact: When sexually abused children are threatened with physical harm or death they often will tell someone.

Myth: Substantial numbers of child sexual abuse victims recant their accusations after telling someone.

Fact: Once children have told someone they were sexually abused, they are likely to maintain their claims.

Myth: Reliable estimates exist on the number of child custody cases that involve sexual abuse.

Fact: Too little research has been done to know the number of such cases.

Myth: Reliable estimates exist on the rate of false child sexual abuse claims made in custody cases.

Fact: They do not. Therefore, a forensic evaluator must assume an allegation of child sexual abuse is as likely to be true as not true.

Myth: Forensic evaluators are competent at identifying false claims of child sexual abuse.

Fact: Many practitioners lack adequate training, knowledge, and skills to perform forensic interviews to help distinguish true allegations from false ones.

If You Think Your Child Has Been Sexually Abused

If you suspect that your child has been sexually abused:

- Do not interrogate or question him or her.
- Listen and be supportive.
- Don't completely discount a child because the allegations involve your spouse, significant other, a relative or friend, and you don't want to believe that he or she could do such a thing.
- Immediately report your suspicions to your pediatrician, the police, and/or your local child protective services agency.
- If a significant other or parent is involved, you should ask the person to live someplace else until the matter can be sorted out and the truth known. In a situation like this, it would not be appropriate for you to allow a visit with the accused offender until the child has seen a professional and arrangements have been made to safeguard the child during visitation. If the suspected offender won't leave, you and your child may have to spend a short time at a motel or with a relative or even at a women's shelter if you have nowhere else to go until the situation is sorted out.

Helpful Hints

If you ask a child the wrong questions at the outset, you may contaminate the process, meaning you may inadvertently feed a child information.

In so doing, even if sexual abuse has occurred, you may ruin the case from the legal standpoint and the offender may go free. Many times parents have come to my office with an audiotape or video tape of them interviewing a child about suspected child abuse. The tapes are filled with leading questions, suggestions, and inappropriate communications.

Questioning in a case of this nature must be done by a well-trained professional. The best place to start is with a child protective services agency or a sexual assault treatment center if your city has one.

Your response to an allegation of this nature is crucial to how your child deals with it. For example, if you become hysterical and make statements such as, "Oh, my god, that's the worst thing I've ever heard. You poor baby," a child's emotional response to the situation is going to be compounded. In one study, more than 100 women who had been sexually abused as children were interviewed. Two factors contributed to the feelings they had in adulthood about the abuse—one was their perception of what had occurred and the second was their mother's response to it.

After you have reported your suspicions to the proper authorities, you should quickly get your child involved in therapy. Children who are abused learn to become victims, and they accept that this is the way their lives are to be lived. When they grow up with that notion, they become "sitting ducks" for spousal abuse, sexual harassment, and abuse in the workplace. The victimization cycle must be broken and the most effective way of doing that is with psychotherapy, in which a child can unlearn being a victim and unlearn victim-like behavior.

Helpful Hint

Children must not be allowed to mature with the belief that it is acceptable to be a victim.

In one case in which a victim never unlearned victim-like behavior, a woman named Leslie was married for 25 years to a businessman who regularly beat her. After the beatings, he would instruct her not to leave their home until her bruises had healed. He would come home the following day and there would be no food in the house because Leslie had followed his instructions, and he would beat her because she hadn't shopped for food. After several years of psychotherapy, she recognized that she should leave the marriage and file for divorce, but she never unlearned her victim behavior. Three years after her divorce, her ex-husband showed up at her door with a basketful of laundry and said, "Wash my clothes." She said, "Okay." He added, "While you're at it, make me lunch," and she said, "Okay."

Sexual Abuse Allegations: True or False?

Ninety percent of sexual abusers don't admit to their crimes. That means that in 90 percent of the cases, someone must determine if the abuse actually occurred. When a sexual abuse allegation is made, there is a victim. The question is, who is it? Is it the child who is at the heart of the allegation or a parent, relative, or family friend who may be falsely accused? In the vast majority of cases, the allegations are true; however, in a significant minority of cases, they are false.

In the past, we relied on the amount o detail a child could provide in an effort to determine if allegations of sexual abuse were true or false. That cannot be done today. Children who have sexual knowledge have not necessarily gained it from direct sexual encounters. Children have access to a great deal of information about sex and sexuality. Network and cable television, videotapes and DVDs, electronic games, the Internet, sex education programs in school, and information exchanged with other children all provide a base of sexual information that may leave a child confused, but informed.

Even daytime television programs are filled with sexual information. I'll never forget my surprise one day when I went home to pick up something, and I decided to make myself some lunch and watch television while I ate. The soap opera that was being aired showed a man and woman in bed, under a sheet. Next to the bed were a bowl of strawberries and a bowl of whipped cream. The couple was describing in graphic detail what they were going to do to each other with the strawberries and whipped cream. The only difference between what was shown in the soap opera, to which children have access, and what can be seen in an R-rated movie is that the couple was covered with a sheet.

Another factor that makes sexual abuse more difficult to determine is that most behavior resulting from sexual abuse can also be caused by ordinary problems. Nightmares, infantile behavior, excessive masturbation, and signs of depression can occur in children regardless of whether they have been sexually abused. Almost all children between the ages of three and six years masturbate, sometimes to excess. It is not uncommon for children who have never been abused to experience nightmares. And children under five may describe acceptable hygiene practiced on them by a parent in a way that sounds like sexual abuse. When children say they have been touched on their genitals, it does not necessarily mean the touching was sexual.

In some cases, children lie about sexual abuse. This is also difficult to verify because children under five usually lack the verbal and conceptual skills necessary for them to undergo adequate psychological testing and to be able to fully cooperate with a professional interview. And the more a child is tested, the more likely it is that the results will become increasingly unreliable.

It is not good practice to use sexually anatomically correct dolls to allow children to show how sexual abuse occurred. If your child says he or she has been sexually abused, don't use dolls to have the child show you how. If the dolls are used inappropriately, prematurely, or sometimes even at all, they may sufficiently contaminate the case so that it may never go to court. The American Psychological Association warns about using such dolls in cases of alleged sexual abuse.

Katherine Kuehnle has descried nine possible reasons why a sexual abuse allegation may range from being totally and completely true to totally and completely false. She points out that the most frequent occurrence of sexual abuse allegations involve a mother who genuinely believes that her child has been sexually abused because she has misinterpreted information.

Almost all false sexual abuse allegations occur during custody disputes. Consequently, when such an allegation is made during a custody fight, everyone becomes concerned about whether it is true.

I recall one case in which a mother, who knew she was in danger of losing custody of her child, used allegations against her ex-spouse to postpone three court dates. First, she made allegations of domestic violence and the court postponed the case to investigate those charges. She then accused her ex-partner of sexually abusing their daughter and the court postponed the case to look into that. Then, one week before the third date, she alleged that her ex-husband had physically abused their child and again the court postponed the case to investigate.

It is extremely difficult for a parent to succeed at initiating a false sexual abuse allegation and be able to carry it out. It would require considerable memorization on the part o a child, and parents cannot successfully coach a child to appropriately answer all the questions of social workers, psychologists, police, guardians ad litem, and the courts. Even if a parent could anticipate all these questions, a child is not sophisticated or clever enough to remember all the answers. As in the case I mentioned above, parents often initiate false allegations to ensure that an ex-partner does not get custody of the children. But this is like playing with fire because if the courts find that the allegations were false, they re willing to take placement away from the parent who made them and place a child with the falsely accused parent.

Children are put in the middle when false allegations are made. When you involve your child in such a lie, he or she becomes a co-conspirator. In foisting this role on your child, you are making him or her a victim of your actions and affecting his or her security needs and moral and ethical development.

In cases where a parent is guilty of sexual abuse, therapy usually elicits some kind of apology to the child. In only 10 percent of these cases do the offenders admit to what they did, so a parent often gives a generic apology, saying something like, "I want you to know that I'm really sorry for anything I did to hurt you." From that point on, the relationship can be carefully rebuilt. If history is then established between the child and parent that is different from the abusive past, the child will start trusting the parent more, feel good about him or her, and enjoy spending time together, even if it is supervised for some time.

If, however, a parent is guilty of sexual abuse and continues to insist that the child is lying, saying things such as, "How can you make up those horrible stories?" or "It's hard for me to love you when you say those kinds of things about me," the relationship will continue to deteriorate. In most of these cases, children still love that parent and, for them, one of the hardest parts of dealing with the abuse is knowing that it occurred and hearing the parent say it didn't. It's almost as if a child can forgive a parent for being sexually or physically abusive, but not for lying about it.

Apart from parents initiating false allegations against one another, other problems can be associated with charges of sexual abuse. As I said earlier, this type of abuse often occurs against children who are under the age of four and have not developed sufficient language skills to explain what has happened.

When very young children are involved, professionals sometimes have difficulty determining if abuse has occurred. I had a case in which the father was accused of sexually abusing the daughter. He had requested visitation and as part of my evaluation, in consideration of that, I invited the child and both her parents to my office. He had not seen his daughter, who was then four years old, for about a year. I allowed the child to pick a seat in my office, which is very long and has 11 chairs, so she would feel that she had some control. She chose to sit closer to me. When her father came into the room, his daughter took one look at him and burst into tears. She wouldn't talk directly to him. She whispered questions to me and I repeated them to him.

When I conduct this type of evaluation, as part of this process, I ask children, "If you could ask your Daddy (Mommy one question, what would it be?" and I ask parents the same thing. But their question is directed at the children. Well, this little girl asked her father, "Tell me about when I was a baby." That's a warm question. Children like their parents to tell them about the silly things they did when they were very little.

During this 20-minute observation, things warmed up and by the end the child showed no fearfulness. When the father left the room and the mother came in to be briefed, before she even had a chance to sit the little girl excitedly told her, "Guess what? I saw Daddy!" Her mother asked the child how the visit had been and the little girl walked to the chair where her father had been seated and patted it with her hand. It was still warm. She put her head down on the seat and rubbed her cheek against the warm spot.

In this case, I couldn't tell if abuse had occurred. It was clear to me that the child was still bonded to her father, and I suggested supervised contacts, moving to unsupervised contacts.

In another case, a family court ordered visitation for a mother who had been accused of sexually abusing her child after a court appointed psychologist found no evidence of abuse. Her ex-spouse, who had custody of the child, complained about the visitation order, and I was asked to do a second opinion evaluation with the child, who was five years old. The child provided a host of descriptions that made it clear that he had been sexually abused by his mother. I found that many crucial details had been ignored in the first evaluation and suggested that her visits be supervised. The court changed the order so that the mother's visits were supervised.

I am convinced that for children in this two-to-five-year age range, many genuine sexual abuse cases are not being pursued because the information is too gray, and a lot of physical abuse cases are being pursued as sexual abuse because the information is also too gray and people aren't sure what children are describing.

In most cases, several different courts may hear sexual abuse cases. The criminal court hears cases when charges have been filed against someone by a district attorney. Family court hears sexual abuse cases containing an issue about visitation or placement being given to the alleged offender. Children's court may hear a case when it involves protective placement or protective orders. It is also possible for a case to be heard in all three courts at the same time.

In a family court setting, because the standard is "best interest of the child" and not "reasonable doubt" as it would be in criminal court, family court judges can deal with sexual abuse allegations that have been rejected by criminal courts. It is not uncommon, however, at the end of such a case for a family court judge to be unable to determine with certainty if the abuse occurred. Most judges are willing to err on the side of protecting a child. For example, a court may order supervised visitation for the accused parent even though there was no finding of sexual abuse in that case. Supervised visitation in a situation like this serves two purposes: it protects the child from the possibility of further sexual abuse and if the abuse did not occur, it protects the accused parent from further false allegations.

Devastating Effects of Sexual Abuse

Extensive research in this area has found:

- Sexually abused children most frequently experience Post Traumatic Stress disorder (PTSD) (32 percent of cases studied); poor self-esteem (35 percent of the cases); promiscuity (38 percent), and general behavior disorders (37 percent).

- The most common symptoms for pre-schoolers are anxiety, nightmares, general PTSD, internalizing, externalizing, and inappropriate sexual behavior.

- The most common symptoms in school-age children are fear, neurotic and general mental illness, aggression, nightmares, school problems, hyperactivity, and regressive behavior.

- Adolescents most commonly experience depression, withdrawal, suicidal or self-injurious behavior, somatic complaints, commission of illegal acts, running away, and substance abuse.

- Symptoms that appear prominently for more than one age group are nightmares, depression, withdrawn behavior, neurotic mental illness, and aggressive and regressive behavior.

- Depression, school and learning problems, and behavior problems are the most prevalent symptoms across ages. Between 21 percent and 49 percent of those studied had no symptoms. Those individuals may have been symptomatic in ways that were not measured, they may not have shown symptoms yet, or they were simply asymptomatic.

- When someone close to a child committed the sexual abuse, there was frequent sexual contact, the abuse lasted a long time, the use of force was often involved, and sexual acts included oral, anal, or vaginal penetration, all of which led to a greater number of symptoms for victims.

- The lack of maternal support at the time a child disclosed the abuse and a victim's negative outlook or coping style also led to increased symptoms for victims.

- It is not clear from the research if the age of an individual at the time of assessment, the age at the onset of sexual abuse, the number of abusers, and the time that elapsed between the end of the abuse and the assessment has an impact on symptoms, but this should be studied.

- As time passed, symptoms abated in 55 to 65 percent of children. Depending upon the study, symptoms appeared to worsen in 10 to 24 percent of children.

- Court involvement also influenced the effects of sexual abuse on children. Children involved in court proceedings showed less resolution and it took them longer to reach resolution. It has long been thought that children who have to testify in court suffer adverse effects from those proceedings.

- Trauma can be reduced by giving children protective settings during their testimony. Children who testified via closed-circuit television, videotape, or closed courtrooms showed fewer symptoms than children who had to testify in open court.

Briere and Runtz identified six areas of concern in reviewing child sexual abuse cases:

- Post Traumatic Stress Disorder (PTSD) is the first. This has been identified as a concern in other studies, as well. These people also suffer from cognitive distortions as a result of their abuse. Their perceptions tend to reflect an overestimation of danger or adversity.

- Sexual abuse victims often experience altered emotions, with depression being the most common symptom.

- Survivors of sexual abuse have disturbed relations with others. For example, they tend to have fewer friends, less closeness with friends and less satisfaction from friendships, it can be difficult for them to adjust socially, and they see themselves as being unworthy of healthy relationships. They also have difficulties with sexual intimacy.

- People who were sexually abused during childhood commonly abuse substances like drugs and alcohol, and are more prone to thoughts of suicide than children who have not endured such abuse. They also tend to be dissociative, that is nonsocial or antisocial.

- Victims of sexual abuse often are involved in activities that reduce tension, such as promiscuity, binging and purging, and self-mutilation.

The effects of sexual abuse don't stop there. Other research shows:

- Histories of physical and sexual abuse are associated with severe psychological disturbances, in particular borderline personality disorder, which is characterized by extreme emotional distress, and behavior, mood swings, and a self image that lead to unstable relationships, problems at home, in social situations, or at work.
- Abused women were less satisfied with their bodies than women who had never been abused.
- 16 to 41 percent of children who had been sexually abused showed overt sexual behavior problems.
- Girls who were abused showed more disturbances in their thinking than boys.
- As I mentioned earlier, people who were abused as children suffer from "sitting duck syndrome" wherein having learned to be victims during childhood, they allow themselves to be victimized in adulthood in relationships, at work, and by service providers.
- Survivors of sexual abuse need to understand how it can affect them because they are at risk of being victimized again.
- Adult survivors of sexual abuse showed a greater tendency toward suicide, eating disorders, and self-mutilation than people who had not been sexually abused.
- Women who were sexually abused have higher anxiety and depression scores, eating disorders and self-mutilation than people who had not been sexually abused.
- Women who were sexually abused have higher anxiety and depression scores, greater life stressors, and greater difficulty recovering from post-partum depression than those who had not been sexually abused. They also did not improve as much as non-abused women.
- Nonoffending mothers of children who were sexually abused had heightened levels of depression and anxiety and were less likely to be close to their children or to bond with their children.

- Sexually abused children have many of the symptoms of Post Traumatic Stress Disorder, with more than half of them reaching the criteria to be diagnosed with PTSD.

- A child's age, the type of abuse, fear of the consequences of telling, and perceived responsibility for the abuse contributed to predicting how long it would take for a child to tell someone about it. The fear of negative consequences had the most influence on older children. Children who were abused by a family member took longer to tell than children who were abused by someone to whom they were not related. In general they took longer to report it if they thought telling would result in negative consequences.

- Delayed disclosure can be caused by guilt, accommodation, self-blame, helplessness, emotional attachment to the offender, mistrust of others, the burden of the secret or successful ego-strengthening experiences. Ego-strengthening experiences are events or achievements that displace the negative experience onto a positive one so the negative experience doesn't have that much of an impact. It's interesting how many sports figures come forward and talk about being abused when they were children. They've gotten strong enough through their successes to be able to talk about the abuse at some point in their adult lives.

Research has shown that there is a relationship between childhood sexual abuse and adult depression and anxiety disorders. But that's not all. Adults who survived childhood sexual abuse:

- Often have physical symptoms such as headaches, gastrointestinal problems, back pain, and muscle pains.

- They have problems with anger control, chronic irritability, unexpected feelings of rage, and fear of their own anger.

- They have feelings of anger that can be internalized as self-blame and self-injury but which can result in violence toward others.

- As many as 36 percent of adult survivors of childhood sexual abuse experience symptoms of Post Traumatic Stress Disorder.

- They show emotional responses through a range of actions that include self-mutilation such as cutting, burning, or hitting themselves or pulling out hair; binging and purging to deal with feelings of emptiness; alcohol or other drug abuse, and an increase in suicidal tendencies.
- Male and female abuse and neglect victims reported higher rates of living with partners outside of marriage, walking out of relationships, and divorce than nonabused people.
- Women who had been abused as children were less likely to have positive perceptions of current romantic partners and to be sexually faithful.
- Men and women who had been sexually abused as children had a harder time establishing and maintaining healthy intimate relationships.
- Frequency of abuse and the number of people who abused a child had a direct relationship with psychological distress of him or her in adulthood.
- Overall patterns suggest that men and women who survived sexual abuse when they were children may experience difficulties with some aspects of parenting, such as establishing clear generational boundaries with their children, being more permissive as parents, and being more likely to use harsh physical discipline.

Researchers have also found that men and women who were abused as children and later reported other incidents of abuse were abused in ways that differed from the original type of abuse. This is called "cross-type recidivism." Researchers specifically point out that children who are neglected at an early age are more likely to be victims of physical or sexual abuse at a later age.

WARNINGS!!!!!!!

- Remember that children under age 4 are unreliable reporters.
- Remember that children's memories do not start to become completely accurate until they are 6 or 7 years old.

- Remember that young children are susceptible to suggestibility.

- Remember that except for an eyewitness and sexually transmitted diseases, all other symptoms attributed to sexual abuse could have been caused by something other than sexual abuse.

- Remember that family courts are wary of sexual abuse allegations that are made just prior to a trial or hearing.

- Protective Services may find an allegation unsubstantiated, not because they believe it did not occur, but because they are dealing with a young child who cannot accurately articulate the allegation.

- Do not interrogate, coach, or repeatedly question your child about the abuse allegations as it will contaminate the information gathering process.

- Do not stay in an abusive relationship.

▼

Chapter

8

The Only Certainty in Life Is Change

One of the toughest elements of divorce is that life can change literally overnight and keep on changing, sometimes with little forewarning. The instability and upheaval this brings keeps everyone off balance and in a constant state of confusion and anxiety. This is troublesome, at best, for adults, but it is completely disconcerting for children.

Relocation cases are a classic example of the kind of rapid and dramatic change that can occur in divorce and custody situations. In many respects, removals are more difficult than any other cases related to custody because they are often precipitated by average lifestyle changes over which you may have no control. If a company relocates to another city, you may have to follow your job, or if you lose your job or change careers, you may have to relocate to find suitable employment.

When children are a consideration, relocation can be extraordinarily trying, particularly if the children have been able to settle into a comfortable routine without major flare-ups between you and your ex-spouse. When one of you has to leave suddenly, your children are once again confronted with feelings of abandonment, helplessness, and fear of loss.

If a loving relationship exists between children and both parents, it is only natural for the parent who is leaving to want the children to make the move too. This is especially true of parents who don't have primary placement. It's also normal for a parent to ask the children if moving is something they would like to do. On the other side, the parent who is staying behind doesn't want the children to leave. Unfortunately, this situation puts children back into the undesirable position of choosing between their parents, and also revives those unsettling questions about where they are going to live and with whom and where they are going to go to school; that is, where they are going to grow up.

Clearly, children can't live in two places at once. So, if you've had a situation that was working relatively well and through no one's fault the system has to be dismantled, one parent is going to end up the winner and one will be the loser, who will ultimately be relegated to the position of visitor. The losing parent must also deal with the fear that his or her good relationship with the children is going to be jeopardized and may even deteriorate.

Everyone involved must deal with feelings of loss and anger, and the parent on the losing side may also confront the grief cycle again. Children are even more upset in this situation because their parents are upset.

Typically, if the primary placement parent intends to move out of state with the children, he or she must file a formal notice to the other parent. Don't succumb to any temptation to just make the move, figuring that once it's done no one will reverse it. You can't move in the middle of the night without anyone knowing because if you do, you will be ordered back by the courts until the matter can be sorted out. And think of what this kind of surreptitious action will do to your children. This takes us back to the issue of secrecy and the burden it places on them. Children will be frightened, worried, and in total turmoil. They will worry about the other parent's feelings and actions, and may ask you such things as, "What will happen when Mom finds out?" or "Is Daddy going to be mad about this?" or "Is Daddy going to be sad when he finds out we're gone?" These concerns are compounded if you decide to move without your ex-partner's knowledge and consent and if you lie to the children, telling them they are going on vacation or that you're only going to stay in the new location for a short time.

What often happens in relocation situations is that the ugliness that parents may have been able to avoid by having worked out acceptable placement and visitation schedules suddenly surfaces. The custody dispute is resurrected and parents engage in pettiness while trying to prove who is best suited to have the children.

People point to minor incidents or negligible visitation infractions, leaving each other saying, "I can't believe you're bringing that up. I never knew that was an issue," or "That was never a problem before." They mention incidents such as a spanking that occurred years before or a time when Dad's girlfriend didn't leave before the children arrived for a visit or a time when Mom didn't tell the baby-sitter to come at a particular hour and the children were home alone for a while. Little mistakes that are generally overlooked for the sake of peace now become issues. Whereas previously you were able to avoid this kind of acrimony and your children became accustomed to a manageable truce between the two of you, now your children see their parents shooting barbs at each other, and they think, "Where did these monsters come from?"

When news of a planned relocation is first presented to the children, the person telling them may not think that a custody dispute will ensue, especially if the two ex-partners have found a way to work together for the children. If the primary placement parent is moving, he or she may figure that primary placement allows for the children to simply make the move. The parent doesn't recognize that the other parent has the right to object.

A case involving four children whose mother decided to move to Arizona heated up when she wanted to take the children with her. The court said that she had no pressing reason to move and that the children should stay in the state in which they were living. After her ex-husband was given placement, she turned on the children, and went so far as to lock them out of her home at Christmastime, denying them access to money they had saved to buy gifts, presents they had already purchased, and all their belongings.

Parents who allow this type of situation to escalate to such dramatic and hurtful proportions sometimes blame their children for the court's decision, accusing them of being in ca-hoots with the other parent and choosing sides. Children can't understand why this happens. If one parent tries to be soothing by giving the children too much information about what's going on, they become even more confused, upset, and directly involved in adult issues. If the other parent does spiteful, destructive things, such as locking the children out at Christmastime, the children eventually become angry with that parent and the relationship grows more strained. Some children move to a position where they don't even want to see the other parent, because of anger or fear of further hurtful actions or because they need to protect themselves emotionally and/or physically.

Move-Away Placement Plan

When parents live in two different cities that are relatively far apart, it is often assumed that the children will not be able to spend meaningful time with one of the parents except during the summer. A popular move-away or different city plan that has been used frequently allows children to see each of their parents for meaningful blocks of time almost every month of the year. Assume Mom lives in Chicago and Dad lives in Miami. Also assume that Mom has placement of the children during the school year. To maximize the time with Dad, he would have the right of first refusal for placement of the children during every long school weekend, for teachers' conferences, national holidays, and so on. The father would be allowed to come to Chicago for up to four one-week blocks of school time with the children during the school year. The children would live with him in a place like the Residence Inn, with sufficient bedrooms, and would engage in all their regular activities while the father assumed all parental responsibilities during that week. In addition, the Thanksgiving, Christmas, and Easter breaks would be split on a 2/3–1/3 basis in the father's favor. Furthermore, the father would have the entire summer, which would be defined as one week after school is out until two weeks before school starts. This would allow the mother to take short vacations with the children if she wanted to.

An arrangement of this nature allows the father to have meaningful blocks of time with children virtually every month of the year without disrupting the school schedule.

Longer Lasting Reactions

In a general mental health sense, if something that has caused an individual to suffer emotionally happens a second time, the emotional reaction will usually recur faster and it will be deeper and last longer. This principle can be applied to divorce situations. If children who came through a difficult divorce and for whom life finally regained some semblance of normality suddenly learn that they have to go through it all over again because of a dispute involving a move, whatever problems they initially experienced will happen faster, will happen with greater intensity, and will last longer. This reaction also applies to adults.

Parents who may have dealt well with their children's emotional problems when the divorce originally occurred may now find themselves dealing with children who are older and whose emotional problems take on characteristics specific to their age group (as mentioned in Chapter 2), and those problems have to be dealt with differently. For example, a child who was six when your divorce originally occurred would have been at an egocentric stage in which the child believed everything was his or her fault and all your energy would have gone into explaining that the child wasn't to blame. If a custody dispute occurs five years later, for example, when the child is 11, he or she is in the middle of the age of anger and you will see a completely different reaction. Your child may say, "You can't do this to me. I'm going to go live with my friends," or "I'm going to run away." A teenager may say, "You've already screwed up my life once. You're not going to do it again."

Another factor that may arise in custody disputes erupting several years after a divorce is that one parent may have remarried and have children through that marriage. It's not uncommon in such situations for the parent who is going to be left without the children in common to say to the remarried parent: "You have other children now. Why can't you give up the ones we had together?" If the other parent loves the children, he or she is going to be unwilling to do that.

A Plan to Make Everyone Feel Better

Don't put your children into any of these positions, especially if you have taken the matter to court, because the court is where the decision is going to be made.

As I said before, when a relocation dispute erupts, one of the first things authorities do is try to determine the necessity of the move. If it looks as if someone is doing it for superficial reasons or to get away from the other parent, the court is likely to say that the parent who wants to move can do so, but the children must stay behind. Remember, courts are generally inclined to leave the children where they are barring any major problems. Very often, when such a ruling is made, the parent doesn't leave.

Sometimes when a move is justified, primary placement may be determined by little details, such as one parent may smoke and the child has asthma, or one parent has a pet to which the child is allergic, or one parent tells the children too much about adult issues such as court proceedings or financial arrangements. If a job is at issue, authorities look to see if a similar job could have been found that would have made the move unnecessary.

Neither of you are to be blamed for the feelings you experience at a time like this, but you can't allow the situation to be controlled by your emotions. Once again, you must think of the best interests of your children. The best approach is to try to work this out to everyone's satisfaction, using visitation schedules that have already been discussed through which both of you can see the children as much as possible.

Many parents agree to this type of scheduling as a way of feeling better about letting children relocate. Even if you don't exercise the visitation plan you choose to its fullest, you will at least have the reassurance of knowing that it's in place and that you can have meaningful contact with your children throughout the year.

The Challenge of Additional Adjustments

All forms of change require an adjustment period, but removals or relocations require additional adjustment time. The most stressful things that can occur in people's lives are marriage, divorce, death of a loved one, loss of or changing a job, and moving. In removal situations, four of those major stressors may be operating simultaneously—the move, the divorce, perhaps marriage if that is the reason for the relocation, and changing jobs.

When you place children in this type of situation, they not only have to recover from the acrimony of the custody dispute, they must also adjust to the move, a new school, new home, and new friends, as well as to the parent who is dealing with these major stressors. This adjustment can take a considerable amount of time, so be patient with yourself and your children. Deal with age-specific problems as they arise and, if necessary, get therapy for everyone involved.

Just When You Thought You Had Enough to Deal With

While all this is unfolding, you may also be grappling with establishing new relationships. Although you may feel at the time of divorce that you have no desire to get involved in another relationship, or that you have little likelihood of doing so, don't discount the possibility of a new relationship.

It is not unusual for dating to start during separation or shortly after divorce. It is also not unusual to be involved in one or more transitional relationships. A transitional relationship is usually short-lived and helps one or both individuals get through a transitional period in life. You may be attracted to someone who has characteristics that your ex-spouse was lacking and you immediately feel an affinity for this person. You may even feel that he or she is the only one for you in the world, but be careful. Rushing into transitional relationships and trying to make them permanent can be detrimental to you and your children.

Helpful Hint

When you start dating, remember the magical wish your children carry with them that you and your ex-spouse will be reunited.

This wish may be strong enough for your children to actively or unconsciously try to sabotage your new relationships. Obviously, if you remarry, your children's fantasy will be dashed, so they perceive that it is in their best interests if you don't remarry.

You may begin by dating a number of individuals, and from your vantage point, this approach has nothing wrong with it. However, your children should not be introduced to every new person you date. They need some stability at this time in their lives, and being introduced to people who may be in their lives for a short time does not contribute to stability. You are best off not introducing children to someone you are dating until you have seen him or her for a long time and the relationship has a serious element to it.

Also consider that children may still have open wounds from your divorce. If you introduce a new man or woman into their lives too suddenly, they may feel as though you are trying to replace their other parent. Your children may resent this, thinking, "I don't want you pretending that you're happy with this new friend when I'm unhappy that you and Mom (Dad) aren't living together."

Too often parents try to push this too fast as a way of compensating to the children for the loss of the marital relationship, but what they're more than likely to do is turn the children off to the new partner. If you add to this the element that you may have a different friend every few weeks, it gets to the point where children become disgusted and say, "Don't drag me through all of this until you've made up your mind." And all the while they are inwardly holding onto their magical wish. Another danger associated with introducing children to every new partner you meet is that if you end up in a custody dispute, the guardian ad litem or judge may ask how you have demonstrated stability when you have subjected your children to one partner after another.

Helpful Hint

Introduce children to a new partner gradually.

The first time your children meet him or her should not be on a week-long trip to Disney World. The initial few contacts should be brief and informal. A formal dinner at a restaurant, for example, may seem appropriate, but it will put a lot of pressure on everyone and may overpower children. Such a meal can be costly, requires everyone to dress up, and carries expectations that good things will result when the outcome may be the exact opposite.

Doing simple things that your children are interested in will increase their comfort level. For example, you might want to take them and this new person for an ice cream cone, or you could visit your new partner's home for 15 to 30 minutes, just to drop something off or to introduce your children to his or her children, if that is the case. In so doing, your children will have a visual image of what this person looks like, but you won't be putting them in a position where they have to establish a relationship. To heighten comfort even further, if your new friend has a pet it should be present when you make your introductions.

After you've done two or three informal things, you can plan something more elaborate, such as a dinner. Taking your children and new friend to see a movie is a good idea because no one has to talk or interact except while traveling to and from the theater.

Wait even longer to display affection toward your new friend in front of your children because they may be accustomed to seeing only their parents act that way and think that is what affection between adults is reserved for. As early as possible, your new partner or you should explain that he or she is not in your life to replace the other parent. Let your friend explain, "I'm just a new person in your life," and tell the children what to call him or her.

Decide what message you want to send the first time your new partner stays overnight and your children know it. If you don't have a problem with your children being aware of the concept of sexual activity outside a marital relationship, you should have no concern about sharing a bed with your new partner with your children present in your home. However, if you don't want your children being exposed to this type of situation, don't have your partner sleep over, or have one of you sleep on the sofa or in a guest room. I remind you once again that children learn what they live. If this is the behavior to which they are exposed, you can't complain when your 19-year-old decides to live with a boyfriend or girlfriend. You can't hold them to a double standard that says such behavior is all right for you but not for them.

Letting your children get to know your friends should be progressive and so should introducing the concept of an overnight stay. Keep in mind your ideas of what you expose your children to and how soon. The overnight stay should not occur until children know this new person well and have spent considerable time with him or her. Remain mindful of your children's feelings, which should take precedence over your own.

I was involved with a case in which the mother brought her four-year-old son to his father's for a visit and they found the father and his girlfriend in bed. This wasn't a situation in which the friend was staying over in the presence of the child; she just didn't leave fast enough. The little boy was extremely upset because this was the marital bed and he was accustomed to seeing his mother and father in it together.

Parents often say they don't want their children exposed to an ex-spouse sleeping with someone, claiming this is immoral, religiously inappropriate, or improper. Not all people embrace those beliefs and you can't hold others to your standards. I recall a judge once telling a mother, "Ma'am, you may not like your children being exposed to your ex-husband living with his girlfriend out of wedlock, but it is more important for your children to see a loving relationship between two adults, considering the fighting between you and your former husband, than worrying about whether they are living together out of wedlock."

Remarriage

If you decide to remarry, how are you going to execute your plans? Some people decide to get married without telling family members, including their children. Although you may think this is romantic, or a way of avoiding outside objections and influences, such an action undermines children's sense of security and whatever trust they have in you as a parent.

Whenever possible, include children in your marriage ceremony. Do not, I repeat, do not forbid your children to attend your ex-spouse's marriage. Parents have actually stopped children from sharing in an ex-partner's joy because the wedding occurred during their placement time! Behavior like this only generates an enormous amount of anger and resentment in your ex-partner and your children.

Helpful Hint

Do not, I repeat, do not forbid your children to attend your ex-spouse's marriage.

Here are other things to keep in mind before you remarry:

- Whose house will you live in?
- Where will the children stay?
- Will there be room for your children in your new home?
- If your new partner has children, who will be staying where?

As I said before, living arrangements are a big issue for children. I am reminded of a girl who told me that each of her parents had "six children." Including herself, there were actually seven brothers and sisters. Five of these children were common to the mother and father and each parent had an additional child from a new relationship. How you handle this type of situation will have a lot of bearing on how your children react and adjust to a new marriage and new siblings.

All These Children

When parents remarry and have additional children, the family will include natural brothers and sisters, stepbrothers and stepsisters, and half brothers and half sisters. Stepbrothers and stepsisters have neither parent in common. Half brothers and half sisters share a mother or a father.

Placement schedules in extended families can be downright confusing for everyone, especially children. Assume, for example, that Mom has two children from a previous marriage, Dad has two children from a previous marriage, and Mom and Dad have two children from a current marriage. The four children from previous marriages will spend time in two households. However, have placement schedules been arranged so that all six children spend some time together?

Placement and living arrangements should be resolved before marriage. As a general rule, try to have all the children together for some periods of time. Consequently, you must consider if you will have room in your new household to accommodate all the children at one time and to make them feel comfortable in both homes.

Until scheduling becomes automatic, your life can feel like a quest for day-to-day survival as you wonder who is going to be at your home on any given day of the week, how many people you will have to feed, how much laundry will have to be done, and who has to be picked up and where. No matter how traumatic it seems at the outset, the situation will become automatic if you work with a good master schedule that is accessible to everyone. When establishing a placement schedule, keep in mind that the fewer transitions you build into it, the easier it's going to be for you and the children to understand and remember.

You won't need to worry about introductions if you and all the children have spent time together before the marriage at zoos, ball games, playgrounds, and so on. You will, however, need to concern yourself with other day-to-day issues, such as who will discipline the children, who will arrange schedules, and who will set rules. Such issues can be volatile and blow up very quickly, so they should not be ignored or relegated to the position of secondary concerns.

You also need to consider sibling rivalry and natural birth order. For example, a child who was the oldest or youngest in the family may no longer hold that position after you remarry. Parents often overlook the adjustment that this repositioning involves. Be advised that there is no easy way to deal with it. Patience, understanding, and communication are crucial but sometimes not enough, and you should not hesitate to seek professional guidance. More and more organizations sponsor support and therapy groups for blended families (as this type of extended family is called), and you may want to take advantage of them.

The Role of the Stepparent

Sensitive issues don't end with figuring out a way to blend and schedule your extended family. One of the most ticklish issues is deciding what to call the stepparent. More hard feelings are created and more time is wasted in court with arguments over one parent allowing his or her children to call a stepparent Mom or Dad than could be imagined.

The use of the label *Mom* or *Dad* for stepparents is not acceptable. Your new partner can be called by his or her first name or Step-mom or Step dad. Allowing a child to call your new partner Mom or Dad suggests that he or she is replacing the natural parent. It is particularly detrimental if a parent instructs a child to call his or her new partner Mom or Dad and not to refer to the natural parent that way but instead use his or her first name. Such instructions are given in order to undermine a parent's role and to reduce his or her importance in a child's life. Courts have been known to transfer placement of children over this issue.

This situation is very confusing and hurtful for children. I had a case in which a five-year-old boy had a natural mother, a former stepmother, and a new stepmother. His father insisted that the child call each of them Mom. This child's solution to reducing his confusion was to call one Mommy, one Mamma, and the other Mommer.

If, however, your children do call your ex-spouse's new partner Mom or Dad, don't assume that they have been instructed to do so. Some children do this on their own, and your ex-spouse has the responsibility of asking the children to discontinue it. If this happens, make your ex-spouse aware of it. He or she will need to explain, once again, that this new partner has not taken the place of a natural parent, and that the term *Mom* or *Dad* is reserved for one's birth parent.

Helpful Hints

Rules of Thumb

- Stepparents should be referred to by their first name and not called Mom or Dad.
- The stepparent does not have a *right* to go to school conferences, doctor's appointments, or similar events.

Disciplining Children

You and your new partner should start by discussing your ideas on what discipline entails, how it will be carried out, and by whom. Resolve any differences at the outset of your marriage. A number of disciplinary measures that do not involve physical punishment

---

Helpful Hint

A stepparent's role in disciplining children needs to be carefully considered and defined.

---

can be used with children, such as time-outs or loss of privileges. Some parents, however, still use forms of physical punishment, such as spankings. Punishments that you rarely or never employed when dealing with your child should not become a norm because your new partner advocates them.

Spanking is not an appropriate form of discipline. Any form of physical punishment has negative side effects. Children who are spanked or subjected to physical punishment learn that when you are frustrated, you hit. Through the use of physical punishment, children learn to avoid the punisher rather than the act for which they were punished, they learn how to escape from the punishment situation, and they engage in behavior that is referred to as counteraggression, in which they strike back at the hitter or someone else.

A more difficult situation arises when your ex-spouse becomes upset when your new partner disciplines his or her children. Some households clearly decide that only the natural parent will discipline the children, especially if spanking is used as a punishment. Although this decision may theoretically resolve concerns about who metes out discipline, parents will find it imprudent at times to reserve discipline for only a natural parent. For example, if a natural parent is out of town and discipline is necessary, the stepparent is foolish to say, "Wait until your father gets home in three days. He'll punish you for this." By the time discipline is finally implemented, a child has already moved on to other issues and the discipline may no longer be relevant. Waiting is appropriate if a child has committed a major infraction that requires some negotiating to determine proper discipline.

If you and your ex-spouse clash about your new partner disciplining your children, all adults concerned should meet to discuss this and find common ground. The last thing you want is for parents and stepparents to be implementing many different types of discipline. Such a situation allows children to manipulate parents and stepparents, to get away with negative behavior, and to undermine parental judgment.

Cementing Relationships

As difficult as some of these issues may be for stepparents, they can take steps to assume a special role. One is to serve as a facilitator, fostering positive relationships between children and their natural parents. As I've said, children should be encouraged to maintain their relationship with the other parent, and to remember holidays, birthdays, and other special occasions. A stepparent can help children select gifts and cards or plan special things for their natural parents.

A stepparent can also serve as a moderating influence when difficulties arise between natural parents. Either or both natural parents can at times lose their perspective, exercising poor judgment, becoming unnecessarily angry, or distancing themselves from a situation. Since a stepparent is a trusted partner, he or she can provide a voice of reason and more objective, meaningful feedback, helping a parent realize that what he or she was doing was inappropriate.

Stepparents, however, can knowingly or unknowingly tip the balance of a relationship between the natural parents in an unfavorable direction. A stepparent may become jealous and devisive about children's relationships with their natural parents or encourage a partner to become competitive over visitation time. This can lead to harsh feelings among a parent, an ex-spouse, and a stepparent. Situations like this are best resolved by having all parties meet in an informal or formal setting, such as a therapeutic environment.

The Other Extended Family

Other family members, such as grandparents, aunts, uncles, and cousins, can also be helpful in smoothing the rough edges of a blended family. Children and adults need to continue relationships with these extended family members after divorce and remarriage. Extended family members should be allowed to continue having a relationship with both sets of parents and the children.

If you have remarried and now have three or four sets of extended family members, time and location constraints may make it impossible for children to have meaningful relationships with all of them. When conflicts arise, relationships with natural parents' extended families should take precedence over relationships with stepparents' extended families.

Change as Children Grow Older

Even after you remarry and deal with all the issues that need to be addressed, as long as your children are children, change will continue. No court order or mediation agreement can successfully be made that will apply to an entire childhood. Changes occur as children get older and parents need to be flexible and understanding.

Very young children need your time and attention with developmental and learning skills. Children in their middle school years have additional needs as they start becoming involved in Little League sports, dance classes, and other outside activities. It is inevitable that some of these events will interfere with placement and visitation schedules. If your visiting time is changed because of activity schedules, don't misinterpret that as sabotage by the other parent. Parents must be flexible to accommodate activities because these activities can be crucial to your child's good health and proper development. However, if activity schedules constantly interfere with placement, sacrifices will have to be made. Either some activities will have to be eliminated or the parent who is missing visiting time should have the children during these activities and be responsible for transporting them to and from the activities.

Other issues arise when children reach their teenage years. Remember, a teenager's job is to separate and individuate from parents. They may be involved in school plays, clubs, or athletics. When both my children were in high school, the four of us rarely sat at the table together for dinner more than once or twice a week. We were just not able to mesh everybody's schedules, considering practice times, meetings, and work hours. The same concerns affect regular placement schedules in divorce situations.

It is not unusual for children to reach their high school years and not want to adhere to alternate weekend placement. This behavior is not rejection by them or interference by the other parent, but is evidence that the children no longer want to spend a whole weekend with a parent. Look at this as a sign of maturation and growth. Once your children reach their teenage years, they don't need to see you as often to maintain an adequate and satisfying relationship with you or to continue the psychological bond you share. After all, children who attend boarding schools, camps, and colleges maintain a relationship with their parents. Don't feel threatened by your child's natural growth—enjoy it.

Chapter
9

Custody Do's and Don'ts

We love our children and should enjoy them, and yet we often contribute to their trials and sometimes their destruction. Each of us pulls an imaginary little red cart behind us, filled with emotional baggage that we collect along life's way. As parents, we heap (sometimes unwittingly and sometimes knowingly) a lot of cargo into our children's red carts, which they have to unload at some point or be left pulling it around for the rest of their lives.

To illustrate the negative impact you can have on your children when problems are not promptly and adequately resolved, I am recounting a case from my files involving a boy named Chris. Not every child whose parents divorce and cannot communicate with one another ends up as badly as Chris. However, even this worst case scenario could happen in your family. While reading this chapter, think about the many situations that have been discussed in this book and note how many of them occurred in this case.

A Boy Named Chris

I met Chris and his parents for the first time in February 1993. They came to see me because of behavior problems they were noticing in Chris and his brother, Larry. Psychological testing was done on Chris and I found that the depressionlike symptoms he was exhibiting were directly related to the ongoing fighting between his mother and father, even though they had been divorced for four-and-a-half years.

Both parents had remarried, but neither had children from their second marriages. Chris's father, who had primary placement of the children, was a retired Army officer and his mother was a homemaker. Their arguing centered around the father's contention that his ex-wife was too lax and unstructured in all ways, including bringing up the children, and she believed that he was too rigid, controlling, and structured.

I told them about the negative effects that divorced parents arguing for five years can have on their children, but they seemed disbelieving. My primary concern was not doing individual therapy with Chris, but family therapy with the group, and I told his parents so. They agreed to begin therapy for themselves and then gradually introduce the boys to the sessions.

Brother Larry

After several sessions with Chris's parents, I began therapy with his brother, Larry. Not only did Larry also appear to be depressed, but he was stuttering severely and had been in speech and language therapy through school for some time. Larry's stuttering increased noticeably whenever he was under psychological stress, but during therapy, when he talked about his parents' arguments, his stuttering became so dramatic that sometimes he was not understandable. His stuttering also increased whenever he was around his parents.

After several months, the stuttering almost completely stopped during therapy. Mild stuttering returned only on occasion when Larry discussed problems with his parents.

Chris

Chris was a 14-year-old freshman in a public high school outside metropolitan Milwaukee when I met him. Early in therapy he told me that he was greatly distressed by the arguments between his parents. They shouted at each other whenever they met and, over the phone, badgered each other incessantly, slammed and threw things, and carried on over the same issues constantly. Every time Chris was with his father, the man continually bad-mouthed his ex-wife; whenever Chris was with his mother, she spent the time in constant criticism of Chris's father. Chris was so distraught over the situation with his parents that he was reduced to tears several times in my office while witnessing them argue over minor differences.

In September 1993, Chris's father called me to say that he had taken the boy to a hospital emergency room because he thought Chris was having seizures. Chris had been unable to recall portions of what had occurred over the weekend with his father, describing himself as having "lost all memory."

Doctors performed a number of tests on Chris, including a brain wave test, to be sure he hadn't suffered any seizures. All the tests were negative. They decided that Chris had had an acute psychotic episode. (Psychosis is a state of mind during which an individual is unable to distinguish reality from fantasy. During psychotic episodes, people separate themselves from reality.)

I had Chris transferred to the adolescent unit of Charter Hospital, where it was determined during his admission interview that he was indeed psychotic. He was unable to identify himself, and didn't know where he was or what day it was. He was unable to identify his parents, and he didn't recognize me, even though we had worked together in therapy for eight months.

Several days later, I asked Chris if he could recall anything that occurred while he was being admitted to the hospital. He was only able to remember one thing from that time period—an argument between his mother and father over how old Chris had been when he had the measles. This answer was very revealing. There was Chris, in a psychotic state in front of his parents; their response was to argue about something inconsequential, and that's what he remembered.

During his first week in the hospital, Chris told me he had a large collection of knives and a gun hidden in his bedroom. Neither parent had been aware of this. He said he had to keep the weapons for protection against whoever was trying to kill him, although he couldn't be specific about who that was. This conversation was further evidence of the psychotic fantasy Chris was experiencing.

He was also having auditory and visual hallucinations, hearing and seeing things that were not real. Chris said he was hearing disembodied voices inside his head telling him, "I will kill you. You can't hide from me. Why don't you just kill yourself? Why don't you just kill your parents?" I was literally chilled by this.

Chris said that because of what the voices were saying, he had thought about killing himself, at one point cutting himself and scraping his wrists with knives from his collection, and had also considered killing his parents. Chris was given antipsychotic medication because these hallucinations were continuing.

Over time, the extremely fragile state of Chris's ego became apparent. Whenever Chris became more anxious, he slipped deeper into a psychotic episode. For example, one day his mother was supposed to bring a jacket to the hospital for him to wear. He was so convinced that she would not remember the garment that he cried uncontrollably during a group therapy session. He then wrapped himself into a fetal position and no one could communicate with him. A staff member went to Chris's room, found the jacket—which his mother had brought while he was with the group—and brought it to Chris, but it was hours before he was able to start pulling himself out of that episode.

It was not unusual for Chris to deny having the hallucinations or delusions two or three days after reporting them. These episodes were so frightening to him that he had to deny that they had occurred to protect himself from them. This alternation between a psychotic state and denial made this case very difficult to treat because unless Chris admitted that the problems existed, we couldn't start to deal with them effectively. Chris's denial of the psychotic events led his father to conclude that Chris had nothing wrong with him, and that he was acting psychotic because he wanted more attention from his mother.

Chris's parents continued arguing during family sessions at the hospital. He responded by curling up in a fetal position in a chair, rocking back and forth and sobbing. His parents ignored this regressive behavior and kept on arguing with one another. I told these people that if they didn't find a way to communicate more effectively with one another, they might permanently lose their child to psychosis or suicide, but they were unable to stop arguing. Chris's father said he recalled the warning I had given them in February about how seriously arguing could affect Chris, but he said he didn't believe it could happen to his child.

After each family session, Chris slipped back into seeing and hearing things, especially the voices telling him to kill himself or his parents. His ego simply wasn't strong enough to deal with what his parents were doing and it seemed to become more fragile every time he was exposed to them.

Chris had the maturity of a nine-year-old, and it was interesting to note that he was that age when his parents actually divorced. His entire psychological development had been arrested for five years while he used whatever psychic energy he had to deal with his parents' arguing instead of continuing his psychological development. Now, with Chris hospitalized, his mother began realizing that she and her ex-husband were responsible for his condition, but his father didn't heed these concerns and he blatantly continued the behavior that had so seriously impacted his son.

Chris was hospitalized for seven weeks, during which time he was discharged twice but came back to the hospital after a day or two because of severe regressive behavior. When he finally was able to leave the hospital, he was unable to return to school fulltime. His ego was still so fragile that he couldn't take part in any activity that required consistent attention and focus.

Chris's father said he couldn't see that any good had come from his son's hospitalization, a response that was both sad and frightening. He criticized the hospital staff as being incompetent and was upset by a social worker who had continually confronted him about the impact his behavior was having on Chris. Instead of heeding the social worker, Chris's father blamed his ex-wife for all the hostility between them.

Chris's mother recognized how dangerous it was to let Chris continue living with his father, but his father would not voluntarily agree to a change of placement. This put Chris's mother in a lose-lose situation, forcing her to decide between leaving Chris with his father, and thereby subjecting him to further psychological damage, or going back to court. She was justifiably concerned that taking the matter to court could lead Chris to regress further and perhaps even cause permanent mental illness. She took a chance, went back to court, and won primary placement of Chris.

Why a Shattered Ego?

Why did this happen to Chris? To answer that, we must understand that the ego is that part of the personality that is the self-concept, or self identity, and that tries to obtain a balance between impulses and conscience. It was very difficult for Chris to gain a strong ego-identity by observing his parents. His mother was unstructured and described her home as chaotic at times, but she was also a caring woman who showed Chris a lot of love.

It was true that Chris's father was rigid and highly structured, and although he loved Chris very much, he had difficulty showing it. When Chris was with his mother, she described his father's approach to life as inappropriate, and when Chris was with his father, he described his mother the same way. As a result, Chris's already weakened ego couldn't find a firm foundation for the growth of his self-concept. Each time he tried to identify with one of his parents for a foundation on which to build his identity, the other parent would shatter and undermine the identity he was building.

Chris became so anxious and depressed about the ongoing fighting between his parents that he began thinking about killing himself to escape having to deal with them. His ego was under constant attack by their hostility toward each other. Eventually, Chris's ego couldn't handle these attacks anymore and it shattered. His mind then allowed itself to become psychotic to prevent Chris from committing suicide.

After Hospitalization

Chris experienced three regressive episodes in the week after he left the hospital, which caused him to be rehospitalized. Once, he became terrified that his mother was going to kill herself because she was so upset over his behavior, even though she never gave any indication that she was suicidal. Another time, he said he felt extremely unsafe in his father's house and had more suicidal thoughts.

His parents responded to this by blaming each other: his mother said she was going to court to get Chris away from his father before he destroyed the boy, and his father drew up a list of "facts" about what he considered to be proof of his ex-wife's incompetence.

Within one month of Chris's discharge from the hospital, his father stopped Chris's therapy, discontinued all his medication, and told him to stop his attention-getting behavior. He took control of Chris's life and began serving as Chris's ego.

Now, more than a year after his discharge, Chris lives with his mother on a full-time basis and rarely sees his father. The only way he was able to keep his ego intact enough so he could start building his way back was to separate himself psychologically from his father. Larry decided to live with his father, which added another sad component to the outcome of this situation because the two brothers seldom see each other.

I sometimes wonder what it takes for parents to understand the effects of their behavior on their children. In Chris's case, two relatively intelligent parents were unable to put their differences aside long enough to prevent their son from becoming psychotic. A number of major issues arose in Chris's case: the ongoing fighting between his parents, which negatively impacted the children; the questions about taking the case back to court; the overall negative impact of divorce on children; the parents' need to express anger taking precedence over love for their children; the impact of parental arguing on a child's social development; and change of placement.

As I have said throughout this book, you can do many things to make your divorce as reasonable as possible so that what happened to Chris doesn't happen to your children. I am giving you a list of do's and don'ts. The more do's you follow, the more likely you will be able to obtain custody or placement. The more don'ts you build into your life, the less likely a court will be to rule in your favor.

Custody Do's

1. **Attempt mediation or collaboration before litigation.** Children and parents have fewer adjustment problems in mediated divorces than in protracted court cases, differences are resolved in less time and for less money in mediation, and parents are less likely to go to court later on. Parents create an atmosphere that is conducive to openly discussing their concerns and disagreements when they give the mediator immunity from testifying in the event the parents do end up in court.

2. **Understand from the outset that two parents living apart will not see their children as often as two parents living together.** Parents typically argue that one of them sees the children more than the other. After divorce, no matter how parents plan living arrangements, they will be spending less time with their children than they did when everyone lived under one roof because the children will be shared by two parents in two separate houses.

3. **Anticipate that two adults living apart will have more expenses than two adults living together.** It is a fact of divorce that a house divided means two separate sets of costs, whether children are involved or not. When children are involved, parents must continue supporting them as well as a second household. Parents must recognize that one parent having more bills to pay than before does not mean the other parent has a lot more money to spend.

4. **Consider a joint custody arrangement rather than sole custody.** Parents who get sole custody of their children often develop a sense of ownership of them to the exclusion of the other parent. This can also lead to problems such as a heightened sense of loss and isolation for children and parents, and greater animosity between parents. Consider

sole custody only when one parent is harmful to the children because he or she is a substance abuser, or is chronically mentally ill, a habitual criminal, or has some other severe problem. Joint custody is generally better for parents and children if parents can find a way to communicate effectively and work together well enough to make decisions about children's education, religious upbringing, nonemergency medical treatment, and other issues.

5. **Be willing to share holidays rather than alternating them.** It is important for children to have contact with both sets of families during holidays, and parents who live in the same city should try to arrange this. Holidays like Thanksgiving and Christmas can be shared so children can see both parents and their extended families for each holiday. This gives children positive memories of holidays, helps to lessen their sense of loss after parents divorce, and makes them feel less anxious and guilty about being with one parent and not the other for holidays. It also gives children the sense of belonging and lessens feelings of isolation when they can see other relatives such as grandparents for holidays.

6. **Be together, with your spouse, when you tell your children about your separation and/or divorce.** Children should not come home from school to find that one parent has moved out of the house without prior explanation or a chance to discuss the matter. It is vitally important to prepare children before the actual separation takes place, and they need to hear about it from their parents together. This sends children the message that even though their parents are getting divorced, they will be able to work together in the children's best interests. Children under the age of six should be given several days notice before a parent moves out because it is difficult for them to understand what divorce actually means and why Dad or Mom is going away.

7. **Provide stability; don't move from one home to another more often than necessary.** It is important to give children stability as soon as possible. A parent may need to move several times during the divorce process—first at the time

of separation, then into temporary quarters after the divorce, then into a more permanent home within a year or two. Don't move more than you absolutely need to because moving children five or six times within two years or less can harm their psychological development.

8. **Be sensitive to your children's needs as well as your own.** Parents often become so bogged down in their own needs during a divorce that they don't recognize or consider the children's needs. This can cause behavioral problems in children, such as withdrawal or acting out in negative ways to get a parent's attention. Your children need your mental and emotional presence as well as your physical presence when divorce is turning their world upside down. Don't ignore them or put their needs off until yours are met.

9. **Plan and consult with each other in advance of placement/ visitation time with your children.** When it comes to school work, athletic activities, camp, recitals, extended medical treatments, out-of-town visits with relatives, or other routine activities, it is essential for parents to communicate with one another before implementing plans. This positively affects children in a number of ways, not the least of which is reducing the stress associated with schedules and shared time. Planning events apart from each other or being at odds over scheduling activities increases acrimony between parents and heightens stress, confusion, and anxiety in children.

10. **Observe time schedules with your children as strictly as possible.** Children already battling feelings of loss and abandonment after their parents' divorce can become even more stressed and fearful when a parent is late for an appointment. Lateness can also add to any hostility that exists between parents. A parent who is going to be late should call, explain why, and say when he or she expects to arrive. Parents who are consistently late should try working out arrangements that will help to decrease the pressure and increase timeliness. One way is to agree that the receiving parent will transport the children. For example, if the children are going to Mom's for a weekend, their mother would pick them up. When the visit is over, their

father would pick them up. The result is less likelihood for lateness.

11. **Be flexible regarding visitation times for each parent.** No placement schedule can take into account all the possible exceptions that may occur, so flexibility is essential. Parents should not count up the minutes, hours, or days that may be lost or gained as a result of being flexible. This will probably be balanced out over the course of children's childhood years. Flexibility can decrease the amount of stress that is inherent in planning access to the children and lead to great cooperation between parents regarding time spent with the children.

12. **Do whatever is necessary to resolve angry feelings toward your ex-spouse.** Some parents can be so filled with disdain for an ex-spouse that it consumes them, much to the detriment of their children and themselves. Children whose parents continue to fight after divorce can become deeply depressed and in extreme cases they can become psychotic and even suicidal. Parents do not have to love or even like one another, but they must be civil to one another in front of their children. This is of paramount importance if you love your children and care about their well being.

13. **Refrain from giving your children too much decision-making power.** Children should not be turned into adults by parents who divorce. Parents should give children only as much decision-making power as is absolutely necessary and appropriate for their ages. Parents should make decisions regarding their own lives and the well-being of their children. Teaching children decision-making skills and responsibility is one thing. Making them accountable and responsible for your life and theirs is entirely different and unacceptable because of the negative impact it has on children's behavior and development. This applies most often to allowing young children to decide whether they will or will not live with a particular parent in a primary placement arrangement. When children up to the age of 12 are allowed to have this kind of decision-making power, they might demand excessive and inappropriate power as teenagers and perhaps even become uncontrollable. Older

teenagers may reasonably have some say in how much time they spend with a parent and when.

14. **Tell your children often that they are still loved and that they are not getting divorced from their parents.** Too often parents assume that children understand that they are loved without frequent reminders. Under the best circumstances children need parents to tell them they love them. When parents separate and divorce, children (even teenagers and adult children) need to be told often that they are loved. The insecurity of divorce leaves children asking if parents stop loving each other will they also stop loving their children? One way of reassuring children is to explain to them that love between spouses is different from the love between parent and child. The love between parents and their children is permanent because parents love their children from birth, whereas adults haven't always loved each other—they must meet and fall in love and they can fall out of love.

15. **Give children therapeutic opportunities if their psychological adjustment appears to be too problematic.** Parents should not run to a therapist whenever a child has an adverse reaction to divorce. However, if adverse reactions last for months rather than weeks, they may have become habitual rather than passing and a child may need to be seen by a therapist. Parents may disagree about whether psychotherapy is needed and beneficial for a child. In general, if either parent believes therapy is warranted, a child should be examined to see if he or she needs therapy.

16. **Create an emotional environment for your children that allows them to continue to love and spend time with the other parent.** Allow children to be in touch with each parent by telephone or other means, such as e-mail, on a reasonable basis. Children often realize that one reason parents get divorced is that they don't love each other. They also recognize acrimony between their parents. As a result, children can be fearful that one parent may see them being friendly toward the other parent and become angry or stop loving them, too. Parents need to let their children know that it is perfectly acceptable and

appropriate to show love and respect for the other parent, despite how the parents may feel toward each other.

17. **Present a united front when handling problems with the children.** Children should not be allowed to manipulate their parents by playing one against the other. Although this rule applies to intact families as well, it is crucial for families separated by divorce not to allow children to manipulate their parents. If this is allowed, it can lead to acrimony and problems with having access to your children, and also teach children that they can achieve a desired effect from someone through manipulation. If a problem arises and Mom and Dad respond to it differently it gives children an opportunity to manipulate the situation. Even if they don't like each other, parents need to be communicating for the sake of their children to avoid being manipulated. Discussions should take place between parents and ground rules for dealing with specific problems should be established.

18. **Encourage a good relationship between the children and the other parent's extended family.** Children should be made aware that it is acceptable and appropriate to love and respect the other parent's extended family—aunts, uncles and grandparents. Children feel pressured and they may question their loyalties when they hear one parent criticizing the other parent's extended family or arguing over whether children should have access to them or not.

19. **Encourage children to remember the other parent on special occasions, allowing them to buy cards and gifts and to telephone.** If children are unable to buy gifts and cards for birthdays, Father's or Mother's Day, and other special occasions without help, parents must encourage and assist them to make sure these occasions are recognized. Each parent needs to understand that the other would enjoy receiving recognition on appropriate occasions just as much as he or she would. Letting children participate in the rituals of holidays and special occasions contributes to their social development, allows them to display affection and regard for both of their parents, and gives them contact beyond routine visits and calls.

20. **Use discretion about the time and frequency of your calls to children.** Parents must recognize that when children are with the other parent they will be involved in family time, quiet time, homework and other activities. Too many phone calls can interrupt routines that are necessary to children's stability, and also worry and agitate children and ex-spouses. Parents need to agree on how often they will telephone the children when they are with either parent, decide how long calls can be, and then stick to that plan. It is not necessary for a parent to have daily phone contact with the children when they are with the other parent unless children want and need that much contact. Otherwise, two or three phone calls per week are usually enough for older children and daily short calls for preschool children.

21. **Recognize that children will feel powerless and helpless and don't demean them, because they are so vulnerable.** When their parents are divorcing, children worry about where they will live, who they will live with, what school they will attend, and who their friends will be. These decisions are often made by parents with little or no input from the children or by a judge to resolve differences between parents. This leaves children feeling powerless and helpless about the outcome of their lives, which worsens if parents fight each other in court over these decisions.

22. **Recognize that children may feel insecure and exhibit regressive behavior; be prepared to get them therapy if these behaviors persist.** Children may become insecure because they feel helpless and powerless over their lives, and because they worry about losing the parent who has primary placement. They think: "Mom already left. How do I know that Dad won't leave, too?" Under this type of stress, children often show signs of regression, including thumb sucking, bed wetting, whining, and tantrums. Therapy is not necessary for children who show this type of behavior for a short time, but therapy may be necessary if the behavior persists for more than two months.

23. **Provide an appropriate role model for your children.** Most children are like sponges when it comes to learning from others, soaking up everything from everyone around them.

Children especially learn from their parents. Parents who are angry, who overreact to situations, are very depressed, or show other types of extreme behavior are teaching that behavior to their children, who may start behaving in a similar fashion. Parents should do everything they can to be on their best behavior for the sake of the children. Parents who can't control or modify their behavior may need therapy.

24. **Allow your children to see where the other parent is going to live after moving out of the house.** Children need to know that the parent who is leaving will have his or her basic needs met, so show them as soon as possible where that parent will live. It will be reassuring to children to see that the parent has a bed, a place to eat, and a bathroom.

25. **Put your differences aside long enough to be able to peaceably attend school conferences and activities.** If parents have a problem dealing with one another it should not become a school's problem. For example, some schools offer only one teacher conference and parents must decide if they will attend together or designate one parent to attend. If they attend together, they must act appropriately without displaying hostility and anger toward each other. Parents must recognize that when their behavior is inappropriate in school, it reflects badly on them and their children. Schools and children need to know that parents can put aside their differences for the good of their children.

26. **Recognize the rights and responsibilities of the other parent to consult school authorities concerning school performance and the right to inspect and receive copies of student records and reports and school calendars and notices.** Children and parents need to feel that they are part of each other's lives. Each parent should continue being aware of children's performance in school and events and activities taking place at school for the good of the children.

27. **Notify the other parent of medical emergencies, and recognize his or her right to have input about surgery, dental care, hospitalization, or institutionalization.** Parents need to be aware of all information concerning the children.

When information about a child is withheld or parents are excluded from participating in the processes mentioned above, it can lead to arguments and court action.

28. **Recognize the right of both parents to inspect and receive copies of children's medical and dental records, and the right to consult with any treating physician, dentist, or mental health professional.** When parents are kept fully informed, they will feel more a part of the children's lives and are less likely to feel the need to take legal action to gain access to vital information about things like school performance, general health, and medical treatments. When one parent does not tell the other this information, or tries to prevent the other parent from getting it, it will weigh against him or her in custody actions.

29. **Recognize that children need substantial contact with the same-gender parent during adolescence.** During adolescence, boys identify more closely with their fathers and girls identify more closely with their mothers. It may be necessary to voluntarily change placement arrangements during this time in your children's lives to meet their developmental needs.

30. **Allow all grandparents to continue having contact with the children whenever reasonable.** Parents may find themselves alienated from each other's in-laws during the divorce process and after it because relatives tend to take sides with the respective parents. Children, however, are not getting divorced from their relatives, especially their grandparents. Children have a special place in their lives and memories for grandparents, from whom they also learn a great deal. When one parent cuts children off from the ex-spouse's parents, it cuts another component of the childhood experience from children's lives. Parents can establish some ground rules, such as grandparents should not criticize the other parent or undermine relationships.

31. **Communicate with the other parent openly, honestly, and regularly to avoid misunderstandings that could be harmful to your children.** Most of the child-rearing difficulties between divorced parents stem from poor communication. When a child tells a parent that Mom criticized Dad or Dad said something insulting about Mom, check it out. Parents

need to communicate about these concerns. If communication between parents is so bad that it is impossible for them to have honest discussions, children will continue manipulating their parents, which will increase the acrimony between the parents and teach the children to be poor communicators as well as reinforcing manipulative behavior.

32. **Make plans directly with the other parent instead of using your children as go-betweens.** Anytime children are caught in the middle of communication between parents it becomes burdensome for them, awkward and stressful. It is unfair to expect children to assume the role of middle persons or messengers.

33. **Live as close to one another as is practical, convenient, and reasonable.** Children are more likely to feel that they have two homes if they can move easily between them, especially if they are old enough to travel on their own by bicycle or public transportation. Older children should be able to go to the other house to get things they left behind, have discussion with the other parent, interact with pets, and so on. Children should understand that they eat and sleep at the home of the parent who has primary placement, except for designated times with the other parent. This reduces the likelihood of them playing one parent against the other.

34. **Maintain household routines as much as possible to keep some stability in children's lives.** Many changes occur in a child's life when parents are separating or divorcing, so as much as possible parents should maintain the basic structure of their lives to give children some sense of stability. Chores, meal times, sleeping routines and regular schedules should be maintained as best as possible. Changes should be kept to a minimum and discussed with the children in advance.

35. **Maintain the same set of rules as much as possible in both homes.** If basic rules differ greatly at each parent's home it can increase children's anxiety. Children will benefit if parents keep rules for meals, bedtime, homework, and general situations as similar as possible in both homes. At the same time, parents must realize that they cannot enforce rules or

maintain discipline when the children are in the other parent's home. Although many parents divorce because they have different ideas about child-rearing, it will benefit children greatly if you can agree on some terms about basic rules that will prevail in both homes.

Custody Don'ts

1. **Don't agree to alternating, 50/50 placement arrangements.** Many parents have tried to work out placement schedules that give each of them equal time with the children such as a Sunday to Wednesday/Wednesday to Sunday schedule, alternating weeks, or alternating every two weeks. The problem with a 50/50 schedule is that it can leave children feeling that their mother has a house and their father has a house, but the children don't have one. This feeling leads to insecurity. Judges have ordered alternating schedules without realizing how detrimental they can be to children.

2. **Don't if possible, allow overnight visitation for infants (birth to 12 months).** Some researchers think it is essential for infants to sleep in the same crib every night, and they advocate frequent short visits with nonplacement parents, but no overnight stays. The nonplacement parent should be allowed to put the child to bed and go through the typical bedtime routine in the placement parent's home. Although this is an intrusion, children are not infants for long, and this temporary solution will provide the child with greater feelings of security.

3. **Don't foster feelings of guilt in children over divorce.** Children, especially young children, often feel guilty about their parents' divorce and assume a degree of responsibility for it, believing they have caused the divorce. Parents who encourage such feelings of guilt will be promoting long-term psychological problems in their children.

4. **Don't allow children 9 to 12 years of age to refuse to visit the other parent.** When children this age are allowed to make this type of decision, they may get the impression,

wrongly, that they will have the power to make other important decisions. Also, a child this age who refuses to spend time with the other parent may be experiencing a loyalty issue and unable to make an objective decision. Allowing a child this age to make such an important decision is likely to lead to problems in adolescence.

5. **Don't allow teenagers to become too parental.** Teenage children often try to fill the role of the same-gender absent parent. Even though the primary placement parent might feel good about having someone at home to lean on, it is not good for the teenager who may assume false feelings of maturity and expect liberties and flexibility beyond what is appropriate for his or her age. Part of the problem is that the teenager stops thinking of himself or herself as a teenager and takes on the responsibilities and persona of an adult. It is very difficult to dissuade a teenager from this thinking once he or she has been filling an adult role for a long time. This can lead to discipline problems and a host of other behavioral issues.

6. **Don't allow children to exhibit too much acting out behavior in response to the divorce. If their behavior gets out of hand, don't deny them therapy.** It is not unusual for children of divorced parents to display acting-out or regressive behavior. It becomes a problem if parents allow it to become excessive because they feel sorry for the child or guilty over what the child has been going through because of the divorce. Parents who think: "He's having such a hard time, let's not make him follow the bedtime rules" will face even greater acting-out behavior later on. Children benefit when parents maintain a consistent, fair structure at home, including setting appropriate limits on children's behavior.

7. **Don't take sides about parenting issues in front of the children.** If a child has a disagreement with one parent, the other parent should remain neutral if he or she was not part of the original problem or discussion. If one parent disagrees with something the other has done, they should discuss it privately. Thrashing out parenting issues in front of children upsets them because they see their parents pitted against each other. It also allows children who are

trying to manipulate parents to see Mom and Dad divided and perhaps enables a child to further manipulate the parents. Children should be told when parents reach a resolution over a parenting issue. If you can't agree, the children should be told how the lack of resolution will affect them.

8. **Don't put the children in the middle when arranging visitation.** Scheduling access to the children should be arranged directly by the parents. Do not burden a child with the responsibility of organizing his or her time with one parent or the other.

9. **Don't communicate with the other parent through the children.** Parents often use children to carry messages to the other parent because the parents are not communicating effectively with one another. This puts children in an awkward and inappropriate position.

10. **Don't fight or argue with or degrade the other parent in front of the children.** It is not uncommon for angry parents to make derogatory comments about the other parent in front of or directly to the children. Doing this further polarizes the parents and puts children in a difficult position, sometimes forcing them to take sides. Children eventually tire of hearing these derogatory remarks and become angry with the parent making them.

11. **Don't plan visitations with the children and then arrive late or not at all.** Angry parents try to hurt each other by arriving late to visit the children or not showing up for a planned visit, but the ones they hurt most are their children. Children feel more rejected and fearful when the parent is late or does not arrive.

12. **Don't withhold time with the other parent as punishment for the children and the other parent.** It is completely inappropriate for one parent to stop a child from seeing the other parent as a punishment for the child or the parent. This is a lose/lose situation that should be avoided. If a parent has a problem with the other parent it should be discussed away from the children. If a child has done something wrong both parents should discuss discipline and be consistent about following through on it.

13. **Don't discuss financial aspects of the divorce (support, maintenance, late or back payments) with the children.** Two parents cannot live as cheaply apart as together, but no matter how frustrating balancing a household budget becomes don't discuss it with the children. Try not to let children see you angry with the other parent over financial issues such as support. This type of parental behavior requires children to deal with an adult problem that they are not emotionally prepared to handle, and it embroils them in the acrimony between parents. When activities and purchases must be postponed, limited, or cancelled because of partial or late child support or maintenance payments, the parent should explain the circumstances to the child in a nonderogatory way. A parent should not say, "We won't be able to go to the movies tonight because you father is such an ass and we can never count on him to give us the money he should." Instead, a parent might say, "It's frustrating to me and I'm sure it's frustrating to you that we don't have enough money to go to the movies. I'll have to see what I can do to get your father to cooperate more."

14. **Don't assume, based on your children's communication, anything about what the other parent has said or done. Check it out.** When one parent believes what a child says about the other parent it is often the start of more legal battles or other problems. Even in intact families, children may tell preposterous stories to parents. If one parent hears something from a child about the other parent that sounds unreasonable, before getting geared up for a fight, verify the child's statement with the other parent. In most cases, unnecessary complications can be avoided by checking with the other parent.

15. **Don't use children as pawns to express anger toward the other parent.** It is unfair to the children as well as the other parent if you schedule activities during time that is supposed to be spent with the other parent, or not allow a child to speak with the other parent on the phone as a way of expressing anger toward the other parents. Parents who do this hurt the children as well as the other parent.

16. **Don't overburden children by requiring them to have too much responsibility for their growing up and maintenance.** When parents become overwhelmed by divorce, it is easy to make children overly responsible for themselves and their environment. Children need to learn to be responsible for their behavior and to carry out age-appropriate household chores. However, when children are put in the difficult position of assuming too much responsibility, they can easily become overburdened. For example, children should not be required to decide what school to attend or whether to have elective surgery.

17. **Don't overburden children by giving them responsibility for maintaining your psychological stability.** Parents can become so caught up in the circumstances of their divorce that they surrender responsibility for their mental stability to their children. In a reversal of roles, children become more like a parent and the parent becomes more like a child (called parentification). The child is put in the position of continually having to console the parent, provide psychological support for the parent, or provide solutions for the parent's problems. This is an excessive burden on the child.

18. **Don't overburden children by making them the focus of arguments between you and the other parent.** Another way children become overburdened is by being put in the middle of disputes between the parents, especially arguments about the children. Overburdened children have greater psychological problems and take longer to adjust to the difficulties associated with divorce.

19. **Don't allow your children to spend too much time with a parent who appears to be or has been diagnosed as being mentally ill.** Children who are required to spend significant amounts of time with mentally ill parents feel less stable themselves. Mentally ill parents should be in therapy for as long as necessary and the therapist should be allowed to report to the guardian ad litem or the court-appointed psychologist. When all three feel visits with the mentally ill parent can be increased, it should be done gradually.

This approach maintains the child's psychological need to maintain stability and parental rights.

20. **Don't separate your children.** It is generally a bad idea to separate the children except in unusual circumstances. For example, if two children are involved in a divorce, the parents might decide that each should have one child. This may satisfy the parents' needs but it does not satisfy those of the children because siblings generally need to stay together. The sibling rivalry that occurs during childhood is a training ground for adulthood. It teaches children how to share, coexist, and deal with controversy. If the children are raised separately, as only children, they will not be exposed to these components of development. Separating them can also heighten their sense of grief as they mourn the loss of a brother or sister.

21. **Don't introduce children to every person you date.** It is hard for children to deal with the end of the marital relationship between their parents, but their burden increases when they are exposed to every new person the parents dates. When a child is introduced to every new date, it can lead to false hopes, unrealistic expectations, and further feelings of rejection. Once a relationship has progressed to the point of becoming meaningful, it can be advantageous to slowly introduce the children to that individual. If possible, parents should date when the ex-spouse has the children, or else meet dates outside the home. This is particularly important when children are young (preteen) and when the divorce is less than two years old.

22. **Don't allow children to see sexually intimate behavior between you and your partner.** Although it may appear to be natural to expose children to intimate behavior between their parents or their parents and new partners, they are not psychologically ready to deal with these observations. Divorced parents and their partners are more likely to be careless about preventing children from observing these behaviors because of the limitations imposed on the dating relationship. Restrict sexually intimate behavior to times of complete privacy.

23. **Don't sleep in the same bed with school-age children except under unusual circumstances.** Parents may think they should let younger children sleep with them to reduce the trauma they experience during their parent's separation and divorce. Allowing children to sleep with parents under these circumstances can cause unrealistic fantasies, expectations, and feelings about the parents. Set boundaries. For example, if you let a young child sleep with you because he or she has been frightened by something, make it clear that you are allowing it that one time and that it is the exception and not the rule.

24. **Don't ask children to keep secrets from your ex-spouse.** It is very disconcerting for a child to be told by a parent to keep a secret from the other parent. This puts the child in the middle again, and encourages the child to be deceptive and to feel guilty about withholding information from a parent.

Be mindful, at the outset of your divorce and throughout the entire process, of one of the primary rules—divorce adversely affects children and it is parents who determine the extent to which they are affected. The more of the do's you follow, the less adversely affected your children will be. The more of the don'ts you bring into your life, the more problems your children are likely to have. Many of the don'ts listed in this chapter were present in Chris's life.

If you are already steeped in divorce- and custody-related problems, it's probably not too late to change the way you are dealing with each other and your children. Few cases are ever really too late for implementing positive change. Children's minds are very malleable and if their parents start changing the way they handle situations, the children will start to change the way they react to them. This change is easier to bring about with very young and middle-school-age children than with teenagers, but they are children, nonetheless, and many of them will respond positively to appropriate changes.

We have now gone full circle in the hope that you have recognized that **WINNING CAN NEVER BE MORE IMPORTANT THAN THE WELL-BEING OF YOUR CHILDREN**.

▼
Chapter
10

Resources Abound

by Colleen Drosdeck and Marc Ackerman

Many types of mental health professionals can become involved in divorce cases and you may have difficulty differentiating one from another. This chapter will help you identify them, and will familiarize you with resources that can help you through the divorce process and its aftermath.

Selecting a therapist can be as difficult a process as selecting an attorney. Many different kinds of therapists are available, and you need to make sure that any therapist you go to is licensed or certified. Before going to the office of someone not licensed or certified, ask why. Being board certified and having a medical license is optimal for psychiatrists. Being licensed and listed in the National Register is most favorable for psychologists, and being licensed or certified is optimal for social workers or counselors.

Most state psychological associations have listings by area of psychologists specializing in divorce-related work. The National Register lists psychologists according to their areas of specialization. Also, ask your attorney for names of therapists with whom he or she has successfully worked. Word-of-mouth referrals for therapists are often the best reference because you know that someone has worked well and felt comfortable with a particular therapist.

The majority of marriage and family counseling is performed by social workers and counselors. When problems become more severe or involve significant concerns about developmental needs or deep-seated psychopathology, contacting a psychiatrist or psychologist is the way to go. If medication is needed for a severe psychiatric disorder, a psychiatrist would be the only individual to contact.

Psychiatrists

The Joint Commission on Interprofessional Affairs, which consists of representatives of the American Psychiatric Association, American Nurses' Association, American Psychological Association, and National Association of Social Workers, describes a psychiatrist as a physician whose specialty is diagnosis and treatment of people suffering from mental disorders. A properly-trained psychiatrist can provide a comprehensive psychiatric evaluation as well as a medical diagnosis, and then integrate a person's personal and medical history with the results of the examination and the tests to determine the best course of therapy and other treatments.

The United States has 37,000 practicing psychiatrists and psychiatric residents. After medical school, most go into a residency program for three years, where they continue their studies and provide supervised inpatient and outpatient clinical services.

Completion of the residency is not necessary for a physician to call himself or herself a psychiatrist. A small percentage request certification from the American Board of Psychiatry and Neurology, for which they must take oral and written exams after several years of practice, but about two-thirds of practicing psychiatrists are not board certified. A psychiatrist certified in psychiatry and neurology may take additional examinations to become certified in child psychiatry and/or forensic psychiatry. These examinations test basic competence, not expertise.

Psychologists

A psychologist is trained to study and measure mental processes and to diagnose and treat mental disorders. Use of this title is regulated by law in all 50 states. Psychologists are licensed to diagnose or treat behavioral, emotional, or mental disorders.

In most jurisdictions, a psychologist is someone who has a doctoral degree in psychology, either a Ph.D. or a Psy.D. The major difference between these two degrees is that the psychologist with a Ph.D. would have completed graduate training that included supervised experience in conducting research and would have conducted a research project as part of doctoral degree requirements. The Psy.D. may have no research experience. Someone with a Psy.D. degree would have completed a full-time predoctoral internship for a full year, usually involving both inpatient and outpatient treatment. If an attorney needs an expert with research experience, the Ph.D. is usually the better candidate. However, if the amount of predoctoral clinical experience is more important, the Psy.D. may have more than a Ph.D. with the same years of training.

There are six major areas of graduate study in psychology: forensic, clinical, counseling, school, industrial/organizational, and experimental. A subspecialty within clinical psychology is neuropsychology. In almost all states, psychologists are licensed generically, not as specialists, even though most psychologists have training as specialists in one of the areas mentioned. Licensing laws, state administrative codes, and professional ethical codes all require psychologists to practice solely within their area of training and competence. You must be careful to retain whichever type of psychologist has the training and demonstrated competence needed to testify as an expert in a particular area.

Finding a psychologist or other expert with the knowledge and experience you need for your case is difficult because as knowledge about areas of forensic practice grew, so did specialization in relatively narrow areas. Many psychologists and psychiatrists who offer general child and family services will not be up-to-the-minute on research and information in forensic child and family services. In a child custody case, you need a forensic expert.

Most of the experts an attorney may want to consult will be forensic or clinical psychologists, who are trained to evaluate and treat patients with severe psychological problems. Most Ph.D.s and virtually all Psy.D.s are clinical psychologists, and nearly all are licensed or eligible for licensure for independent practice.

People often ask what the difference is between psychiatry and clinical psychology. About 80 to 90 percent of what they do overlaps. However, the major distinction is that psychiatrists can prescribe medication and psychologists can administer, score, and interpret psychological tests. Psychiatrists have moved more toward the biological or organic aspects of mental health care and their expertise in prescribing medications has become a more central part of their work.

In the past, psychologists generally were not allowed to admit people to psychiatric hospitals. Patients were usually referred to psychiatrists, who could hospitalize them. Today, depending on the state, psychologists are increasingly allowed to admit patients to hospitals in conjunction with a psychiatrist or on their own.

Not all psychologists are trained to administer all psychological tests. This is especially true with regard to neuropsychological tests, which examine the central nervous system. Most psychologists can administer a screening test for brain damage, but few are skilled in the kind of neuropsychological testing that can establish, for example, which part of the brain is involved and how serious the deficit is. If these details are important to your case, your attorney should question the psychologist about his or her areas of expertise. It is best to have a board-certified neuropsychologist to do this kind of testing.

Counseling psychologists are trained to work with less severely mentally ill people. Most counseling psychologists are inadequately trained to administer, score, or interpret projective tests, but they generally perform well when dealing with ongoing problems with day-to-day living. School psychologists are trained to evaluate, treat, and consult on educational problems of children and adolescents. They are trained in evaluating and dealing with learning problems. Industrial/organizational psychologists are trained to apply principles of psychology to business settings. Experimental psychologists are primarily teachers and researchers.

As I said before, most licensing of psychologists is generic, but some psychologists meet requirements set by some states for listing in the National Register of Health Service Providers in Psychology. Those requirements are:

- Currently licensed, certified, or registered by the state/provincial board of examiners of psychology at the independent practice level of psychology.
- A doctoral degree in psychology from a regionally accredited educational institution.
- Two years of supervised experience in health services in psychology, of which one year is in an organized health service training program and one year is at the postdoctoral level.

More than 18,000 psychologists are listed by the National Register. Whenever clinical or health expertise is relevant, an attorney would do well to retain a psychologist listed in this registry.

Social Workers

Social workers may have either a bachelor's or master's degree in social work and are trained to help people in the context of social and economic affairs. For example, a social worker may find a home that meets a person's special social, psychological, and physical needs. Many social workers are also able to evaluate children's developmental needs, parental emotional and economic stability, and each parent's ability to fulfill a child's emotional, social, and economic needs.

All 50 states, the District of Columbia, Puerto Rico, and the Virgin Islands license or certify social workers with master's degrees. Some states also license or certify those with bachelor's degrees. Because many people who have no educational background in the field are hired to do social work, it is necessary to ask about a social worker's training.

Social workers may receive certification through the Academy of Certified Social Workers (ACSW), within the National Association of Social Workers (NASW), and may use ACSW after their names once they are certified. Certification requires:

- Graduation from a school of social work accredited by the Council on Social Work Education.
- Two years of full-time paid social work practice beyond a graduate social work degree, or an equivalent amount of part-time professional practice.
- Regular NASW membership.
- Submission of three professional references.
- Successful completion of the ACSW examination.

Social workers who meet the requirements for ACSW certification can be listed in the NASW Register of Clinical Social Workers.

Social workers are not used as expert witnesses as often as psychologists and psychiatrists, but their expertise is sought in some cases. Social workers, for example, have testified in a number of appellate court cases involving child sexual abuse.

Professional Organizations

An essential part of an expert's qualifications is the list of organizations to which he or she belongs, particularly if membership is based in part or whole on a formal peer review rather than simply on payment of dues. "Fellow" status in professional organizations is predicated on such a review.

Psychiatrists

American Psychiatric Association (www.psych.org) represents about 70 percent of psychiatrists in the United States. Members must be physicians with some training and experience in psychiatry and pay annual dues. Fellow must have been members for at least eight years and have made significant contributions to psychiatry and to the association.

American Board of Psychiatry and Neurology (www.abpn .com) grants certification in psychiatry, neurology, and child psychiatry based on examination.

American Psychoanalytic Association's (www.apsa.org) members are psychoanalysts as well as psychiatrists.

American Academy of Psychiatry and Law (www.aapl.org) is an organization of psychiatrists interested in the practice of and training in legal psychiatry. It does not certify. Any member of the American Psychiatric Association who is willing to pay the membership fee may join.

Psychologists

American Psychological Association (www.apa.org) limits full membership to psychologists with doctoral degrees (or master's degree associates for five years) who pay membership fees. Specialty areas are represented by separate divisions. Fellow status is granted to those who have made "unusual and outstanding contributions or performance in the field of psychology."

American Board of Professional Psychology (www.abpd.org) confers diplomate status on psychologists in the areas of clinical, counseling, school, industrial/organizational, and neuropsychology based on examinations.

American Board of Forensic Psychology (www.apa.org) provides certification of psychologists in forensic psychology based on examinations. The American Board of Forensic Psychology and American Board of Professional Psychology have coordinated efforts in the areas of forensic certification.

American Psychology–Law Society (www.ap-ls.org) is a division of the American Psychological Association. Membership is open to those who pay the membership fee.

Social Workers

National Association of Social Workers (www.socialworkers.org) is the primary membership organization for social workers. Membership is open to "professional social workers" who pay the dues.

Academy of Certified Social Workers is an administrative unit of the NASW Academy of Certified Social Workers and certifies master's degreed social workers who meet the criteria listed earlier.

National Organization of Forensic Social Work (www.nofsw. org) certifies as diplomats social workers who are heavily involved in providing social work consultation in the legal process. Certification is based on a review of training and experience, written work samples, and oral examination. All applicants must have at least a master's degree in social work and three years of post-master's experience.

Other Organizations

American Board of Medical Psychotherapists certifies psychologists, psychiatrists, social workers, and others with substantial knowledge and experience as medical psychotherapists.

American Orthopsychiatric Association (americanortho @gmail.com) is an interdisciplinary association for psychologists, psychiatrists, and social workers. Fellow status is offered to members in good standing for at least five years.

American Academy of Forensic Sciences (www.aafs.org) promotes education and research in forensic sciences. Its members are organized into sections, with most mental health experts in the section of psychiatry and behavior science.

* * *

One of the biggest differences in divorce work between the first and second editions of this book is the advent of web sites, e-mail systems, computer available resources, and internet accessibility to virtually everyone. There are a number of resources available for families who are in the process of divorcing or who already have obtained a divorce and are looking for assistance in how to deal with many of the issues.

Current Resources on Child Custody/Divorce

The Americans for Divorce Reform estimates that "Probably, 40 or possibly even 50 percent of marriages will end in divorce if current trends continue." Statistics have shown that divorce greatly increases, two- or three-fold, the incidence of all kinds of bad effects on children of divorce. Some of the negative effects include: psychological problems, juvenile delinquency, suicide, undereducation, and teen motherhood. The conflict that arises between the parents during and post divorce frequently results in more problems for the children than the conflict that arose during the marriage. The detriment is still increased in children of "low-conflict" divorces. Problems related to divorce persist into early adulthood and affect the marriage and mating choices of children of divorce.

As a result of the abundant statistics, identifying the detrimental effect that divorce can have on all individuals involved, a plethora of information has been generated on the subject to ease people through the process. Current books and online resources offer reliable and invaluable information on a variety of subjects, including general overviews of how the process will unfold, legal aspects of divorce, and beneficial resources for children. The following list of books and online resources, organized by category/topic, may prove beneficial to any individual who is going through or has been through a divorce.

Resources that Provide Support for Parents

Online Resources

Our Family Wizard: https://www.ourfamilywizard.com/index.cfm. This site is aimed to minimize the stress between parents that may result from verbal communication and is designed to help work out differences for the children's sake.

ParentCenter: http://parentcenter.babycenter.com. A site that will distribute a customized, informative, and fun weekly newsletter, which will include information and news specifically tailored for each family.

The Centers for Youth and Families: http://www.youthandfamilies.org. The mission is to provide specialized prevention, intervention and treatment services that promote emotional and social wellness for children and families.

Children, Youth and Family Consortium: http://www.cyfc.umn.edu/welcome.html: This website is a bridge to a wide range of information and resources about children and families, which connects research, teaching, policy, and community practice.

Making Lemonade—The Single Parent Network: http://www.makinglemonade.com. Provides resources for single parents in all phases of single parenting; including, divorce, bill problems, credit repair, and falling in love again.

Parents Without Partners: http://parentswithoutpartners.org. An international organization that provides real help through discussions, professional speakers, study groups, publications, and social activities for families and adults.

Family Education: http://life.familyeducation.com/divorce/parenting/45564.html. The company's mission is to be an online consumer network of the world's best learning and information resources; personalized to help parents, teachers, and students of all ages take control of their learning and make it part of their everyday lives.

Safe Kids: http://www.safekids.com. This site provides a family's guide to making the internet a fun, safe, and productive place for children.

U.S. Department of Health and Human Services: http://www.insurekidsnow.gov. Alerts individuals to services that may be available to children and teens, including doctor visits, prescription medicines, hospitalizations, and much more.

Commission on Domestic Violence: http://www.abanet.org/domviol/home.html. Works to mobilize the legal profession to provide access to justice and safety for victims of domestic violence.

Published Material

Armstrong, Kristin. *Happily Ever After: Walking with Peace and Courage through a Year of Divorce.* New York: FaithWords, 2007.

Benedek, Elissa P., and Catherine F. Brown. *How to Help Your Child Overcome Your Divorce: A Support Guide for Families.* New York: Newmarket Press, 2001.

Clapp, Genevieve. *Divorce & New Beginnings: A Complete Guide to Recovery, Solo Parenting, Co-Parenting, and Stepfamilies.* New York: John Wiley & Sons, 2000.

Coloroso, Barbara. *Parenting through Crisis: Helping Kids in Time of Loss, Grief, and Change.* New York: HarperCollins, 2000.

Covy, Karen A. *When Happily Ever After Ends: How to Survive Your Divorce Emotionally, Financially and Legally.* Naperville, IL: Sourcebooks, 2006.

Emery, Robert. *The Truth about Children and Divorce: Dealing with the Emotions So You and Your Children Can Thrive.* New York: Penguin Group, 2006.

Everett, Craig, and Sandra V. Everett. *Healthy Divorce.* Hoboken, NJ: Jossey-Bass, 2003.

Gemelke, Tenessa. *Stay Close: 40 Clever Ways to Connect with Kids When You're Apart.* Minneapolis, MN: Search Institute, 2005.

Hooper, Anne. *Getting Your Children through Divorce: A Parent's Guide to Separation.* rev. ed. London, UK: Robson Books, 2005.

Kent, Richard, and John Steinbreder. *Solomon's Choice: A Guide to Custody for Ex-Husbands, Spurned Partners, and Forgotten Grandparents*. Lanham, MD: Taylor Trade Publishing, 2006.

Long, Nicholas, and Rex L. Forehand. *Making Divorce Easier on Your Child: 50 Effective Ways to Help Children Adjust*. New York: NTC Publishing Group, 2002.

Lowenstein, Liana. *Creative Interventions for Children of Divorce*. Toronto, Canada: Champion Press, 2006.

McKay, Gary D., and Steven A. Maybell. *Calming the Family Storm: Anger Management for Moms, Dads, and All the Kids*. Atascadero, CA: Impact Publishers, 2004.

Information Specifically Designed for Fathers and Mothers

Online Resources for Fathers

Dads Rights: http://www.dadsrights.org: provides information on how to minimize the horrible effects of divorce on children by disclosing what every single father should know during the process of divorce.

National Center on Fathers and Families: http://www.ncoff.gse. upenn.edu: the primary goals of this organization are to expand knowledge on father rights, family efficacy, and child well-being; all within multiple disciplines, through research and development.

Published Material for Fathers

Clavel, Paul. Dad Alone: *How to Rebuild Your Life and Remain an Involved Father after Divorce*. Montreal, Canada: Vehicule Press, 2004.

Hoerner, Thomas, and Patrick David. *The Ultimate Survival Guide for the Single Father*. Richmond, VA: Harbinger Press, 2004.

Knox, David, and Kermit Leggett. *The Divorced Dad's Survival Book: How to Stay Connected with Your Kids*. New York: Perseus Publishing, 2000.

Mandelstein, Paul. *Always Dad: Being a Great Dad during and after Divorce*. Berkeley, CA: Nolo, 2006.

Marguiles, Sam. *A Man's Guide to a Civilized Divorce: How to Divorce with Grace, a Little Class, and a Lot of Common Sense*. Emnaus, PA: Rodale Press, 2004.

Published Material for Mothers

Ellison, Sheila. *Courage to Be a Single Mother: Becoming Whole Again after Divorce*. New York: HarperCollins, 2001.

Engber, Andrea, and Leah Lungness. *Complete Single Mother: Reassuring Answers to Your Most Challenging Concerns.* Avon, MA: Adams Media, 2006.

Karst, Patrice. *The Single Mother's Survival Guide.* Darlinghurst, New South Wales, Australia: The Crossing Press, 2000.

Oberlin, Loriann Hoff. *Surviving Separation and Divorce: A Woman's Guide to: Regaining Control, Building Strength and Confidence, Securing a Financial Future.* 2nd ed. Cincinnati, OH: Adams Media, 2005.

The Ability to Co-Parent after Divorce is Essential. Resources to Help Individuals Effectively Co-Parent

Online Resources

Shared Parenting Information Group: http://www.spig.clara.net/body.htm. The mission of this organization is to promote responsible shared parenting after divorce and make available information, research, and resources to all concerned.

Center for Divorce Education: http://www.divorce-education.com. This is a corporation created to educate the public, the court system, and the law and policymakers about divorce-related issues, with a goal of minimizing the negative impact of divorce for families.

Shared Ground: http://www.sharedground.com. Parenting plans made easy; computer software that allows parents to communicate effectively by tracking recurring events, identifying scheduling conflicts, and much more.

National Association of Counsel for Children: http://naccchildlaw.org: The mission of this association is to improve the lives of children and families through legal advocacy.

Published Material

Adler, Robert E. *Sharing the Children: How to Resolve Custody Problems and Get on with Your Life.* Bloomington, IN: Authorhouse, 2001.

Lyster, Mimi. *Building Parenting Agreements That Work: How to Put Your Kids First When Your Marriage Doesn't Last.* Berkeley, CA: Nolo, 2005.

Lyster, Mimi. Child Custody: *Building Parenting Agreements That Work.* Berkeley, CA: Nolo, 2000.

Sember, Brette McWhorter. *How to Parent with Your Ex: Working Together for Your Child's Best Interest.* Naperville, IL: Sourcebooks, 2005.

Stahl, Philip. *Parenting after Divorce: A Guide to Resolving Conflicts and Meeting Your Children's Needs.* Second Edition, Impact Publishers, 2008.

Thayer; Elizabeth, and Jeffrey Zimmerman. *The Co-Parenting Survival Guide: Letting Go of Conflict after a Difficult Divorce.* Oakland, CA: New Harbinger Publications, 2001.

Thomas, Shirley. *Two Happy Homes: A Working Guide for Parents & Step-Parents after Divorce & Remarriage.* New York: Springboard Press, 2005.

Wittman, Jeffrey. *Custody Chaos, Personal Peace: Sharing Custody with an Ex Who Is Driving You Crazy.* New York: Penguin Group, 2001.

Resources Aimed to Aid Children through the Divorce Process

Online Resources

Children's Institute: http://www.childrensinstitute.net. This program works for children by developing and promoting prevention and early intervention programs, evaluating children's conditions and programs, training professionals, and forming community partnerships to inspire and implement positive public policy.

Kids' Turn: http://www.kidsturn.org/kids/main.htm. A program that was developed to help kids learn about divorce through allowing them to read what other kids feel about divorce, playing games, and doing activities that teach them about this process.

Lemons 2 Lemonade: http://www.lemons2lemonade.com/default.htm. This web site teaches children how to handle life when things go sour between their parents; including, how families change, why divorce happens, how to handle problems, important questions kids have, and much more.

Kids Guides: http://kidsinthemiddle.kidsguides.com. Find everything you need for kids; including information on child care, educational toys, parental control, summer activities, and much more.

Girl Power: http://www.girlpower.gov/girlarea/general/divorce.htm. This site identifies important aspects for kids to remember while their parents are going through a divorce.

Published Material

Charles, Norma. *All the Way to Mexico.* Vancouver, BC, Canada: Raincoast Book Distribution, 2003.

Ford, Melanie, Annie, and Steven, as told to Jann Blackstone-Ford. *My Parents Are Divorced Too: a Book for Kids by Kids. 2nd ed.* Illustrated by Charles Beyl. Washington, DC: American Psychological Association, 2006.

Foster, Brooke Lea. *The Way They Were: Dealing with the Divorce of Your Parents after a Lifetime of Marriage.* Foreword by Ian Birky. New York: Crown Publishing Group, 2006.

Gallagher, Mary Collins, and Whitney Martin. *Ginny Morris and Mom's House, Dad's House.* Washington, DC: American Psychological Association, 2005.

Gregory, Nan. *Amber Waiting.* Illustrated by Kady Macdonald Denton. Calgary, Alberta, Canada: Red Deer Press, 2006.

Kanyer, Laurie A., and Jenny Williams. *25 Things to Do . . . when Grandpa Passes Away . . . Mom and Dad Get Divorced . . . or the Dog Dies: Activities to Help Children Suffering Loss or Change.* Berkeley, CA: Parenting Press, 2003.

Lowry, Danielle, and Bonnie Mathews. *What Can I Do? A Book for Children of Divorce.* Washington, DC: American Psychological Association, 2001.

MacGregor, Cynthia. *The Divorce Helpbook for Kids.* North Fremantle, Western Australia: Impact Publishers, 2004.

MacGregor, Cynthia. *The Divorce Helpbook for Teens.* North Fremantle, Western Australia: Impact Publishers, 2004.

Marquardt, Elizabeth. *Between Two Worlds: The Inner Lives of Children of Divorce.* New York: Crown, 2008.

Masurel, Claire, and Kady MacDonald Denton. *Two Homes.* Cambridge, MA: Candlewick Press, 2003.

Moore-Mallinos, Jennifer, and Marta Fabrega. *When My Parents Forgot to How to Be Friends.* Haupauge, NY: Barron's Educational Series, 2005.

Moser, Adolph. *Don't Fall Apart on Saturdays! The Children's Divorce-Survival Book.* Kansas City, MO: Landmark Editions, 2000.

Peters, Julie Anne. *Between Mom and Jo.* New York: Little, Brown, 2006.

Prestine, Joan Singleon, and Virginia Kylberg. *Mom and Dad Break Up.* Greenville, WI: School Specialty Publishing, 2001.

Ransom, Jeanie Franz, and Kathryn Kunz Finney. *I Don't Want to Talk about It: A Story about Divorce for Young Children.* Washington, DC: American Psychological Association, 2000.

Ricci, Isolina. *Mom's House, Dad's House for Kids: Feeling at Home in One Home or Two.* New York: Simon & Schuster, 2006.

Rubin, Judith Aron, and Bonnie Matthews. *My Mom and Dad Don't Live Together Anymore: A Drawing Book for Children of Separated or Divorced Parents.* Washington, DC: American Psychological Association, 2002.

Seward, Angela, and Donna Ferreiro. *Goodnight, Daddy.* Buena Park, CA: Morning Glory Press, 2003.

Spelman, Cornelia Maude, and Kathy Parkinson. *Mama and Daddy Bear's Divorce.* Morton Grove, IL: Albert Whitman, 2001.

Winchester, Kent, Elizabeth Verdick, and Roberta Beyer. *What in the World Do You Do When Your Parents Divorce? A Survival Guide For Kids.* Minneapolis, MN: Free Spirit Publishing, Inc., 2001.

Information Concerning the Legal Aspects of Divorce

Online Resources

Divorce Online: http://www.divorceonline.com/articles/fnew.html. This site provides free articles and information on the financial, legal, psychological, real-estate, and other aspects of divorce; additionally, you can turn to the Professional Referral section of Divorce Online to locate professional assistance near you.

Divorce Source: http://www.divorcesource.com. Not only a resource for vital divorce related information, but it also carries a supportive atmosphere through The Interactive Support Community and The Chat Rooms; you may want to think of the site as one enormous on-line divorce support group that caters to people facing divorce (or related issues) who desire pertinent information and want to share questions, find answers, and learn from other's experiences.

Divorce Support: http://www.divorcesupport.com. A web site that provides divorce information on family law topics such as; divorce, child custody, visitation, child support, Alimony, and property division.

Find Law: http://www.findlaw.com. Find Law offers services on how to find a lawyer for your legal issue.

Flying Solo: http://www.lifemanagement.com/flyingsolo. A resource for life transitions, including separation and divorce.

Crown Financial Ministries: http://www.crown.org/Tools/budgetguide. asp. This site allows individuals to track the amount of money spent in a month and then compares it to the guidelines shown; allowing individuals to adjust their budget to make it balance if need be.

Parenting and Custody Calendar: http://www.kidshare.com. An online tool that allows you to easily schedule and track parenting time as well as monitor compliance with your custody arrangement, because often just monitoring compliance is enough to cause a change for the better.

American Bar Association: http://www.abanet.org/family. The members are dedicated to serving the field of family law in areas such as divorce, custody, military law, alternative families, elder law and children's law.

Center on Children and the Law: http://www.abanet.org/child/home. html. This site provides technical assistance, training, and research that addresses a broad spectrum of law and court-related topics that affect children.

Child Custody Pro Bono Project: http://www.abanet.org/legalservices/ probono.childcustody.html. A site that seeks to enhance and expand the delivery of legal services to poor and low income children involved in divorce, adoption, guardianship, unmarried parent, and protective order matters.

Published Material

Schepard, Andrew I. *Children, Courts and Custody: Interdisciplinary Models for Divorcing Families.* New York: Cambridge University Press, 2004.

Sember, Brette. *No-Fight Divorce: Spend Less Money, Save Time, and Avoid Conflict Using Mediation.* New York: McGraw-Hill, 2005.

Sember, Brette. *The Divorce Organizer & Planner.* New York: McGraw-Hill, 2004.

Tesler, Pauline, and Peggy Thompson. *Collaborative Divorce: the Revolutionary New Way to Restructure Your Family, Resolve Legal Issues, and Move on with Your Life.* New York: HarperCollins, 2006.

Watnik, Webster. *Child Custody Made Simple: Understanding the Laws of Child Custody and Child Support.* Claremont, CA: Single Parent Press, 2003.

Webb, Stuart, and Ronald Ousky. *The Collaborative Way to Divorce: the Revolutionary Method that Results in Less Stress, Lower Costs and Happier Kids—Without Going to Court.* New York: Penguin Group, 2006.

Index

A

Abuse, 42
Academic performance, 26
Ackerman Plan, 98
Alcoholism, 41
Arbitration, 68–69
Attorney(s), 51–60
  acting as own, 60
  dirty tricks, 56–58
  switching, 58

B

Bad schedules, 100

C

Child support, 9, 90
Collaborative divorce, 64–68
College-age children, 24–26
College education, 125
Confidentiality, 81
Cooperation, 149
Court, 59, 88
  appeals, 90
  contempt of, 89
  orders by, 43
  going back to, 88
  temporary orders, 69
Custody dispute, 72
Custody evaluation, 76
Custody study, 76

D

Discipline, 195
Domestic violence, 159–165
Do's and don'ts, 207–223
Drug abuse, 41

E

Early childhood, 17
Emotional abuse, 165–167
Endangering children, 44

F

Family conference, 133
Family violence, 159–164
Finances, 130

G
Grandparents, 49
Guardian ad litem, 72–74

H
Hague Convention, 91
Helpful hints, 14, 23, 30, 37,
    39, 44, 45, 47, 48, 50, 55,
    60, 61, 69, 78, 81, 85, 90,
    97, 105, 109, 113, 114,
    117, 120, 121, 124, 128,
    136, 138, 140, 143, 146,
    158, 170, 171, 189, 190,
    193, 195, 196

I
Informed consent, 80

J
Joint custody, 37

K
Kidnapping, 91

M
Maltreatment, 152–182
Master schedule, 109
Mediation, 61
Mental illness, 39–41
Middle childhood, 18, 21

O
Obstructing visits, 43

P
Parenting plan, 111
Parents' rights, 121

Phone calls, 127
Physical abuse, 42,
    154–159
Placement, 48, 134
    holidays, 101
    separating children,
        105
    young children, 96
Presents, 129
Psychiatrists, 225, 229
Psychological abuse,
    165–167
Psychologists, 226, 230

R
Records, 124
Refusal to visit, 148
Religion, 126
Relocation, 85
    schedules, 107, 186
Remarriage, 192
Resources, 231–239
Right of first refusal, 105
Role reversal, 31
Rules, 107

S
Schedules:
    Ackerman Plan, 98–99
    bad, 100–101
    different cities, 107, 186
    general rules, 101
    supervised, 83
School events, 104, 122
Separating children, 105
Sexual abuse, 42,
    167–181
    evaluating sexual abuse,
        169

Sleeping arrangements, 140
Social worker, 228, 230
Sole custody, 37
Stepparent, 194–195
Supervision, 83–85
Support, 9, 90

T
Teenagers, 21–24
Temporary orders, 69

V
Vacations, 129
Violating orders, 43